M000224308

# HURDLES
# IN THE DARK

## ELVIRA K. GONZALEZ

ROARING BROOK PRESS

New York

**A note about language:**

I've included words and phrases throughout this book that reflect the regional slang of Laredo, Texas. I wanted to honor the language I heard and spoke growing up in my border town. In some cases, this mix of Spanish and English has its own distinctive pronunciation and spelling. Laredo is a proud and unique community, and I hope the inclusion of our slang helps you gain a sense of the place I once called home.

Published by Roaring Brook Press
Roaring Brook Press is a division of Holtzbrinck Publishing Holdings Limited Partnership
120 Broadway, New York, NY 10271 • fiercereads.com

Our books may be purchased in bulk for promotional, educational, or business use. Please contact your local bookseller or the Macmillan Corporate and Premium Sales Department at (800) 221-7945 ext. 5442 or by email at MacmillanSpecialMarkets@macmillan.com.

Library of Congress Cataloging-in-Publication Data

Names: Gonzalez, Elvira K., author.
Title: Hurdles in the dark / written by Elvira K. Gonzalez.
Description: First edition. | New York : Roaring Brook Press, [2024] | Includes
   bibliographical references. | Audience: Ages 14–18 | Audience: Grades 10–12 |
   Summary: "A YA memoir about survival and strength by Elvira Gonzalez,
   a Mexican American track star who found freedom from poverty and violence
   by training to become one of the top athletes in the U.S."—Provided by publisher.
Identifiers: LCCN 2023028103 | ISBN 9781250847850 (hardcover)
Subjects: LCSH: Gonzalez, Elvira K.—Juvenile literature. | Women triathletes—
   United States—Biography—Juvenile literature. | Track and field athletes—
   United States—Biography—Juvenile literature. | Hurdling (Track and field)—
   Juvenile literature. | Track and field—Coaching—Juvenile literature. | Mexican
   American women—Biography—Juvenile literature. | Minority women activists—
   United States—Biography—Juvenile literature.
Classification: LCC GV1060.72.G66 A3 2024 | DDC 796.42092 [B]—dc23/
   eng/20240224
LC record available at https://lccn.loc.gov/2023028103

First edition, 2024
Printed in the United States of America

ISBN 978-1-250-84785-0
10  9  8  7  6  5  4  3  2  1

This book is dedicated to all the girls and women around the world fighting for their dreams in the face of adversity.

Don't. Give. Up.

Success is to be measured not so much by the position that one has reached in life as by the obstacles which he has overcome.

—Booker T. Washington

# FOREWORD

**This book began inside a juvenile detention center. I was sixteen** and locked away in a jail for kids. I felt alone. Trapped. Scared. Especially when nothing seemed to be going the way I dreamed. Things were far from perfect, and the adults in my life were going through their own struggles, too.

One day, the other girls in juvie and I secretly gathered to talk about our lives. We learned about the challenges each of us had to face. Among each other, we found people who listened. People who cared. A ray of hope came over me. Like a match struck in a dark room. This exact moment made me hopeful for my future. I realized I wasn't alone after all. There were others just like me who had faced so much adversity. The problem was, up until that point, I had never heard stories like theirs or my own. That day, I became inspired to write a book. I wanted other girls like us to know they weren't alone.

I had no idea what it would take to write and publish a book. No one in my family ever attended a university. Spanglish was my first language. I barely passed high school English. I didn't know I was struggling with dyslexia. I wasn't exposed to literature outside of schoolwork. In my hometown, a city with a population of nearly a quarter-million people, we didn't even have a single bookstore. Our literacy rates ranked dead last in the entire country. Despite it all, I did love to write. I've kept a daily journal ever since I was seven, and something about storytelling provided an outlet to express my feelings.

When I began to write the first pages of my story in juvie, my goal was to share this story with you and that this big dream of mine would become a reality. Somehow, someday. Now, more than fifteen years later, the book is out!

In your hands, you are holding my story through Kristy's perspective, in her most authentic teenage self. My high school journals and earlier drafts were used to complete this manuscript.

Throughout this book, there are memories, experiences, and decisions I made that I originally planned to omit from sharing with you because I felt afraid, embarrassed, and ashamed. However, I realized to honor my truth and give a voice to those with similar experiences, I needed to tell this story the way it happened. Without filters. Without my adult perspective. I hope that by sharing these very personal, often difficult, and sometimes traumatic experiences, I help you better understand what it was like for Kristy and other kids like her.

If at any point during the reading of this book you feel negatively impacted by the topics explored or if you yourself are struggling with your own hurdles or traumas, I encourage you to reach out to a mental health professional, trusted family member, or a friend. If you don't know where to start, there are a few resources at the end of the book.

You deserve the support and the tools needed to overcome whatever adversity you are experiencing. Your life and your story matters to me and to so many people around the world.

Your friend, Elvira

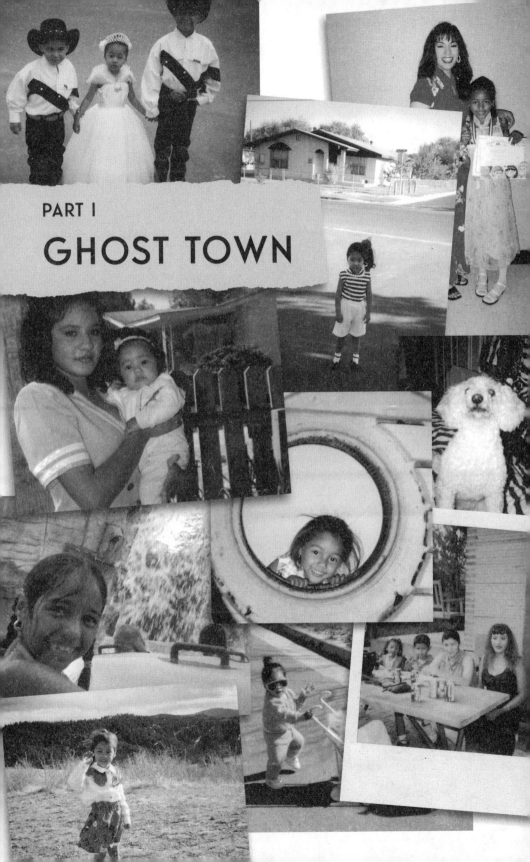

PART I

# GHOST TOWN

# RUN

**For some middle schoolers who compete in track and field, ribbons** and gold medals might be the main goal, but for a barrio girl like me, it's a lot more than winning first place.

It's a fight for survival.

"Stick!" I yell, sprinting through the first triangle mark on the track, entering the exchange zone. I extend my right hand to pass the baton to Velma Reyes. She's our second leg in our 4×400 meter relay.

*Clean handoff.* We're up by thirty meters, but those girls from the north side schools are turning up the heat. After all, they're the relay champions every single year. I wonder if we'd have a fair shot at winning if we didn't train on a makeshift dirt track and only practice twice a week.

"Let's go, ándaleeee!" I shout from behind, pushing out each syllable and imagining my voice moving her body forward like the wind would blow a leaf. She dashes away in the lead as I wobble into the infield, my legs feeling like Jell-O. I collapse on my knees trying to catch my breath.

I look up at Ma and she gives me two big thumbs-up. Standing next to her in the bleachers is Miss Marissa, my former elementary teacher who encouraged me to try out for the school track team six years ago.

"You're awesome!" Miss Marissa yells. She's got a knack for discovering hidden talents on the playground, but had she visited our barrio, she would have figured out sooner. We're all quick at getaways, runners who bolt from danger.

*Black. Silver. Go!* Our team chants our school colors as Marcela, our anchor, comes out of the second turn and into the homestretch. Ahead of her, a girl from a north school. To her left, a girl from another north school. Marcela can't hit the gears and power through to first or second place. She's boxed in.

"¡Vamos, Marcela!" I yell hoarsely, but the sounds of my teammates singing *Dame más gasolina* muffle my words.

A block party has broken out on our side of the bleachers. We got singing. Dancing. Clapping. So what if our sports teams can't beat the teams in the north side in relays or in any other sport? We roar like leopards, just like our school mascot. We're known to cheer louder than any other team and we're proud of it. Meanwhile, on the opposite side of the bleachers, there's no dancing. No singing. No shaking their hips. Why do they clap so proper, with their backs straight and chants faint? *Que chafos.*

Our coach rallies around us, "Buenas, ladies!" She's proud we finished strong.

"Time to celebrate, eyyy!" Ana, our third leg screams, and we pop open bags of Hot Cheetos.

I'm relieved it's a wrap, cuz this past school year I was in way too many sports teams: The school track team. A club track team. The school cheer team. A club cheer team. I can't wait to chillax for a few weeks before summer track begins.

"Bye, guys! See y'all at school mañana." I wave to my teammates and turn to Ma.

"Look!" I wave my third-place ribbon at her, pumping my arms up and down.

"You ran so fast, mija!"

"Nambe. I got super tired at the end, though. Couldn't feel my damn legs," I say, dragging my feet like a flat tire. I gave this race everything I got, cuz Ma raised me to give it my best. Quitting isn't an option.

"Ma'am . . ." A man wearing a striped collared shirt and white tennis shoes interrupts us. ". . . You must be this track star's beautiful sister," he says in an accent, not the staccato type like me and Ma picked up from the barrio. Our accent sounds like an accordion that rises and falls with the vowels. His sounds more like a mix between Tejano and a Texas twang.

Ma chuckles. I think she loves whenever people mistake her for my older sister. Sometimes, she even goes along with it and forgets to tell people she's not actually twenty-two. She's thirty.

Crossing my arms and pursing my lips, I clear my throat and say, "Nah. She's my mom."

"Oh!" he adds with one eyebrow raised, shaking Ma's hand, and then reaching for mine.

I stare at my fingers covered in chili powder. *Oops.* I rub my hands furiously on my shorts, but the red dye from the powder has seeped into my skin like a tattoo. "Ay, sorry, sir," I apologize, snapping my hand out anyway.

"Great to meet you." He shakes my hand, squeezing it firmly. "I'm a track and cross-country coach at Anderson High School," he says, making Ma's spine stiffen up straight as a pencil.

He's a coach at one of the top local public high schools in the north side of town, a thirty-minute drive from our barrio, in an area where rows of Spanish-style houses with smooth stucco exteriors, arched doorways, and tiled roofs stretch for miles. The only time our family has ever strayed there is to gawk at the big, fancy Christmas lights once a year, conjuring daydreams of what it would be like to grow up in one of those homes.

"Here. Take my info," the man adds, reaching into his pocket and giving Ma his business card.

Ma holds the card up, scrutinizing every inch. "Mira, look." Her eyes glisten as she reads the black lettering.

## ANDERSON HIGH SCHOOL
### Coach Richard
### Assistant Coach
### Track & Field / Cross-Country

"Miss Gonzalez," he starts to say, not realizing me and Ma have different last names. "Don't take this the wrong way, but your daughter . . . look at how she's built. She was born to be a runner. She's going to be real damn fast. One of the fastest around here. I tell you that."

*Thanks but no thanks.* My head snaps. I don't like the way he's looking at me or Ma. Or maybe I'm overreacting, but it's sorta weird.

"Mija, did you hear what the man said?" Ma pulls me under her busty chest.

I look up, faking a smile. "Sí, Amá."

"Kristy's always been athletic since she was three," Ma answers back, recalling the time she caught me climbing and leaping off furniture at my dad's house shortly before they split up and we moved down the street into Ma's childhood casita. Eventually, after Ma got her first job at a nursing home as a palomita and saved enough money, she begged the only gymnastics center in town to allow me to enroll at their gym despite my age.

"She must get it from you," the man responds flirtatiously. Ma blushes, smiling wide, something she seldom does cuz of her crowded teeth. "And . . ." He points directly at me. "What do you think about coming to our school next year?"

"I'm a sixth grader, sir." I still got two more school years before I reach high school. And who the heck thinks about life that far ahead? All I really know is that I wanna play sports. I wanna go to school with my friends at South Middle. I wanna be a punk singer when I grow up. And I will always love to eat bean-and-cheese tacos every single day.

"Well, I'll tell you more about our school anyway. We got the best of everything you can imagine. Sports. Academics. Coaches . . . ," he brags on and on. Everyone knows that the north side schools, Anderson and Union, are the best public schools in town.

I nod my head. *Bet they don't have bleacher parties like us, though.*

"You go and think about it, oh-kay?"

I shrug my shoulders, looking in the distance as my teammates load onto the bus. *I could never ditch my best friends and teammates.*

Ma's lips purse. "Ay. Kris-ty." She says my name in two broken syllables, making me feel guilty about not wanting to end up at a north side school.

"Sure. I guess . . ." I fiddle with the black jelly bracelets around my wrist, fearing I'd be forced to swap my metal studded belts, pink hair extensions, and fake eyebrow piercing for white wigs and elaborate, handmade colonial dresses. Just like Las Marthas that attend the north side schools. They're a group of high school girls that are members of an exclusive society for the most prominent families, many of whom trace their lineage back to the founding Spanish families of our town.

Every year during our city's annual George Washington Celebration, Las Marthas are paraded around on patriotic floats along the Rio Grande as they're officially debuted into the community while the rest of us wave at them like celebrities.

I've heard that could never be a barrio girl like me, anyway. I'm not a descendant of those elite families, and we can't afford a thirty-thousand-dollar dress. That's more than Ma makes in a year, and I don't even know how to eat with a fork and knife properly. But whatever, who needs cutlery when you can eat the world's best tacos for breakfast, lunch, and dinner? I'm a morena, a prieta, and I wouldn't change it for anything.

"I'd take care of your daughter. You have my word."

"Thank you!" Ma guards the business card close to her body, igniting memories of seeing her reread letters from her father, Enrique. He writes us monthly from prison, promising to move us out of the barrio and into one of his houses.

*Someday, mija. Just pray to God it will happen soon.* He signs off each letter, like a dangling carrot. I think he gave Ma hope for years. But it's been nearly a decade now, and I'm beginning to believe that Ma wishes she would have never met him in the first place.

These days, Ma works longer hours at the bar, stashing wrinkled dollar bills inside a massive zebra vase with the hope that one day we'll have enough money for a house. Somewhere we can build our own refuge.

I pull Ma's arm, trying to get her attention. "Let's go. C'mon," I plead, peering into Ma's wide, dark brown eyes. She desperately wants to move us out of the barrio, and knowing how strong-willed Ma has always been, she's probably already thought about a million more ways she can accomplish this.

We say goodbye to Coach Richard and make our way to the parking lot, where Ma comes to a full stop. She stares into my eyes, gripping my shoulders.

"Yes, Amá?"

"Mija, one of these days . . ." I swear if she could, she would patent this sentence. ". . . We will have enough money to buy our own house. Just you. And. Me. I promise," she says, pressing on my shoulders with each syllable, transferring her big hopes into my little bones.

# SOUTH MIDDLE

"Who was that?" Mr. Dally, our band conductor, demands, and our entire seventy-member band turns to the back of the room. I freeze, looking straight ahead at him. He's scanning our drum line, scrutinizing our wrists.

I should know this song by now. We've been practicing during class for months. But I'm lost most of the time. Secretly, I attempt to get by just listening to the rhythm of the music.

"Umm," I say, my hand slowly rising, but someone interrupts.

"Me, sir." My friend Rodrigo, our section leader, raises his drumstick high up in the air like he doesn't already stand out. He's the tallest kid in our entire middle school. People in the administrative office sometimes confuse him for a high schooler or sometimes even a parent until he speaks. He has a soft, gentle, and innocent voice. That's why people sometimes call him Big Bear.

"Nambe, my hand slipped," he says, taking the blame. Rodrigo knows I can't read music. He's attempted to teach me during lunch period way too many times to count, but I don't think I'll ever be as good as him. He's turned out to be one of our best drummers.

"Alright, alright." Mr. Dally doesn't get mad. He hardly ever does. He just shakes his head and continues, "Mighty Leopards. Please, don't forget to submit the name of your bus partner for our end-of-year school field trip. They're due next week. Have a great weekend!"

I pull the steel snare drum harness over my head, feeling relieved. One, cuz band practice always makes me nervous; I don't want to mess up. Two, cuz I swear these metal harnesses weren't made with boobs in mind. My chest gets crushed. But I can't quit. I promised myself that I'd pick up the drums. I'm dying to start my own punk band even though most people at school listen to norteño, reggeaton, or cumbia music.

Just a few more years and I'll have every instrument needed to start my band. For the past few years on my birthday and Christmas, Ma's been surprising me with one instrument at a time, overcrowding the cramped room she and I have been sharing for so many years.

"Hallelujah!" I shriek when class breaks, thanking Rodrigo silently. He's always looking out for everyone.

"¡Ay, güeys!" Mario, our bass drummer, yells out to the drum line. "We all get on the Scream ride or what?"

My stomach drops to my feet at the thought of being strapped in a roller coaster harness, shooting upward like a rocket over two hundred feet. Might as well end up practically over the clouds and into outer space, overlooking Six Flags Fiesta Texas in San Antonio, Texas.

"Hell to the no. What's wrong with you, dude?" I reply, looking mortified.

Mario teases me. "¿Tienes miedo?"

"Duh I'm scared! Look at me . . ." I tug at my extra-small black T-shirt that still fits one size too big. "That thing they strap you into would not fit me properly. Like my shoulders would pop right out and I'll be launched over the moon and never make it back to earth," I joke, peeling my eyes away and letting them land on Rodrigo's face.

He's usually the payaso one of the group. But right now he's biting down on his lip, scratching his head.

With my index and pinkie finger up and the rest of my fingers down, the international sign for *rock on*, I ask, "What's up, dude?" Something is wrong.

"Que onda, rock star," he replies, smacking his lips.

"You don't wanna go to Six Flags?" I ask.

"Nambe, es que I can't get on that ride," he explains, throwing one of his drumsticks across the room, aiming for his backpack. It misses. Not sure what he means that he can't ride it. Is he scared of roller coasters? I don't know.

"We can hide together when we get there. Actually. No! Even better. We'll get lemonade slushies and watch these mensos scream at the top of their lungs," I whisper so no one can hear me, thinking how much better it would be to have someone to talk to while all our friends get on Scream. I mean, this is way better than blasting off with my feet dangling in the open air, yelling, *Please, oh God, I don't wanna be blown to outer space.*

He smiles and nods his head in agreement. "Órale. Let's be partners on the bus ride y tirámos rollo?"

"Deal." Our fists collide. I'm paired up with the best traveling partner. Rodrigo always makes me laugh. In a few months, we'll be cracking up on our two-hour drive up north on Interstate 35.

I walk out of campus, into the parking lot, and head toward the school buses. From the distance, I see Isela, my best friend of four years, waving at me. Her head is bobbing with her iconic red bandana and pigtails that flap back and forth as she prances.

"What's up, ruca!" our hands slap. We got a secret handshake that takes thirty seconds too long, and we love every second of it. "Do you have cheer or track practice after school today?"

I shake my head. "Nah."

"Cool. Cuz this vato from my fourth period wants to race you. Le dije that I got five dollars on you."

"¿Ahorita?" I stare down at my feet and scrunch my forehead. I'm wearing skate shoes and the soles have worn off.

Isela looks at me dead serious. "Al chile, güey. I already told him you race on the spot." I mean, I do, but I can't miss the bus home. It leaves in fifteen minutes.

"Pretty please? I really need the five dollars. No te agüites."

"Okay. Fine." I give in, pointing at the metal gate across the parking lot and then to the welding building. It's about one hundred meters long, the same distance I've ran at track meets before. "From there to there. That's todo. Okay?"

Isela grins. "BRB!"

A minute later, she returns with a group of cholos, telling her that we got no shot cuz girls can't outrun boys. *Whatever.*

Isela leans up against me, crossing her arms. "Son puros haters. Pos, we'll see," she blurts out confidently.

"Like tomorrow?" I say sarcastically cuz I need to bounce.

Then, one of them comes forward—my competitor.

"I'ma race you and win, wacha," he says to me, pulling up his baggy-ass pants, tucking in his gold chain with a cross, and unbuttoning his polo shirt, revealing his neck tattoo that pokes up right below his jawline.

I roll my black-and-red plaid jeans above my knees and say, "Try!"

"¡Ándale, Pelon!" his friends encourage him.

I get in a running stance, a standing start. My feet shoulder-width apart. My left leg slightly out front, bending at the hips.

"¡Vamos! Dale shine," Pelon tells Isela. He sets up his legs parallel on the ground, shoulder width apart. *Doesn't he know he's already losing?* Our body's natural reaction when standing like that is to rock back and then launch ahead, instead of pushing forward from the front foot, losing precious time. I suppose only a runner would know that fact.

Well, he does have one advantage over me. He's aerodynamic cuz he's got a razor shave, almost bald head. That's why they call him Pelon.

"Ready?" Isela puts her hands up, making sure we're good to go. I nod, noticing a crowd of students starting to gather around us. *Keep your eyes ahead.* I stare down to the welding building, the finish line. *Boys may be physically stronger, but Ma says I can do anything if I don't give up.*

"Get set . . . go!"

I bolt out quick.

"Ala. ¡No mames!" Pelon's voice trails off behind me. I think I'm reaching the welding building in first place, but I don't dare look back. A runner never looks back. Only forward.

*Go. Go. Go.* I sprint like he's running right up on me up until my hand touches the red-orange brick walls and I throw my arms up in victory. *YES!*

Pelon shouts, "Sobres. I need a head start next time, ruca!" and comes to a stop, pulling up his jeans that sag under his waist, exposing his white boxers.

In the distance, Isela is jumping up and down cuz she just won $5.

"I gotta go, guys!" I pick up my backpack and run to catch the bus before it leaves without me.

I hop up the steps a few seconds later, making it just in time.

Plopping down in the back of the bus, I sigh and catch my breath. *Close call.*

"Eyy, shh. Chhh," I holler at Tommy, my barrio skater friend, sitting four seats in front of me. "What's up with that?" I lean to the center of the aisle, pointing to the front. I notice Mr. Garcia—our usual bus driver—stepping off the bus, and another person replacing him. I can't make out who it is.

"You missed the announcement. We got a new bus driver today. Mr. Garcia feels bad. His head hurts."

"He's out of the Vicks?" I ask cuz he often says to us kids that gooey gel fixes everything. Headache. Toothache. Cold. Even an injury. You name it.

Tommy replies, "I don't know, but dude . . . he didn't even pull out the Vicks this time, must be gacho bad."

I chuckle even though I know I'm not supposed to.

He keeps going. "Yeah, the new driver is Isela's dad. Seems like he's chill."

*Ay, why didn't Isela warn me?* Now I'm freaking out. "Really?!"

Although Isela is my best friend at school, she's never visited me at my house. Actually. None of my friends outside our barrio have, either. It's prohibited. I think I got it from Ma. She makes me lie whenever Mike, her boyfriend of two years, or her coworkers ask where we live.

The truth is, Ma grew up in the same bare-bones casita her entire childhood and we only moved back when Ma and my father separated when I was three.

I run up to the front of the bus before we pull out of the campus parking lot, and quickly ask, "Hi . . . are you our bus driver today?"

"Kristy, ¿cómo estás?"

*Oh no.* He recognizes me, and now my worst nightmare is minutes away from becoming a reality. He's gonna tell Isela where I live! And maybe she'll think her perception of me was totally off.

This is how I feel each time someone close to me is about to uncover the truth . . .

And the truth is . . . I live in a two-bedroom house with twelve of my family members. There's my tías. My tíos. My abuela. My abuela's abuela. My second cousins. And all the adults except for Ma are unemployed and barely speak English.

Our casita sits on a plot of land that sags deep into the earth like ancient bones crumbling to dust in a neighborhood called Ghost Town, a barrio where clapboard shacks are united by generations of la misma sangre.

"I'm . . . good. Umm." I try to think of something. Anything that can take me off this bus, immediately. But nothing genius comes to mind while I'm in a panic except, "I just moved and now I live like a few blocks from my old house. Just wanna let you know."

He takes out a dust-covered binder resting on the dashboard. "Aver. Aver . . . ," he says, moving his index finger down a list of passenger names and addresses, while my eyes anxiously follow. My pounding heart drops slowly down to my feet.

Pointing at my name and address, I rush to say, "That's not mine anymore. It's different."

With horror, I imagine Isela's dad pulling up to our house and questioning everything about it.

How am I supposed to explain the assortment of animals we

have and how I ended up with three stray dogs, roosters, and even a goose?

Why our front yard looks like a tornado spewed debris across a junkyard? Why my great-grandmother Florencia rocks back and forth in her metal chair barefoot all afternoon with her six-pack of beer, selling our clothes without our consent? Her prices start at $1, but if you're a great haggler, you can take any item for only twenty-five cents. It's how she funds her drinking. And cuz she's drunk and suffers from dementia, she falls often, sometimes splitting her head open. And when she's not in an ambulance or selling our clothes, I'm dodging her flying chancla that she launches at me like a Frisbee when she's upset. What about the old plywood shack in our backyard where Tía hides immigrants cuz she is a coyote?

How could I possibly explain any of this?

Isela's dad grabs his yellow pencil from his chest pocket, turns it upside down, and erases my address. "¿Cuál es ahora?" he asks.

I shrug my shoulders and throw my hands up in the air, "¿Qué sepa? I don't know it. Se me olvidó." *Is it even possible to forget your own address?* "But I'll show you where I live as we get closer . . . ," I explain as I slink backward, away from the front of the bus. Even though I don't know anyone at South Middle who's *rich*, I worry Isela will judge me if she sees where I live.

"Okay. Está bien."

Relieved, I slump in the back seat, thinking about Ma wanting to leave the barrio so we can have a better life. But I don't know if life would be better. Maybe it would be nice to have our own house and even my own room, too. Then I wouldn't have to lie about where I live, and I could invite all my school friends over.

Half an hour later, after the last kid gets off the bus, I make my way to the front again and direct him to the "right" direction. "Allá. Over there. That's where I live now." I point ahead to no house in particular.

"Here! Here! Here!" I pretend he passed it since there's no way a giant yellow school bus could back out when the streets in the barrio are so narrow.

"Le digo a mija you made it home okay. Hasta luego."

"Aww, thanks. Bye!" I jump off the last step of the bus and amble toward the red brick house, the prettiest house in our barrio, wishing Isela's dad would just drive away faster. But the bus idles as he watches me.

I try to think quick on my feet.

*Aha!* I approach "my fake house" and pretend to knock, but I slip and accidentally bump my knuckles on the door. *Please no one answer.*

I wave at Isela's dad, reassuring him everything is good.

"¿Quién buscas? Who are you?" a viejita answers suspiciously.

"Umm . . . Umm . . ." I turn back to the street. Isela's dad has driven off.

"Perdón. Wrong address . . . ," I lie to her, and she slams the door mumbling, "Van a ver, niños." I'm gonna get it. She probably thinks I was one of the cholos playing the ding-dong ditch prank as usual.

Quickly, I turn to walk away. But just as I'm leaving, I hear barking and notice stray dogs coming my way.

It's always the same thing. Running from crazy stray dogs. Usually, I would run to the nearest vehicle, jump on the hood, and wait until someone comes to save my freaking life. But I'm close enough to my house that I just might make it if I run fast enough.

"MAAAAA," I scream at the top of my lungs as I run toward my actual house. By now, Ma should be getting ready to head to work.

She's got a double shift tonight and needs to take inventory. She won't be back home until 5:00 a.m. tomorrow.

I hop our chain-link fence and run past Julietta, Florencia's forty-year-old daughter. I heard family members say she suffered from a neurological disorder, that one day she was celebrating her quinceañera, and the next day she lost some of her ability to communicate.

Eventually, I can't hear the dogs coming after me anymore when I see Julietta out in the front yard. She's known in the barrio for waving at every passing car with her black headphones sitting over her ears, playing her favorite Selena Quintanilla song on repeat.

*Bidi Bidi Bom Bom . . .*

"¡Vamos a bailar! Let's dance." Julietta giggles with her stomach protruding from her Selena T-shirt. She's shaking her hips, shifting her weight from her right foot to her left foot. Julietta is dancing to Tejano music.

I smile, cracking up.

"¡Ay, Kris! I thought something te pasó. ¿Qué tienes? Why were you screaming like a crazy person?" Ma comes rushing out.

I turn to Ma and say, "Those freaking dogs were chasing me again!"

Ma is annoyed that I frightened her para nada. "I left some food for you inside the fridge. I gotta go into work now. I'll call you later to check up on you. You better not get into trouble. Okay?"

"Hmm-hmm." I nod as she hugs me and does the sign of the cross on my face. "On the father . . . the son . . . the holy spirit . . ."

"Amen," I add, kissing her hand softly, knowing that I'm going to stay up real late tonight and eat Hot Cheetos until my stomach hurts.

# THE BARRIO

**It's a Sunday. Ma's only day off from work.**

"Start packing your bags cuz we're moving today," Ma announces in bed like it's nothing.

"Like for real, for real?" I ask in disbelief. Like is it actually happening?

Just two months ago, Ma made it clear at the track meet she really wanted to move us away from Ghost Town.

"Yup!" Ma cheerfully responds. *WOW!* She is really making it happen.

"Oh my god!" My eyes open wide. I jump out of bed, feeling both sad and excited. I gotta say goodbye to everybody in the barrio. I'm out the door in a flash.

For the last time, I ding the cast-iron doorbell hanging on my neighbor's fence.

Tita, who runs a Mexican tiendita for the entire barrio out of her living room, comes out in her usual floral huipil that flows down to her ankles. She hands me my daily snack for one dollar—a strawberry heladito and Flamin' Hots with pickle juice.

"Gracias," I say, licking the edge of my frozen ice pop before it melts in the South Texas heat. "Tita . . . I'm moving today." I reluctantly break the news.

Her chest heaves up as she brushes her gray hair with her fingers, exhaling deeply. "No te olvides de nosotros," she pleads.

Even though Tita is eighty years old, she is known to be mighty strong. Every morning, she carries big buckets of ice and boxes of Mexican candy to run her tiendita. How could I forget her? She's like my third abuelita who adopted Linda, Ma's best friend, after Linda's parents abandoned her.

I shake my head hard. "No. Nunca."

"Kristolla!" Linda storms out in her polo shirt and jeans.

She's the only person in the world who calls me that even though my first name is Elvira. I was named after my father's mother, who I haven't seen or heard from since I was three. And Ma gave me my middle name, Kristelle. Ever since I could remember, Ma has only been introducing me as Kristy.

Sometimes I secretly think Ma wishes I wasn't an Elvira. But so do I. Elvira doesn't even exist.

"Ey, Linda, ya . . . my mom and me are leaving soon," I tell her, trying to eat my snack quickly, making it sound like we're moving to another country. I mean, it might as well be. The north side is a whole different world.

Linda wraps her arms around Tita. "Ay, Kristolla, my mom is gonna miss you so much. Come back to visit her. Don't forget about us. Okay?"

"I'll come visit all the time for reals!" I promise them, feeling sad and remembering the sweltering nights when Ma and I went over to her house to hang out. Tita would be in the living room catching up on her favorite telenovela and Ma, Linda and I would be playing lotería on the front porch until sunrise.

I used to listen to them talk for hours as they shuffled the deck of cards and played their tables for nickles and dimes. Sometimes they bonded over conversations about their biological fathers. About who they were. What they were about and why they weren't in their lives. Other times they strategized for their upcoming basketball tournaments with their friends, a group of young gay women who called themselves Las Machas.

One of my favorite moments from Tita's front porch was watching Las Machas play ball and thinking how cool they were to be themselves and not care what anyone thought about them. To me, the Machas were strong, athletic, and courageous. I wanted to be just like them—fearless.

Tita attempts to speak English, "Comeee . . . back. Ok-ay? I miss you." Her eyes glisten.

"Okay, gotta go, Tita!" I say, tossing the paper cup inside the garbage like a basketball, and sprint away down the street. I gotta hurry to make sure I say all of my goodbyes before Ma says it's time to go.

I make my way to the monte, three blocks away. I come up to a dead end and leap over a railing and into the scrublands. Carefully, I step over cacti and spiny twigs. "Where the heck are you guys?" I yell, surrounded by the thick, sharp brush of the vast desert.

"Hey, negra! Cáele." I hear one of the cholos answer back somewhere out in the monte. Our playground isn't like most. Much of the area is covered with honey mesquite trees that got wicked long thorns that stick out of their branches like bee stingers, easily able to puncture through layers of clothes and skin. It's painful.

I follow his voice and the smell of smoke and find the cholos and my three primos. They're on their bicycles.

"Simon, vatos!" Pancho shouts. "¡A ver quién se atreve!" He's daring anyone who has the guts to launch off their makeshift kicker ramp that they've built using cinder block and plywood. It won't be just any bunny hop. The ramp is right in front of a tree limb they lit on fire so you gotta fly through a cloud of smoke and hope the flames won't burn your ass.

"You guys are super dumb," I say, cringing cuz someone might get hurt.

Pancho, sporting his long Spurs jersey with khaki pants and already a faint brown mustache, says, "Miedosa." He thinks I'm a scaredy-cat.

"Nada que ver." I roll my eyes and say, "I'm moving today, guys."

"Pos, that's good! Maybe you will meet girls who wanna play sports in your new barrio cuz girls can't play with boys here. Don't forget!"

Javi teases me all the time. I've had to deal with it for so long cuz he's my second cousin and lives under the same roof as me.

It used to be him, his two brothers Manuel and George, and both of his parents in the room next to me and Ma. His dad used to be my favorite uncle. But one day Tío Manuel left his family and disappeared. Eventually, everybody found out he secretly fathered kids with different women. We never saw him again.

I thrust my palm inches from his face. "Talk to the hand," I say, giving him the middle finger. *Girls can play with boys!* I think to myself, even though I end up getting hurt all the time.

"Now we don't have to go back for you mensa. You're too slow!" Javi adds, and they all burst into laughter.

It brings me back to last summer, when the flashing lights and sirens rushed into the monte. The cops were after us cuz Javi and the other cholos had broken into an abandoned trailer home on our way back from a baseball game. Most of them had bikes and those who didn't jumped on the diablitos, riding off into the night and leaving me behind on foot to save my own life from la chota. I had to think fast, so I slid my flaca body underneath a car and waited until the coast was clear.

Soon enough, I won't be their accomplice, and Javi won't have to worry about me getting caught up in their trouble anymore.

*Trouble.* This is what has been worrying Ma for years. If we keep living in the barrio, I might end up dropping out of high school, joining a gang, getting into drugs, getting arrested, or getting pregnant before I graduate high school like many kids in our barrio.

"Yeah . . . yeah . . ." I trail off, nodding my head, feeling upset but trying not to show them or else they will call me a crybaby. I turn my back on the smoke and leave the monte, wondering if I'll ever see them again. I spent my entire childhood playing sports with them, learning to stand my ground as a girl and trying to prove to them that I'm tough, too.

Back at home, I wave at Tío Cesar, who's in the backyard making a carne asada. Cesar is Ma's older half brother who used to be in and out of prison. Either for hosting the local cockfights in our back shed or dealing drugs right out front in our yard.

"Hey, flaca," he says, greeting me with one of his iconic gritos while removing his sombrero like a vaquero. "Your abuela is coming out with the tortillero soon."

Myra, my abuela, walks out with the best homemade tortillas in the world. She leans into me, giving me a big smooch. "Móchate. I want many kisses," she demands in Spanish, leaving her thin lips traced on my cheek in bright red lipstick. Today, she's wearing her 1960s go-go style, which includes thick eyeliner, pastel eye shadow, and a bouffant wig. She's known in the family for her colorful, eclectic style that ranges from traditional Indigenous dresses to pencil-thin eyebrows and lace headbands like she's from the 1920s.

Myra places the tortillas on a long wooden table outside and dances to Tío Cesar fiddling with the accordion. He's playing rancheras. "No sé porque tu mamá te quiera llevar . . ." She doesn't know why Ma wants to take me away from here.

I shrug my shoulders, wishing I could explain to her. But I don't think she will understand. I gotta be honest with myself. There's a part of me that is scared to leave. Ghost Town is everything I've ever really known. But at the same time, I've always wondered what it would be like to have my own room, sleep in my own bed, have some privacy, and live in an actual house that isn't falling apart—a house I'm proud to call my home.

To distract myself from the sadness, I yell out for Heary, my goose. "Where are you, pajarito?" That's if he can hear me. I doubt he can. I don't think he has any ears. That's why I named him Hear-y.

*Hraff-Hraff-Hraff.* Here he comes, running from underneath the small trailer in our backyard where my abuela sleeps.

Myra and Tío start to freak out. "Ay, nambe, Kristy. It hurt and bite," my abuela protests in broken English. Everyone in the barrio is scared of Heary and his bright orange, snappy beak cuz he will nibble on your butt when you least expect it. But it's been four years since I got him, and he's become family.

"Take it with you," Tío Cesar dice.

"I wish . . . ," I respond, daydreaming about the day Heary came into my life.

It was on Easter Sunday. My dad scooped me up from Ghost Town and we cruised down to the local ranch that sells dyed Easter pollitos with feathers of all kinds of colors. Pink, green, blue . . . It's a tradition where I'm from.

That's where I met Heary, buried in a pile of pollitos.

I was told he wouldn't live for long. I didn't know why, but I promised to take care of him. Then, on the fourth day, I accidentally dropped Heary in a bucket of water, removing his hair dye. Months went by and he grew bigger and bigger. After a while he started honking out of his narrow beak. It turned out Heary was never a chicken or a hen. He was a goose!

"He's staying in the barrio," I add, wishing Ma would let me bring him with us. But she pushes back every time I ask, saying, "What would people say if we brought this animal to the North Side? We're moving to a civilized place now." Whatever that means.

I say goodbye to Heary along with the rest of our other animals and hop on the trampoline for one last last time.

*I'm a rockeettttttttt.* I shoot up high in the air, above our sagging roof that lets the rain into our home. I spent so many nights on this trampoline, lying on my back, looking up at the stars with my cousin Samantha. She dropped out of eighth grade this year and now she isn't allowed to leave the house. But when we used to hang out, we would stare at the sky for hours listening to the local radio station until we fell asleep. Tío's roosters would wake us up as the sun would start to rise.

"Kris!" Ma yells from inside the house. "What's taking so long? We're leaving in a few minutes. Hurry up."

*I guess this is it.*

My gaze scans the backyard until it stops at our lemon tree, where I have a little ofrenda of my old dog Bubbles. She was my best friend when I was a little. I told her all my secrets. When she died, I had no one to talk to. So I turned to a paper and pen. She inspired me to write my first journal entry.

Suddenly, flashbacks flood in. *I don't wanna leave this place with all these memories.*

There was once a time when me and my primos made some moolah over the summer by offering spooky tours of the barrio at night. We pushed kids in HEB shopping carts while my cousins narrated the history of Ghost Town. According to some elders, our barrio was built on top of an abandoned cemetery and is frequently visited by La Llorona, La Lechuza, and El Chupacabra. Mexico folklore that scared everyone and their abuelas.

Soon, these memories will only be a part of the past.

I walk inside our casita, down our railroad hallway, and to the living room. I count all the pieces of gum stuck on the concrete floor, darkened by time and heavy foot traffic.

"Bye, Julietta . . . I'll come back soon, okay?" She's sitting on the couch where she sleeps looking through the broken windowsill.

"Where going?" Julietta mumbles.

"To my new house."

She sits up, her lips quiver. "Why? This home."

"Cuz I have a new one," I reply, trying to fix the cardboard taped over the cracked window one last time. It's been broken for many years, inviting critters and rainwater into our house as if our casa was Noah's ark.

"And you, you can stop looking at me like that now." I squint at the Virgin de Guadalupe shrine hanging above Florencia's rusty coiled mattress adjacent to Julietta's couch. She's passed out with an empty beer can on her hand.

La Virgin has been a powerful symbol for our household. Every year, our family even hosts the Matachines, with their colorful glass beads and intricately sewn sequins. But I've never felt the magic like everyone around me.

"Kristy!" Ma screams from inside our room.

"I'm coming, hold on!" I shout, rushing back to our bedroom.

"We gotta go. Carry your dolls to the car." Ma has wrapped the porcelain dolls that I've been collecting for so many years. She says someday these dolls will be worth more money than we could ever imagine.

I take my dolls to the car but return to my bedroom one last time.

"Ready? Vamonos." Ma makes it sound like moving is no big deal.

"Almost . . . just one second."

"Are you excited to get your own room soon?" Ma asks, attempting to cheer me up.

I should be happy we're leaving and that I won't have to sleep next to her anymore. We've outgrown our room and our tiny bed.

Ma says we're gonna have a better life on the north side. But what is better? I can always come back, right?

"We gotta go now. Stop taking so long," Ma says, standing at the door.

"Mami, just wait a sec . . . please!" I linger behind, feeling sick.

For a few seconds, I stand there in silence looking around. The room Ma and I have shared for over ten years is now empty.

I take a deep breath, trying to ignore how I feel, and run out the door.

"Lista?" Ma says from the driver's seat, wiping the red lipstick from my cheek.

I slump in the passenger seat. "Mmm-hmm."

We drive away in Ma's Honda. I don't dare turn around and look at our casita. Our familia. Our barrio. Becoming smaller. Farther. Disappearing in the distance.

We pass my dad's place, which is starting to look more and more like an abandoned house with each passing year.

"Have you talked to your dad?" Ma asks. She hasn't spoken to him since we moved out of his house.

"Nah." Back in the day, we used to meet every Sunday for breakfast tacos, but now I hardly ever see or hear from him. I try to forget how things used to be between us. He gets pretty busy working at the oil rigs. "He's probably busy working or something."

"You should call him sometime, Kris."

I nod, saying, "Hmm-hmm." *Why can't he call me?*

"Kris . . . you're gonna love our new house. Just wait until you see your room . . ." Ma changes the subject.

Suddenly, I get a dose of excitement. "Really? Like for sure I'll get my own room?"

"Yup," Ma answers back without a doubt.

I stare out the window, noticing how different the neighborhoods change once we make it to the north side. "The skate park!" I point out. "Honk, Ma! Hurry." It's a habit to honk whenever you drive past the skate park.

"Hey, guys!!!" I yell, sticking my head out the window, and wave to all the skaters.

"Now you'll be closer to your stinky friends," Ma jokes. "Nomas báñate."

I lean back in my seat, slowly starting to feel optimistic about the future.

"Ma, what happened to those girls?" Just a few blocks from the park, there's a group of people congregating on the sidewalk in front of a gas station. They're holding up signs, chanting something I don't know.

*Brenda Cisneros. Yvette Martinez.* Each sign has the name of a girl. Pictures of two young women with the words MISSING are printed on the signs.

"They went missing across the border."

"Why?"

"I don't know, Kris. Why do you ask these questions?" Ma sounds irritated.

"I'm just asking, duh." I glance at the rearview mirror, looking at the sad moms standing there in the sizzling sun. *I hope they're okay.*

We keep driving north, closer to our new house, soon to be our home.

"Whoaaa!" My eyes open wide, "These houses are freakin' huge!" North side neighborhoods have houses that look like museums, with each immaculate home and big yard on display, not a mismatch of unkempt colored shacks and chain-link fences in disrepair.

"We're almost there, mija." I feel Ma's anticipation as we pull into a neighborhood where there's rows of green grass and blooming flowers.

It's nearly silent. Like a ghost town, except it's far from *my* Ghost Town. There are no kids running outside. No carne asadas.

No cumbia music blasting from inside the houses. No gritos. Only manicured lawns and dazzling cars in driveways leading up to enormous houses. How could a neighborhood so quiet feel so loud?

Ma pulls up to a white stucco house and says, "Kris?" distracting me from daydreaming about playing outside with the cholos.

"Yeah?" I turn to Ma as her face lights up.

"This is our new home. Look."

"Oh my god!" I let out. Our new spot is built with arched windows. A stoop leading to the double door entrance. "It's . . . it's amazing, Ma!"

Ma unlocks the door and I run inside mindlessly screaming at the top of my lungs like I just won the lottery. My voice echoes inside the empty house.

"Kristy! Stop screaming. You can't scream like that. The neighbors can hear you."

"Okay. I'm sorry, Amá." I jump silently up and down, opening the stainless steel dishwasher, relieved I don't have to wash dishes by hand. I've never seen one in real life. I mess with the brand-new kitchen sink. It's not like our yellow portable rusty sink we're used to.

"Pick your room, ándale. I'm taking the big one with Mike."

"He's living with us?" I ask, surprised.

"Yes. We bought the house together." That's probably the only way she was able to afford the down payment.

"Fine." I guess. He's been Ma's boyfriend for two years.

I lie on the brand-new beige floor, making carpet angels. I close my eyes, imagining how I'll decorate my room. How I'll rock out when Ma is working. How I'll play the radio super loud. How I'll start my garage band like many of my favorite bands did before they became super famous. All my dreams may actually come true now.

When Ma goes outside to unload our things, I let out a loud screech. "Yes! Woo-HOOO!" My voice fills up the house. Maybe, just maybe, our new life will be the best damn thing to ever happen to me.

# NORTH SIDE

**"Do you want to end up homeless?"**

"No," I reluctantly reply. *I don't wanna end up on the streets, but I also don't wanna end up in jail for breaking in. I mean, is it illegal to break into your own house?*

Ma nods at her hands stacked on top of each other like a cheerleader spotter ready to lift a flier. "Then? What are you waiting for?"

I look up at my bathroom window five feet above our heads. It's tiny. Not sure if I can squeeze in without removing one of my ribs.

"I'm ... I'm ..." I look back at our neighbor's two-story house terrified—their windows overlook where we're standing. I hope they don't think Ma is out of her mind for sending me climbing up the wall.

"Ugh! Fineeee," I give in.

I lift my left knee up high, placing my foot on her palms. Taking a deep breath, I try to overcome my fear of heights. *"Squeeze your belly. Make it Tight. Don't panic. Breathe."* I recall my cheer coaches' words every time I was a flyer.

I begin the count, "5 ... 6 ... 7 ... 8 ... 1 ... 2 ..." On the count of *three, four,* I press my foot down on Ma's cupped hands and pop up high in the air. My right leg wobbles a little as it hangs in the air. *Stick it!* I try to balance without collapsing down to the ground.

"Reach!" Ma orders. Her arms at full extension as my fingertips skim the cracked open windowsill.

"I got it. I got it," I say, looking below, then sliding the window fully open.

Ma's barely able to say, "Pull, mija." Her arms are trembling.

I struggle to lift myself upward, banging and scratching my knees against the stucco wall. With all my strength, I manage to pull up and rest my elbows on the window frame. My feet dangle while I take a breath and rest my ribs on the sill.

I peer inside our house. It's a big leap, and it makes my heartbeat fast. "Too high, Ma. I can't."

Ma grunts. "Nothing is too high, goddammit. Just jump, Kris!"

I force a breath out, and I take Ma's orders. *I can do it.* The fear of being kicked out. Without our stuff. Ending up on the streets, homeless—it's too much for me to think about. So I push off my toes against the wall and wiggle my torso upward.

"Good job!" Ma says as I slide my body inside my bathroom.

Just an hour ago, I took a long, hot shower. It's one of my favorite things about living here. Gone are the days when Ma needed to boil water in a giant menudo pot just so I can have a warm rinse.

"I'm in!" Like a cat, I land on my feet and sprint to the front door, letting Ma in.

"Help me look for the keys." Ma misplaced her set somewhere in this giant house.

"Okay . . . but I really gotta go to school. I'ma be super late," I remind her in case she's forgotten school starts in a few minutes.

"We're not leaving until we find the keys!" Ma insists.

Lately, Ma has been reluctantly driving me back and forth to South Middle, an hour-long round trip. But I refuse to attend one of these North Side schools near our new home.

"Like I said . . ." Ma is really frustrated right now.

I guess it makes perfect sense.

Earlier this morning when we were halfway to school and Mike was on his way to work, he called her cell. He told Ma we weren't allowed to return and locked the doors. I don't know what's going on, all I know is that it can't be good.

"Ma? Do we have to move again?"

"No! We aren't going to be kicked out of our own home. As if . . ." Ma reassures me everything will work out.

"Pero why can't we just go back to Ghost Town? I don't wanna be here." This place doesn't feel like home anymore.

Not when I gotta turn on the radio on full blast, hide in the closet, cover my ears, and pretend I can't hear Ma and Mike during their screaming matches.

No matter how nice this house is or how hot the showers are, it will never feel like home if Mike and Ma always fight, and he doesn't want us here. Even if our casita in the barrio was always falling apart and breaking. Like the front doorknob. The fridge. The windows. The roof. The walls. At least it was everyone's house. It didn't belong to nobody. Everyone was welcome.

"Because we can't! I worked too hard for this. Don't you under-stand?" Ma feels I don't appreciate her, but I just wish she kept her promises. It was just supposed to me and her.

For the next few days, Ma anchors us inside the house like we're glued to the floor. The fights don't stop and I find myself back in a dark closet, wishing they could be happy again.

Then one day, everything changes. I hear Ma screaming and I can't take it anymore.

"UGH!!!" I tear out from my hiding place, charging toward Mike. "Stop! You better fucking leave my mom alone."

"Go back to your room!" Ma tries to hold me back. But I'm seeing red.

"Nooooo!" I run toward her boyfriend, pushing past Ma like an angry bull. But he's bigger and stronger. His body is like steel, and somehow I end up on the ground.

"Don't you EVER touch my daughter!" Ma has had enough.

She locks us in the bathroom and tells me, "Pack your bags. We're leaving right this second."

Not long after, we end up in a two-bedroom apartment much closer to the skate park. I can literally walk there.

"This is much better, right? Now it's really just you and me." Ma smiles as she signs the lease agreement.

It's the last week of seventh grade and I'm running late to school.

"Wake up!" I shake Ma. She's fallen asleep on the couch wearing her work apron that smells of stale cigarette smoke. I know she got home really late and stayed up drinking with her coworkers in our living room.

"Ma! Hurry. I'm gonna be late!" I shake her again, annoyed.

"Kris, take the car. Drive yourself."

"I can't drive."

"You already know how to drive," Ma says, half asleep.

Yeah, I do. She taught me how last year. But I only know how to drive to the corner store and back. Not to the other side of town! And I'm just *thirteen*! If I get caught, I will be sent to the local juvenile detention center. *No thanks.*

"MA! Please ..."

I don't know what's up with her lately.

Maybe she's depressed cuz of the breakup with Mike, but that was a few months ago. Or maybe she's stressed cuz someone apparently took out a credit card under her name and spent thousands of dollars and she can't afford to pay the bill. Or maybe she's just tired of working double shifts. Who the heck knows? Ma hardly tells me anything when it comes to her feelings.

"C'mon, Ma. It's my last week of school. And today is my field trip. We're going to Six Flags." I nudge her hard, trying not to move her too much from my excitement.

"I'm tired," Ma drowsily says. "I can't be driving you all the way over there anymore, Kris."

I know it's far to drive to the south side, and I feel bad Ma has to spend all this time driving me around, but I'm not the one who made us move here. I already left Ghost Town, I don't want to have to leave my school and all my friends, too. Especially when I'm close to finishing middle school. Plus, Isela warned me that the fresas from the north side will call me a naca, a low-class, poorly educated person if I moved there.

After I bug Ma for a few minutes, she sighs and finally gets up with her mascara smeared under her puffy eyes and shuffles to the car.

"Remember to stick with your friends when you get there. Don't walk alone."

"Duhhh. I know. I'm not dumb."

"You just never know ..." Ma makes it sound like someone is going to kidnap me in the middle of a crowded theme park.

I stare out the window, checking to see if any of my friends who live near school are walking there now.

"Ma, mira." I point at yellow tape that barricades a house just across from campus, bloodstains splattered on the driveway. Police scope it out like a crime scene.

"Ay, something bad happened," Ma says while I feel a tight knot inside my throat.

"That's Rodrigo's house!" He's gotta be at school by now, though. We're supposed to be partners on the bus later today.

When Ma stops at campus, she does the holy cross on me like it'll shield me away from harm. "Don't forget your prayers, okay?"

"Mmm-hmm, bye!" I rush to band hall, where the room is full, but the air feels colder than usual. It's awfully quiet.

"Did you hear what happened?" one of our band members turns to me to ask.

I shake my head. "No, dude . . . what happened?"

"Big Bear got shot. He's dead." I drop my book bag. Cover my mouth. I can't breathe. I can't think.

The rest of the day at Six Flags is a blur, like my brain erased it all. When I get home, Ma calls me from work to check in on me.

"Ma, I wanna move schools."

"What? Are you sure, Kris?" Maybe Ma is right. The north side could be a better fit for us. I could become a cheerleader, excel in school and sports. Live the life Ma always wanted for me, a life of opportunities.

"Yeah. For reals." I need a fresh start.

I'm moving on, away from everything and everyone I've ever known.

PART II
# THE KIDNAPPING

# GROUNDED

Ma is frantic.

Three pairs of stilettos. Seven dresses in different colors. Two fake Louis Vuitton handbags and a bunch of costume jewelry, scattered in every direction. Ma has managed to turn our living room into an explosion of multiple dressing rooms.

"I just can't decide what to wear," she admits, pacing back and forth and looking at me as if I'm her personal stylist.

I shrug my shoulders and arch my eyebrows. "Just wear whatever." I'm not actually paying attention. I'm too busy daydreaming about starting my freshman year at Anderson High School. That's just four weeks away. Soon, I'll meet new skating friends. Well, that's if I get home at a decent hour from cheerleading practice.

Twenty minutes later, she sucks in her belly and pouts her brown lips. "How does the length look?" Ma finally decides to go with a little black dress.

I give her a half-hearted thumbs up with a lopsided smile. "Cool!"

"Never mind, then," she says, rolling her eyes cuz she knows I'm not really helping.

It's true. I'm not the best daughter to ask about style. I've learned to keep my personal thoughts on what to wear to myself. There hasn't been a single time where I gave Ma my honest take on style and she didn't sigh and say, "No sé porque te pregunté." She doesn't know why she bothered to ask.

I dress like a "freak" according to the girls on my cheer team at my new high school—Anderson High. I just really love wearing my wristbands, studded belts, and pink clip-on extensions. It hurts to feel like an outcast because of what I wear. But I won't give in to what they say just to fit in.

"Help me feed your brother, ándale," Ma says, grabbing a baby bottle from the refrigerator and stuffing it into the diaper bag. Meanwhile, Rafael, my four-month-old brother, begins furiously crying.

She snaps her fingers at me. "Vamos. We gotta go." I can feel her frustrations growing even more now that Rafael is screaming, but I don't budge.

"Chinga, we gotta leave in ten minutes. We can't be late." She makes it sound like we're never late. Actually, we're always late. Where I'm from, punctuality is rare. It's not rude to be late. When you say you're on your way, you might as well warn everyone that you've sent that memo an hour ahead just in case. But even then, we're the last people to show up anywhere. Ma is also always one of the last to leave. She and her friends talk mucho chisme. I think both tardiness and gossiping should be a local sport. And if that ever happened, Ma would be crowned a champion.

"You think I don't know that?" I sass, hoping she'll ground me. "I don't even know why you wanna go across. It's not safe there anymore." The reception is just a few blocks over the International Bridge that separates the Mexican and US border.

Long before our local newspaper began to publish articles about the Drug War, Ma and I used to visit across all the time. There was La Feria, the Mexican version of carnivals. There was our favorite park along the Rio Grande, where Ma would snap photos of me with her Kodak camera. There were Ma's dentist appointments where she could afford her braces since they were half the price compared to back home. Now everyone and their mothers around town know it's not like how it used to be.

Every single day, we are reminded of violence surging through our sister city of Nuevo Laredo, Tamaulipas. Drugs. Shoot-outs. Cartels. Kidnappings. The violence is so horrific that their last police chief was executed the first day on the job. All of which has made Ma think twice about traveling across for all the fun stuff we used to do. For some reason though, wedding receptions are safe? *I guess.*

Ma says it's not like anything could really happen to us. Bad things only happen to people caught up in illegal activities, and she would never break the law. She even likes to scare me by saying that if I ever commit a crime, "Tu vida va estar over. F-O-R-E-V-E-R." I don't know if she finds joy scaring the hell out of me, but that's what stops me from getting into any kind of trouble.

"It's fine, Kris." Ma scoffs at me.

I really don't want to go. Plus, the idea of driving across the Rio Grande and over the border into Mexico to celebrate her coworker's wedding sounds like such a waste of time. I honestly could care less about these people getting hitched, or anyone getting hitched, really. I mean, what's the point? Ma says I'm amargada, but I swear to God I'm not bitter. It all feels like a big theatrical show that a family puts on for friends. It's a show-who-has-the-biggest-wedding. To me, it feels too rehearsed. Not authentic. And I've heard on the radio that half of married couples end up divorced. I mean, more than half of my friends are raised only by their mothers.

"Amá, I hate weddings . . . ," I admit. Maybe I am just jaded, cuz all of this makes me feel like love isn't real. Anyway, I'd much rather skateboard than go to any wedding. ". . . And I just don't feel like going."

"You don't ever want to do anything anymore." Ma sighs, exasperated.

"So?" I tug at my hair and roll my eyes. She's right, though I won't tell her that. I guess I'm still hung up on the idea that nothing has gone according to plan. Back in Ghost Town Ma promised me we would live in a house as soon as we leave. Just us. No one else. And now we live in a small apartment, and I have a new family—my brother's dad's family. I don't even think they like us. The truth is I really think Ma just wants to fit in with a different family than the one we grew up with back in the barrio.

"Come on, Kristy. Let's go! You don't have an option."

"Nambe, why don't you ask your new family? I don't wanna go." I slam the door to my bedroom, lock the door, and crank the stereo to the highest volume.

Ma's heavy footsteps reach my door. She rattles the doorknob and shouts, "You are grounded if you don't come out right now!"

"Whatever. ¡No me importa!" I scream back. I'm totally okay with being grounded.

"Fine!" she relents. I envision her throwing up her hands and surrendering. "If you're gonna stay back, you better be home when I call you! Si no . . ." She walks out the door with a warning.

Ma is the type of mother who routinely conducts check-in calls.

Like, sometimes she'll call several times during her shift. She's the type of mother who calls to let me know when she's coming home, and she calls to tell me she's staying out longer. She's the type of mother who worries so much it's *annoying*. As if anything will happen to me. *Nothing bad* ever happens to me.

I peek out the window, checking to see if Ma is gone. *Woo-HOO!* I grin and run through the apartment, scrambling to find a pair of matching long white sock socks, an oversize sweatshirt, baggy pants, and torn boxers that I borrowed from my friend Tigro.

Minutes later, I pull my hoodie over my long brown hair that's tucked in behind my sweatshirt. I grab my skateboard and head out the door to the skate park, which is about a mile away.

Walking on broken sidewalks down McPherson Street, I swing my arms wide. I pinch my chin up. I square my shoulders. I straighten my spine. I take longer strides. I need to look and act as manly as possible. Or else I might attract some creepy men who could pull up and say, *Chh-chh . . . Needa ride, kid?* and I'd have to make a run for it.

I hear my shallow breathing as cars zoom past me, worrying about the time I nearly got pulled into a stranger's car. I was alone when a black sedan rolled up and stopped beside me. A man got out of the car, trying to convince me to get inside. I fled to the nearest house, pretending it was my own. It was the last time I wore shorts and a tank top at night. I never told Ma cuz if I did, she would never let me walk alone again.

*I'm a boy. I'm strong. I'm invisible.* The last person anyone would try to abduct is someone who looks like trouble. When I see the lights of the park, relief sweeps over me, and I sprint the rest of the way.

"Ey, Kristy! Wassup . . ." I'm excited to hear my friends Tigro,

Tommy, and Jerry greet me with open arms. They're super cool. I feel like I can be myself around them. They don't treat me any different even though I'm the only girl that skates here. I feel like this is where I belong.

"Let's play a game of skate!" I say, challenging the boys.

I come in last place, but they don't talk any trash. Plus, I kicked most of their asses at a skate competition last summer. I came in second and won some badass purple trucks.

We skate for a couple of hours and jam out to hip-hop and punk music. The air cools my sweaty skin as I kick and push, gliding across the park. I practice my favorite trick, the kickflip body varial, over and over again. I have no regrets about skipping the wedding for this.

Suddenly, Tigro yells, "Runnnnn!!!" Flashing red and blue lights flood the park, forcing us to scatter into the night. I hide underneath a quarter pipe with a few other skaters. Apparently, a new midnight curfew is being enforced for the first time ever.

"Shhh. Be quiet. Don't move . . . ," Tommy whispers as we huddle on top of each other like sardines in a can. I'm trying to hold my breath, but the stench of sweat and body odor invades my nostrils. Ma was right. *We freakin' stink.*

The beams from la chota's flashlights expose our hiding place.

"Go! Go! Go!" I yell, and we sprint off again, shouting at the police to leave us alone.

My friends run one way toward the ditch, where it's dark and full of bats and creepy noises. I dash for home with my skateboard in my hand. I make it back home safely and quickly check the caller ID. I'm nervous Ma has already completed her check-in call. Thankfully, she hasn't yet. *Hallelujah.*

I heat up some bean-and-cheese tacos and eat them in my

bedroom. I write in my journal, feeling like this is the best summer of my life. All I want to do is skate all day, every day. I place the house phone under my pillow. Ma should be calling any second now. And when she does, I'll just pretend like I've been home all night. For all she knows, I've been at home safe and sound, grounded until she gives me back my freedom.

# SOMETHING BAD

*Bang. Bang. Bang.*

I duck my head underneath the sheets. *Who is that? What is that?*

"Ma-mi?" I say out loud, scared. No one ever knocks after midnight. I try a second time. "Ma?" Nada. I peek my head out of the sheets, just enough my eyes can read the clock hanging on the wall.

It's 2:35 in the morning. *What the heck?* Ma never fails to announce when she's come back home. I check the phone and scroll through the missed call log just in case I didn't hear a call. Maybe Ma called to say she forgot the keys to the apartment. Or something.

*Nope.*

No missed calls. No voice messages. It's not like her.

The loud thuds are coming from my bedroom window, and I spot a dark shadow. It's standing . . . very still. I can't make sense of the silhouette. It's tall. Wide. It sure doesn't look like Ma's curvy body.

Instantly, my throat gets tight, and my heart palpitates. *What did Ma say if a stranger ever knocked and she wasn't home? Don't open the door.*

*Bang! Bang! Bang!*

The sharp sounds force me out of my bedroom and straight into the kitchen, clutching the house phone to my chest. *C'mon. C'mon.* I punch in Ma's cell phone number as fast as I can. But my fingers aren't moving as fast as my brain is thinking. *Answer. The. Phone. Por favor, Amá.*

"Leave a voice message after the tone," Ma's voicemail comes on.

I dial again, and again.

My fingers tremble cuz my call won't go through, and the stranger outside our apartment keeps knocking louder and harder.

"Mamiiii," I cry out between my short, shallow breaths.

I whisper into the phone speaker, "¿Dónde estás? Come. Hurry. Someone's pounding on the door. I'm so scared. Please. I need you."

The knocks have transitioned from my bedroom window to the front door, and I think I'm going to faint. *Maybe someone followed me home from the skate park.*

*Check who it is.* I dare myself to scope out who it may be.

I have a bad feeling in my gut, kinda like when I feel like my life could be in danger. Like walking alone in the dark where I usually can escape and run. But how will I be able to run if danger is standing directly in my path? It's like the beginning of a horror movie. It feels like a trap, but Ma always says, "the only way to overcome fear is to face it."

I walk over to the front door and stand on my tiptoes. I look through the tiny peephole. *If it's an intruder, I need to dial 911.*

"Oh my god! Seriously?!" I exclaim, annoyed and relieved.

It's Javi—my cousin. He's in his boxers, looking at me like he's seen a ghost.

"Dude, what the heck is wrong with you? You scared me!" I say, swinging the door open.

Javi and I haven't seen each other in almost a year. We didn't even have a proper goodbye when I last saw him in the monte. And he's like a brother. Ma basically raised him right alongside me. But once we started fresh on the north side, we slowly drifted away from our family in the barrio. Since then, things have changed.

Samantha got pregnant at fifteen and now she and Javi have both dropped out of school. To make matters worse, Javi has moved on from petty crimes to more serious ones. He's been in and out of juvenile. Ma says if he doesn't change his ways, he might end up in prison in a few years. I think Ma feels like she failed them and she's worried if we remain close, the same things could happen to me.

"Hey, ummm . . ." is all Javi says.

I roll my eyes and walk over to edge of our balcony, gripping the rusting green railing. I can barely see Tía's car parked beneath a broken lamppost. She's in there, sitting alone in the dark. "Tíaaaa!" I wave her down, wondering why they're here.

Her head pops out the window. "¿Te dijo?"

I turn to Javi to ask, "Tell me what?"

He looks at the ground, his chin presses down his chest. He says something. But I can't really hear him. "Huh?" I nudge his shoulder. I don't think I heard him correctly.

"I said something bad happened to your mom," he blurts out in a single breath.

"Bad?"

"Yeah, really bad," he says flatly.

"Like just really bad? Or bad bad?"

"What's the difference?" Javi asks, looking confused.

I make a hissing sound and sigh, "Ayyy, never mind. Why do you try to freaking scare me all the time?"

"But . . . ," he tries to say before I interrupt him.

"Ugh. I bet she's fine. Stop playing with me. It's not funny." Maybe Ma twisted her ankle. Maybe her car broke down. Nothing bad bad can actually happen to Ma.

"I'm not," Javi replies in a serious tone.

"How? My mom is with Rafael. She's super careful around the baby."

"Your mom came to our trailer to drop him off before she went across. He's there."

Tía honks the horn and shouts, interrupting us. "Vámonos. Take her. We gotta go. Right. Now."

"We're leaving!" he urges me out the door without letting me know what he's talking about.

"Wait . . . ," I try asking but Javi and Tía are acting strange, and now they want to take me away? "Where to?" I fumble with my words as Javi grabs me by the arms, pulling me downstairs.

But he won't answer me. We just dart down the stairwell so fast I feel like we could tumble down and break a bone. It's as if we're fleeing the danger we used to face in Ghost Town, back when police sirens and javelinas in the monte chased us.

We make it to the bottom of the stairs unscathed and I jump into the back seat of Tía's beat-up truck. Javi hops in the front, and within seconds, he passes out snoring. If he's able to fall asleep, it must not be that serious. Right?

Tía says nothing. She just pulls out of the driveway and drives like a maniac.

As we pass through each uneven intersection, the back of the trunk rattles. It gives an eerie sound, and I don't like it. I'm getting a little panicky, especially when Tía's eyes drift to the rearview mirror ever so often. Her dark brown eyes are written with sadness. It's like she's telling me something, but what?

Instead of asking her questions, I just sink into the back seat and try to undo this lump in my throat that feels like it's grown to the size of a watermelon. Soon enough, I won't be able to breathe.

Fifteen minutes later, we arrive on the same block where Tía's new trailer home is located.

"Allá están," Tía says, pointing to the right side of her trailer home.

There's a crowd of people standing on her front porch. All dressed up for a night out. Short miniskirts. High heels. Long-sleeve polo shirts. Cowboy hats and snakeskin, leather boots.

I squint my eyes. I recognize them. They're Ma's coworkers from the bar who would've been at the wedding with Ma.

"What are they doing here?" They must know where Ma is.

Tía doesn't answer, so I get out of her truck and walk straight into the crowd.

"Hey!" I speak.

They turn around. Their mouths drop wide, unsure what to say or do with me.

"Dile."

"No, you tell her."

"Oh my god, it's Kristy." I can hear a couple of whispers in the back. *Do they know that I can literally hear everything?*

Everyone seems to be talking in secrecy, but no one is saying exactly what happened to Ma.

"Where's my mom? Why are you guys here?"

"Kristy!" Vivian, one of Ma's coworkers, pushes through the crowd.

She reels me toward her muscular body, squeezing me so hard, way too tight for my scrawny body. I shy away and try to let go, but Vivian manages to hold me tight. "What's happening?" I demand an answer, noticing dark circles under her almond-shaped hazel eyes.

Vivian's hands shake. I can feel her pulse pounding. "I'm sorry. I'm sorry," she keeps repeating. She's freaking out.

"What? Why? Tell me!" *Why won't anyone answer me?*

Vivian says, "It happened across. After the wedding reception."

I start shaking my head and try to back away from her. "What happened?"

"There were men in masks. Maybe four or five. All dressed in police uniforms." Vivian bursts into sobs.

Immediately, I recall the stories like this in the newspaper. Corrupt policemen or cartels impersonating la chota across the border, pulling people over. Kidnapping them. Then they force the victim's family and friends to pay a ransom—or else they make people disappear forever.

I interrupt her, "Did you guys pay them?"

"No. We couldn't."

"Why?" I start to freak out.

Vivian makes a gun sign with her hands, then points her index finger directly at her skull, and says frantically, "Because they had us at gunpoint."

I cover my mouth, unable to say another word.

"I smacked the guy who put a gun to my head and ran. Your mom tried to do the same but . . ." Vivian begins trembling. "She didn't escape. They caught her."

"I can't . . ." I just shake my head at her. I'm having trouble understanding if this is real.

Vivian continues, "She was screaming for help like crazy. Then, when gunshots went off, I couldn't hear her anymore."

I feel in my heart that, if any of this is true, I am certain that I'll die. I tug at Vivian's long arm as she towers over me. "Are you playing?" She's barely able to nod or stand still without quivering, and this is when it finally hits me. I'm living a nightmare.

"No, párale! Please. Stop!" I beg, shaking my head, *no, no.* How could this be real life? My heart feels like it stops for a moment. Then it starts pounding, harder than ever, pounding inside of me like it wants to burst out of my chest.

I can barely hear Vivian talking. "Sorry I didn't go back to help her. I thought they were gonna shoot me. I didn't wanna die. Please forgive me . . ." A stream of her tears lands on my skin.

All I can think about is that Ma is dead and now I'm gonna be orphaned. And so is Rafael. *Life isn't fair.*

A long and loud shriek escapes from my mouth. Noises I never thought were capable of coming out of me. I stomp the ground three times like I want the earth to crack open and swallow me whole. The world beneath me crumbles.

"Mami!" I scream into my hands and cover my face. My hands tremble. My head spins. My knees buckle. I hunch forward, holding on to my stomach. I feel like I got sucker punched. *Help me!* I feel like I'm dying.

# MISSING

**I lock myself in Tía's bathroom and weep.**

*Mami, are you there? You said you'd make a sign if you died. Show me, please.* Years ago, Ma swore to God she'd make a sound to let me know she's watching over me like an angel. *Just make a sound but don't scare me.* I close my eyes for a second. Tune in to every sound.

Silence.

My hands press together in prayer and plead, "Please, Amá, answer me. I promise I'm gonna believe in a god if you come back. Next time, I'll even come with you anywhere, and I won't sneak out. I'll behave. Just come home. Don't leave me."

"Kristy!" I hear my name and my eyes pop open.

But it's just Tía saying, "Abra la puerta. Unlock the door."

"I'm in the toilet. Wait . . ." *Stop crying*, I tell myself. *No one can see you cry.*

With the back of my hand, I wipe my tears and tap the bottom of my eyes a couple of times. I've read that's how you stop your eyes from getting all big and swollen. I don't wanna scare Tía with my sad, drooling sobs.

Tía jiggles the doorknob. "You need to come out, ándale," she whispers through the door.

"One second . . ." My face is looking a lot worse. Now my cheeks are turning red. *Stop.*

"Pos es que some detectives are outside. They're asking for you," Tía announces.

I come out of the bathroom hoping no one can see the terror in my eyes.

"Hello. I'm Mr. Rodriguez and this is my partner, Mr. Martinez." Two men in black polo shirts and blue jeans greet me in Tía's living room, under the dim, flickering light.

"Ummm . . . ," I reply, wondering if they are who they say they are. *Show me your badge. Who do you work for? Are you really law enforcement agents? Then why are you wearing jeans? Shouldn't you be in uninforms? How can I trust anybody?* "Hi . . ." I look at my feet instead of their eyes. I don't ask anything cuz maybe that's only in movies and I'll look dumb if I do.

"You're gonna have to come with us . . . ," Martinez says, pointing at the front door.

Moments later, Rafael and I end up in the back seat of an unmarked car. I caress Rafael's soft, wrinkly palm. His reflex grabs on to my thumb. Weirdly, his touch makes me feel less alone. *We're in this together, brother.*

We all make it up to our apartment, and quickly, Rodriguez and Martinez storm inside like two robbers in the night.

"Miss Gonzalez, where's your mom's bedroom?" one of the detectives asks, and I point to the hallway that connects both Ma's and my room. They are on opposite sides. Just eight feet apart. Way too close for my liking.

I crane my neck to peer in Ma's room to see what they're up to. I mean, what could they possibly find that will help figure out what happened to Ma?

"Find anything?" I dare to ask. My question makes Martinez jump. I caught him off guard. He struggles to keep Ma's jewelry box in his hands, but it slips and crashes on our tile floor, shattering into tiny pieces. All of Ma's fake pearls scurry to all corners of the bedroom like silverfish.

"My mom is gonna be so pissed!" I blurt out. Ma hates when I mess with her things cuz too often I accidentally break them or forget to put them back.

Instantly, I drop to my knees and cup as many beads as my hands can hold on to, never dropping one. The detectives stand there, unsure how to react. It doesn't even matter what they say or what they don't. I can't hear a word cuz all I can think about is Ma and her favorite broken necklace. I gather all the pieces into the living room and try to put them back together while the detectives ransack Ma's bedroom.

I carefully pick them up one by one. Maybe it's a way for me to distract myself from my own apartment turning into one of those crime investigations like on TV. The thought of Ma ending up on an episode makes me wanna puke.

Now they're looking through our living room. Then the kitchen. Then the bathroom. One of the men approaches me and asks question after question: "Do you remember what your mom was wearing? Anything out of the ordinary before she left? Did she call you?"

"I don't know. I can't remember," I repeat over and over, while I imagine digging into my brain, trying to find the answers. All of a sudden, it's like my brain isn't working properly. Looking around my apartment doesn't help either. It's a mess. Furniture drawers removed. Papers scattered on the ground. Receipts from Ma's purchases gathered in a pile. Old mail and Ma's address book opened.

I don't know why, but I start pacing back and forth. All I can hear are voices in my head telling me I should be doing something. Not just standing still listening to these men interrogating me.

"Please sit," Rodriguez asks. I think I'm making them nervous.

I gaze at Rafael. He's still strapped in his car seat. I walk over toward him and caress his face. *It's just you and me, little brother. I won't leave you alone, promise.* His eyelids flutter. I've woken him up. He's starting to cry.

"I gotta feed him, sir. He's probably hungry," I say to one of the detectives as I microwave the last bottle of milk that Ma prepared for him yesterday.

"Drink up, baby," I whisper into Rafael's ear, and try to hold the bottle in the same angle Ma does it every time. When Rafael slips back into a sleep coma after his meal, Rodriguez says he needs to be up-front with me. I hope he's gonna say they've got an idea. *Please, just don't say my mom is dead. Just not that.*

"Tú sabes bien how bad things are over there, right?" I nod and wait impatiently for the rest, but he asks me another question instead. "Do you know why your mom traveled *across*?"

"She went across cuz her coworker Carlo got married, and the reception was over there." I shoot him straight, true answers.

He presses me even further. "Why didn't you go with her?"

I wonder if I should tell them the truth or a partial truth. I just don't think they'll understand why I was mad at Ma. "She grounded me." I worry they can sense I'm not divulging the entire truth.

"What for?"

"Cuz ..." I pause and look over my shoulder to see Rafael. Ma's voice makes its way into my head. *You're so unappreciative. Why can't you just help me a little more with your brother?*

Ma and I are more like sisters, so it's normal for us to get into heated arguments. I feel guilty our last interaction was so bad. I wish I could take it all back now.

"I didn't feel like going with her. I suck at dancing cumbias," I lie. Accordion, tamboras, and maracas are engrained in my DNA. I was born to dance in a looping rhythm.

"Can you guys just tell me where she is?" I beg them.

"Here's the thing, Miss Gonzalez," Rodriguez says, keeping me on the balls of my feet, uncertain where any of this is heading.

"We don't actually know where your mother is, pero we do suspect that she's been kidnapped or by now ..." He pauses and inhales before saying that she could be dead.

I squeeze my eyelids shut. *I'm dreaming. I'm dreaming. I'm dreaming. No, she can't be kidnapped or dead.* Disturbing images flood my imagination. Maybe Ma's somewhere in a rural part of Mexico. Hostage. Scared for her life. What if Ma's eyes are wide open? She's lifeless. Her beautiful, long hair covered with dirt and maggots eating her smooth, brown skin. I know I shouldn't be imagining horrible things, but I can't help it. They just hijack my thoughts like kidnappers do. I hide my eyes with the seams of my T-shirt and begin to cry.

"But why? Why us?" I ask, even though I don't believe these men could give me these answers, despite how it works in movies. "Can't you guys call the Mexican government?" I say. What good is this investigation if they aren't doing the best they can?

Martinez doesn't hesitate to answer my question. "No. It's a huge mess over there, *mija*," he replies, calling me like I'm his daughter. *¿Mija?* I could be orphaned. How dare he call me that. I purse my lips together, and I think he can tell I'm bothered.

"Sorry, we can't trust the government to help us over there," Martinez explains even further to me.

"Y do you know if your mom had any friends that seem como out of the ordinary o no?" Rodriguez asks.

"Like?"

"Like did anyone stand out?"

"No," I reply. I can't think of anyone. That's cuz Ma has a lot of different friends. Mostly from the bar. She's been in the bar industry for a decade. She meets a lot of people as a bartender. The last bar she worked at, before Rafael was born, was just down the road from the International Bridge, where a lot of businesses are located. The perfect cantina where both locals and visitors could pop in for a beer and live music. Ma doesn't have enemies at work. At least not that I know of.

"Why would anyone wanna hurt my mom?"

The detectives mumble something underneath their breaths. And then, seeing my confusion, Rodriguez chimes in a little louder, "Mexico is a cartel battlefield . . . and now it's happening here, too."

Instantly, Rodrigo's death and all the recent front-page headlines about cartels flash in my mind. He's right. "But what's that gotta do with my mom?"

Martinez pulls out the last unopened kitchen drawer. "We're try-ing to figure out if your mom had any involvement with what's hap-pening across. Your mom has a lot of friends. Many different friends."

He comments with a get-a-hint tone. I'm baffled he would insinuate that. That's not my mom. *"What?"*

Both men turn to each other and respond, "You just never know. People get caught up in the wrong crowds these days."

I shake my head immediately. "She's not involved. My mom would never do that. I know her." I do. I live with her. They don't know my mom the way I do.

"I understand. You're probably right." Rodriguez evaluates what I've said, but then reiterates, "Pero we just can't make a conclusion ahorita. That's all we're saying."

"She's my mom. She would never get involved in that kind of stuff!" I say out loud, assertive on the outside, but secretly doubting everything I know about Ma.

*My own mother? What if she's been living a double life? Was the bar a front? What if one of her customers was involved with a cartel? What if she was framed? What if someone put drugs in the car she was in?*

Martinez looks around the apartment for things he might have missed, and passively says, "We just want to rule out that possibility." *No.* My mom saved every penny so we could move out of our casita in Ghost Town. They're *wrong.*

"But we will make sure you and your brother are okay," Rodriguez tells me.

He looks over at Rafael "I *am* making sure he's fine." I'm his big sister, and I'm not gonna let anything happen to him. Rafael is my job. But: "What if you guys travel to Mexico and look for her yourselves?" Surely this will make more sense than relying on any corrupt Mexican authorities.

"We don't have jurisdiction across."

"What's jurisdiction?"

Martinez explains that it means they just can't go across the border and look for her. My nose flares, and my fists clench. *Fuck jurisdiction.*

In the back of my mind, I can hear Ma's pep talks—the ones she's always given me, going back to my first race in first grade. *Go and win.* It never mattered to Ma if I was racing against eleven-year-old girls as a six-year-old, or if I was competing in a skateboarding competition against a field of boys, Ma would never let me back down.

I feel a surge of adrenaline flooding my veins. It makes me feel invincible. If I could just run to the same location where Ma was last seen, maybe I'd discover clues about her disappearance. Maybe I will be the one to find her. "If you guys can't find my mom, then I will!" I slam my fists down on the table.

"Sit. Sit. Just sit." Both men hold me down by the shoulders, insisting I calm down.

How can I? I won't. They can make me sit. They can keep me quiet, but I won't calm down.

Not until Ma comes back home.

# MAN ON FIRE

**It's been nine hours since Ma was last seen.**

I open the blinds in the living room, hoping they will reveal a different picture outside. I wish there were reporters flocking our front door, asking me for an interview on national TV. I'd plead to everybody watching. *Please, help me find my mom! I need her to come back home.*

The reality is . . . there's no cameras. No reporters. No press conferences. No crowds. No places to speak on Ma's disappearance. I worry it might be cuz Ma is a brown-skinned woman from a middle-of-nowhere border town working as a bartender and not some blue-eyed white woman who's rich or famous.

I stare into the clear blue sky, wondering if I should stand on a street corner and hold a sign with Ma's face with the word MISSING just like all the other local women who have vanished, too.

Suddenly, a shrill ring shatters the silence, and I dash toward the house phone. I grab it, my heart pounding. The green light blinks.

**PRIVATE. PRIVATE. PRIVATE.**

Private calls only mean one thing: Someone wants to disguise their number. *What if . . . what if it's Ma?*

Both detectives huddle around our second phone line out in the hallway. *SHHHH.* They murmur as they lift their fingers toward their lips. Martinez's eyes lock with mine. It's as if he's communicating to me that I need to be a grown-up now.

"You're gonna answer it on the count of three," Martinez orders me. *Do I need to? I guess I don't have an option.*

Riinnnngggggggg.

Martinez's hands ball up in fists. "One . . . ," he begins to count without any further instruction. Like, what am I supposed to say?

"Don't tell anyone we're here. Got it?" Rodriguez quickly adds.

I nod. "Hmm-hmm." I feel my heart beating so fast. *I'm literally gonna faint.*

"Two!" Martinez's middle finger comes up.

My head feels like it's spinning. *I don't think I can do this. What if I mess up? What if I drop the phone? Do I really gotta do this? Is it too late to say that I can't? Is there a panic button?*

I lock eyes with Martinez again, and I wish he could read my mind. That all I can think is, *You answer it! I'm too scared.*

"THREE!"

I pick up the phone and I let out a soft, shaky, "Hell—hello?"

There's a stillness that comes from the other end of the phone that gives me goose bumps. "Hellooo?" I repeat a little louder.

A woman's voice cracks, "¿Estás bien?" and my whole body clenches tight.

"Ma?" I feel myself breathing faster.

She whimpers, and it makes me cry, too.

"Mijaaaa . . ." Ma's voice stretches into broken syllables. I've never heard Ma cry before. "¿Cómo está tu hermano?"

I glance at Rafael, unaware of what's been happening to our family. "Sí, Amá. He's asleep." I try to ease her anxiety, but mine just heightens even more. "Ma, what's happening? Why are you only speaking in Spanish? Where are you? Are you coming back soon?" I ask questions back-to-back, expecting Ma to give me the answers the detectives can't.

But Ma doesn't give me any answers, instead she says she's gotta tell me something very important.

"Escúchame sabes que," she says urgently. I listen in closely, clutching the phone, as if the harder I squeeze, the easier this will all be. I can hear her shallow breathing. "Sabes que los amo mucho."

"Yes, Amá . . ." I get flashes of us arguing gacho bad, but I know she's always loved me. "Why are you saying this?"

"Si me pasa algo, por favor cuida a tu hermano. Acuérdate de mí y le dices a tu hermano de mí." She makes me promise I'll tell Rafael about her and I'll take care of him if anything happens to her. Ma says that I'll be a great big sister. "Sigas fuerte." Stay strong.

"Ma, we won't forget you. I promise." I can feel Ma trying not to cry, so I hold back my tears.

"Are you gonna die?" I barely muster the courage to ask. The only times people talk like this are when someone is on the verge of life or death. Never in a million years could I have imagined talking to Ma about death when we are both still so young.

I wish we could go back in time. I shouldn't have given her that many gray hairs and made her angry. I'm a bad daughter, and if Ma dies, I'm gonna regret every horrible thing I did and said to her.

This could be the last time we speak to each other, but I just can't express how I truly feel. We've never talked about "feelings." And now I don't know how to let them out. Usually, I'm supposed to be made of stone. Nothing can hurt me.

"Ma?" I press her, but she doesn't answer my question.

"Mira, estas personas quieren mucho dinero," Ma manages to say instead.

I look at the detectives. They turn to each other. It's as if they knew exactly what would happen today. They give me a nod and motion me to speak, but what am I supposed to say next? *Whoever is there, let my mom go! I have detectives here with me.* I just wish I could say that to make everything go away. But I can't risk Ma's life. Would that even scare them?

"How much money?" I say in one breath, but Ma just keeps repeating that she loves me, sounding defeated. Her life is coming to an end. "Ma! Tell me."

A man's voice interjects, "¡No voy a negociar esto de nuevo¡ ¡Cuarenta mil dólares! ¡Rápido! ¡Dile o si no todos se mueren!" The man is firm on the amount of ransom. He wants it fast. He wants it now. If not, everyone dies. *Who's everyone? Me too?* His tone and words scare me to death.

"No! Por favor, señor." Ma pleads for a lesser amount of money. She tells him we don't have that kind of dinero. She hasn't gone back to work yet since she gave birth to Rafael. She was supposed to be going back next week. The man goes back and forth with Ma, bargaining for her life. Finally, she gets him down as low as he will go.

He's stern on the amount: $40,000 for her freedom. That may as well be a million dollars. Who the hell has that much money, especially in this town?

"Ma!" I interrupt. "Tell him that we need you. Rafael is a baby. Please. Dile. You can't die." *Don't cry. Act tough. But I really do need my mom and I'm scared to lose her.*

"No!" he shouts at Ma. He doesn't seem to care.

Ma sighs, saying that I can raise the money. To ask her customers, the super wealthy ones who have tipped Ma for her services. "Son mis amigos, te van ayudar." Ma reassures me that they are her friends. They will help me.

Ma says she will always be proud of me, no matter what happens.

"I'll get the money, Ma. No . . . no . . . no," I interrupt Ma from her deep sobs, reassuring her, "No. Don't worry. You're gonna come back soon. Okay?"

"¡Y no le llames a la policía! Te lo ruego."

I glance over at the detectives. *I gotta lie to Ma.*

"Nah, I swear to God. I won't. The police don't know, and they won't."

"Tienes vienticuatro horas."

I look at the clock that hangs in the living room. It reads 1:00 p.m. Twenty-four hours to raise $40,000 isn't much time.

"Te amo, mija y . . ." Ma's words get cut off midsentence.

"Ma? Maa? Maaamiiii?" I check the caller ID. The call is disconnected.

My tears pour out faster than I can speak. "Can you guys trace the call and find out where she's at?" I ask the detectives.

"No, sorry, we can't do that," Martinez replies.

"No . . . You have to, sir!"

Rodriguez says, "We can't actually trace the call."

"Why not?" I say, thinking about how they do it all the time in the movies.

"They're not dumb enough to do that. They probably called from a number that can't be traced."

I'm furious. "Well, they are that dumb to think we have forty thousand dollars!" That's the equivalent of what Ma makes in *two years*.

I run to my bedroom and smash my head against the pillow. I kick and punch the mattress. *I hate my life right now! I hate myself! I hate these kidnappers! I hate the detectives! I hate everything! Life isn't fair.*

I punch and punch till I got no energy left. I just lie on my side, staring at the portraits of me and Ma hanging on my walls, and I start to think about a scene in the movie *Man on Fire*. Don't these detectives have the power to unleash a firestorm of apocalyptic vengeance against everyone responsible for Ma's kidnapping, just like Creasy did for Pita when she was kidnapped in Mexico? Why can't the detectives be Ma's saviors? Why should I have to save her? I'm just a kid.

*She believes in me. Stay strong.* Ma's last words dance around my mind, though. If I'm able to secure the ransom and save her, then everything will go back to normal. Rafael and I will have a mom, and someday, we can live in our own house again and have the life I always envisioned.

I squeeze my eyes shut for a moment to get away from reality. But I know. I can't hide. I can't run away. There's no escaping this. I gotta face it. I just gotta run toward it. Even though Ma didn't want to raise me in the barrio, it taught me to be headstrong even when facing fear.

*BE STRONG!* I feel my heart pumping. It's pounding inside my ears like a drum. It's like facing the crazy stray dogs. Scary men in cars. The sound of the police. It's like in a race, running against competitors on a track. Everyone looks faster and stronger than me. I'm afraid that I might not run fast enough. I might even come in last. But once the starter pistol goes off, I gotta dig in deep. I gotta look straight ahead at the finish line, never to the side or behind me. I gotta give it my best. Don't let whatever is chasing me take me down. It's all like that right now, except I'm not competing against anybody—just the clock.

I don't want a medal or a first-place finish. I just want Ma back.

"Okay. I'm doing it! I'ma get the money," I say out loud, watching the seconds hand tick away on the clock.

# COLD-CALLING

**I pick up a paper and pen and create a list.**

Ma's contact book has lots of numbers, like a gazillion, and I somehow gotta find the names of the people Ma said could help us. I find them and write down my top three friends from South Middle, all of whom I've known since I was little. I wave the paper to the detectives. "I'm gonna call these people and ask them to help me."

First, I call Linda, Ma's childhood friend.

"¿Qué pasó, Kristolla?" She answers on the first ring. I give her the horrible news and ask her if she could help me.

"Don't go anywhere. Stay right there. I'm coming to you right now."

Linda arrives shortly after. She's trying to make sense of everything when the detectives explain to her what's already happened. Five men approached the vehicle. Ma held at gunpoint. She was kidnapped. They want a ransom.

She replies, "We don't have a lot of time. Let's go. Let's go. Let's go," and jumps straight into action.

"But how do I tell them?" How do you cold-call anybody? Ask

them to give money to a teenager? I hardly know Ma's customers, but knowing her, they probably know a lot more about me.

"Nomas tell the truth." Linda encourages me to be honest, but the problem is, will they even believe me?

I dial Ramiro first. Ma's customer that tips her crazy good.

"¿Bueno?" a man answers in Spanish.

I take a deep breath and rehearse in my head what I'm about to say. "Hi, my name is Kristy, and my mom's name is Carolina. She's a bartender at Coyote Cantina," I tell him, attempting to sound like an adult.

"Oh sí, hello! I'm back in town. Is she back at work again? Let her know I'll be there mañana."

I wish I could stop this dude midsentence. Tell him there's no tomorrow for Ma if he can't help pitch in for the ransom. "Actually, ummm." I pause. The last thing I wanna do is scare the hell out of him. "I'm calling cuz my mom is in trouble. She was kidnapped across last night and she called earlier to say to give you a call. We're raising money for the ransom so they will let her go. Do you think you can help us? Please?"

I did. I said it. I didn't stutter. "Hello?" I ask. "Are you there?"

Desperately to get his attention, I add, "She can pay you back right away. I promise." I'm worried and embarrassed that my coldcalling might sound like I'm a troublemaker making up some elaborate story to get a fix or something.

"Hellooooo?" I repeat again.

Finally, he speaks. "Perdón, pero no puedo." He can't help me. The call drops.

Disappointed, I turn to Linda and tell her, "He didn't even explain why he couldn't help." I try not to drown my thoughts in more sorrow, so I call the next person on my list. It's another of Ma's customers, and again, they hang up on me.

"It just sounds too unbelievable," I say to Linda.

"Ya sé, but it's the truth," Linda says, but then she brings up the recent kidnapping cases across. Maybe it's not that they don't believe me. Maybe it's cuz no one wants to get involved, especially when you're wealthy and you could be the next target.

I'm frustrated, but I dial the final person anyway.

No answer. "Ugh!"

"Maybe call your friends?" Linda advises.

I start to think about my friends. Would they let me down? Can I handle rejection from my own friends? They won't be my friends anymore, but then again, I can't expect them to help me with the ransom. They live in the barrios, too. None of us grew up with money.

"Hey, dude, it's me Kristy," I start out each call in case my friends already forgot about me. It's been over a year since we last spoke. They probably think I'm a traitor for leaving them for a north side school, and now I'm begging them to help me save my mom.

My friend Nathan is the first one I try. I'm relieved he remembers me, so I press on. "So . . . um . . . something really messed up happened. My mom got kidnapped and I need a huge favor. Think your family could lend me money? My mom will pay you back. Te lo juro," I say in two breaths.

"Dude! For reals?" Nathan responds.

"Yes, swear to God."

"Sobres, Kristy. My family has your back. We'll ask our neighbors and family for help, too. No te preocupes. Cáele."

One by one, I go through my list of friends, and each time I'm given the help we desperately need. Every single person is willing to pitch in whatever they can.

"Linda! They all said yes!" I deliver the good news.

"I'll drive Kristy to gather the money from her friends." Linda lets the detectives know that we got it from here.

"Call us if you guys need anything." Rodriguez hands Linda his card before they finally leave. Linda, Rafael, and I are on our own.

Before gathering the ransom, we drop off Rafael with a relative. "Mami's gonna come back soon. I promise, baby." I kiss him on his forehead goodbye.

Sitting in the driver's seat, Linda asks, "¿Lista?"

"Let's do it," I reply as if we're in a relay competition.

"¡Vamos!" Linda presses on the gas, her eyes locked ahead. We head south, just a mile from the Mexican border.

"What if they think I'm using them?" I dare ask Linda as we approach the south side of town. Worried they might wonder how I could just leave South Middle and never come back to visit them like I promised I would. I mean, it's only been one year, but we all used to talk on the phone or in person every week since I was six. I did what I thought Ma wanted me to do. Move on from our past and start fresh.

"It's not like I don't like them, Linda . . ." I explain to her why I haven't kept in touch. "I've just been busy with sports and my new friends at the skate park."

I tell her half the truth cuz if I tell her about Ma wanting to leave the past behind, I might hurt her feelings and Tita's, too. I promised them I would visit their yellow casita often.

"But the last thing they told me was that I'm gonna turn out all mamona, like the chicks in the north side . . . ," I reveal, asking myself if I've become one of them.

"Ayyy, Kristolla . . . ," Linda begins by saying.

"I'm serious. They're gonna hate me, right? Like, how could I ask for help out of nowhere?"

"No. Never. Sometimes I don't hear from my close friends for months or even years and they're still my friends."

"Really?"

"Yes. Nambe. Don't worry." She helps me feel a little relief, but I also worry about potentially putting my friends in danger.

"Wouldn't you do anything to help your friends out? Especially if something bad happened to their mom?" Linda asks. She knows me. I'd give anything for my friends.

I unbuckle my seat belt, looking out the window.

"¡Dale!" Linda encourages me to go.

"You sure it's fine?"

"Pos sí, they already said yes. Just go and talk to them." She gives me an extra push.

I shut the door behind me and immediately feel the blazing Texas sun on my skin and in my eyes.

Linda sticks her head out the window. "Your mom would be so proud of you, mija!"

I'm standing right out front of Isela's front door, chewing my nails. I wonder how she'll react when she sees me.

Isela's father comes out and says in Spanish he's happy to see me again.

"Ven adentro," he welcomes me inside.

"Hey . . ." Isela comes out from her bedroom and squeezes in under her father's armpit.

"It's been a while, dude," I remind her as if she doesn't know.

"I told them what happened," she says, looking up at her father. "We're gonna help you."

Isela's mom comes out of the kitchen. "Sit, mija." Her gentle voice eases up my hunched shoulders. "Allá," she adds, pointing at a flower-print couch that's got a couple of punctured holes.

Isela says, "I've been praying a diosito that your moms comes back safely." She fiddles with her crucifix necklace. Her eyes gaze softly at a Virgin de Guadalupe statue.

I feel warm inside, cuz Isela is the same girl I had always called my friend, sweet and thoughtful, even though during school she acted just as tough as I did.

"No tenemos mucho dinero, but we borrowed some from the neighbors," her father says, placing a white envelope in my cupped hands. I tuck it in under the elastic band of my shorts, feeling a little guilty that they had to borrow money on my behalf.

"That's very nice of you guys. Thank you! Means so much to me and my mom. I'll pay you guys back. Promise!" I got no clue how much money is inside, but it doesn't matter, all that does matter is that they got my back.

I run out of their house, waving the envelope at Linda. "We got some money!" As I'm trying to unseal it in the passenger seat, Linda stops me.

"Open it once we got all the other money, no?"

I shrug my tensed shoulders, "I guess . . . ," and stuff the envelope in the glove compartment.

Sprinting like my feet are on fire, I run toward the next house down the block and I end up at Nathan's house.

"¡Hola!" Nathan's mom opens the door in her pink rollos, pieces of her hair tightly rolled like Fruit Roll-Ups. She's cradling her newborn. With her free arm, she leans in to give me a hug. Awkwardly, I hug her back.

Nathan comes out of the backyard.

"Is she involved?" he inquires like a detective, wondering if my mom is caught up with the wrong people.

"No. I promise. It's not like that," I reassure him, especially after what happened to our friend.

Days after Rodrigo died, chisme spread like wildfire. People speculated his father was living a double life and the cartel was after him. Rodrigo wasn't the target. With all the cartel violence spilling over from across the border, people have become unsure of what to believe.

"But you never . . ." Nathan tries to say I never know, but I cut him off.

"She's not. I swear to God. Can you help me or nah?"

He nods at his mom. "Dale."

She hands me a few wrinkled hundred-dollar bills and coins in a Ziploc bag. "This's our savings. It's para tu mom."

I don't want to take her money, but she insists that I do. I feel like a burden.

"Okay, but I promise to pay you all of it back," I tell her, and stick out my pinkie finger toward her face.

"No te preocupes." But it's hard not to worry when I know how much money this is for their family.

After Nathan's house, I make my way to the Riveras' house where my other school friends live—Velma and her brother Julian.

"This is from our family. It's a gift." Ms. Rivera says, giving me a bag full of stacked cash. My hand can barely wrap around it. I have no idea how they were able to get so much money in less than ninety minutes. But I don't ask questions.

I sprint back to Linda's truck as fast as I do at my track meets. The speed of my feet determines Ma's future.

"Someone from your mom's bar called," Linda announces when I return to the truck, explaining how a man heard about Ma's kidnapping ordeal, and kindly donated money for the ransom.

We haul it to La Sanber, where Coyote Cantina is located among all of my favorite restaurants, seedy automobile shops, run-down motels along Highway 35, which leads directly to the International Bridge—the gateway to Mexico, where Ma is being held hostage.

Even though the only thing separating my hometown and Mexico is the narrow Rio Grande. Nuevo Laredo feels foreign to me. Maybe it's the random gunshots that explode in the air like cuetes during the ringing of the New Year. Or maybe it's cuz I was born in Laredo, Texas. I speak Spanglish. I've never mastered both languages, but to my family, the raza runs deep in our blood. Now with Ma missing across, all the beautiful memories Ma and I once shared in Mexico are shattered. It will never be the same again.

I jump out of Linda's truck and bolt straight past the doors of Coyote Cantina just like I used to as a little girl. Back when I was cheery and happy, and Ma would wait for me with a giant baked potato.

"Hey, Kristy," the hostess greets me with a different tone. I feel a little uncomfortable cuz by now, I think everyone knows what happened to Ma.

"Hi."

"I'm sorry about your mom."

"Thanks," I reply sheepishly. I still don't know how to react when someone feels bad for me.

The hostess walks me back into the main area of the cantina. She brings me to Ma's coworkers, who greet me. Many of them were at Tía's house just a few hours ago.

They huddle around me like they do at funerals. More condolences. I swear if I hear another sorry, I'll scream my lungs out. To them, I probably already seem like a walking orphan cuz kidnapping victims hardly make it back alive.

I give them a toothless smile. "Thanks," I say, staring at my feet.

The hostess brings out a small black bag and whispers, "Here's the money."

I take it from her, quickly taking a glimpse inside and attempting to guess how much it may be, even though I know I shouldn't just yet. I just can't help it.

"Wow . . . that's a lot of freaking money."

"A guy named Angel left it. He owns a car wash down the street. He said he hopes this helps bring your mom back," the hostess says. Thankfully, there are generous people in our community.

Suddenly, as I try to guesstimate the amount of money left, Ma's coworkers dig deep into their maroon aprons.

"Here, take this." One by one, they begin to stash the tips they made today inside the bag.

Marta, Ma's old boss begins to pray. *In the name of the father. The son. The holy spirit. Amen.* Once she's done, she sends me off to Linda as if I'm going to war. I'm heading onto the battlefield, a soldier fighting for Ma's liberation.

"Look, mira!" I carry on with Linda. She quickly flips her Motorola phone shut.

"Who was that?" I ask her.

Linda attempts to tell me, but she is distracted by what she sees in the rearview mirror. I turn my back. It's Claudia, Ma's friend and coworker.

"Tell her we're in a hurry, ándale."

I roll my window down manually, rushing to explain to Claudia that we gotta get going. It's 8 p.m. and we're running out of time. There's only seventeen hours left until the deadline.

"Oye ¿cómo están tú y tu hermano?" Claudia asks.

"We're okay," I reply even though I know if I pause to think about how I'm really feeling, I'll probably cry gacho bad and I don't have time to cry right now.

Then she offers to take care of Rafael.

"Thanks, but he's already with family."

She must really empathize with how bad Ma may be feeling, being a mother herself. Once, she had to leave her child behind in Mexico. It wasn't until recently that coyotes like Tía smuggled him into the States. They're still waiting for real or fake papers, though.

Linda sighs, and I know what that means. I turn to Claudia to tell her we really must go, but she's pointing at the black object and asks, "¿Qué es eso?"

"It's a recording device," Linda answers, annoyed.

I add, "We're gonna record the calls if Ma or the kidnappers call." Linda and I don't wanna miss anything important or get anything wrong.

Claudia nods her head, and quickly pulls out a twenty-dollar bill from her back pocket. "Toma esto."

I take her money and feel grateful that she's helping us out, especially knowing that she hardly has any money for her and her three-year-old son. We wave her goodbye.

"She's super metiche." Linda says Claudia gives her coraje cuz she's nosy.

"Yeah, she asks too many questions." I turn away from Claudia's receding figure, back toward Linda. "So what were you gonna tell me?"

# RACING AGAINST THE CLOCK

**"Your mom called,"** Linda finally reveals the identity of the person she had just spoken to and my heart stops.

"What? What did she say?"

"I don't wanna scare you," Linda says. Her eyes look at the road, and though she says she doesn't want to scare me—she does anyway.

"Why?"

"She said that the kidnappers know what you're wearing."

I inspect my clothes, and ask, "Did they describe them?"

Linda says no, but that she for sure knows they are watching us. Somehow, I start to think, *That's BS.* If they were really following us, they would've known that the detectives had been at the apartment earlier.

"I already called Mr. Rodriguez and Mr. Martinez. I told them we're good right now." Linda reassures me we got nothing to worry about. The detectives are one call away. We just need to raise the ransom.

"Linda?" I begin timidly. "I need to stop by my dad's place."

"When's the last time you saw him?" Linda responds, making the detour and heading toward his house.

I gotta think hard. "Hmm, I don't know." Maybe it was two or three years ago. Back when I had pink hair extensions and a flat chest. Ever since I became a teenager, we hardly speak to each other.

In the distance, there's a lonely house with a front yard buried in tumbleweeds that have grown up to my knees. Mesquite trees surround the property. The same dried-out trees whose rough branches I once grazed with my fingertips.

Once upon a time, I used to be a rocket. An object launching upward, fast into the sky, and safely landing in my father's arms. Back when Ma and I lived here, when we were a family. The last time I stepped foot inside my father's home was eleven years ago. The day Ma and I left him. Now this home is just an old, jagged memory.

I unbuckle my seat belt and let out a deep sigh. Linda notices my apprehension and looks at me to say, "Just tell him it's an emergency cuz it is."

"But how?" I reply, unable to come up with the right words.

"He's your father!"

He is, but I hardly know him now.

*Never beg for anything. Never rely on a man. Especially for money!* Ma would often remind me. She was militant about me becoming an independent, strong woman. I wonder if Ma would give me permission to break that rule in this situation.

I gather the courage to ask him for help. Slowly, I exit the vehicle, scanning my father's front yard. I've heard sometimes he sits outside, drinking cans of Budweiser until he passes out, but not today.

*Just run back. You don't need his help. You can raise the ransom without him.* Then there's this opposing thought. *I need all the money that I can get. Doesn't matter from who or where it comes from. I just desperately need it. I just gotta swallow my pride and do it. For Ma. For Rafael. For our future.*

"¿Hola?" a woman's voice stops me in my tracks. I turn to the side and it's my father's neighbor, and a little boy playing with a soccer ball.

"Mira. That's Milo's daughter," I hear her whispering, tugging at the boy's arm.

*Yes, it's me.* I wave hello to them. A few other neighbors peek out of their blinds. I guess I'm supposed to wave to everyone else, too, like I'm in a parade. A parade for beggars. Even my father's rooster crows louder and louder the closer I get to the front door, alerting my father of a potential intruder. But I'm not a robber, or a trespasser. This used to be my home, too.

I'm standing at the door, noticing the beige paint peeling off and remembering how everything was once new. Everything about his house reminds me of the past.

*Okay, fine.* I dig deep and find the courage to knock.

"Ey, que onda," my father pops his head out of the door, greeting me as if we saw each other just a few days ago, when really, it's been years.

"Hey, sorry to bother you, but could you lend me money?" I ask him, barely explaining what it's for. He doesn't ask me about the details of Ma's kidnapping ordeal or how I feel or if I need more help.

"Here. Take it." He offers me three hundred dollars and I stuff the cash in my shorts.

"Thanks, Dad! I gotta go now. Pero I'll talk to you soon." I dash as fast as I can, weaving through the tumbleweeds and past all of the old memories.

"Drive! Drive! Drive!" I hop in the passenger seat, buckle my seat belt, and hunch over my knees, trying to conceal my face as if the paparazzi was out to snap photos of me asking my father for money. "I never wanna do that again, ugh!!! It was super awkward."

Linda brushes me off. "Ay, Kristolla. He's your father!"

Yeah, he is, but what does that even mean? What's the definition of a father, anyway? I wish things turned out differently. I picture how it could have been. He would be standing at his front door, his arms wide open. I'd tell him what happened to Ma. He would reassure me everything is gonna be okay. He would become a superhero, jump into action, and rescue Ma himself.

"I don't even know him anymore," I reply, feeling disappointed. For the first time in my life, I wish I had a father. A real father.

When we finally reach the apartment, I'm clutching all the money tight underneath my armpit. "We gotta count the money!" I turn back telling Linda as she trails right behind me on the stairs.

Once I get inside the apartment, I remember Ma's secret stash. An emergency fund of coins inside the zebra vase. All of which came from Ma's tips.

I take it, trying not to drop it. It's heavy.

Dropping on my knees, I carefully flip the vase upside down until all the jangling coins bounce off the floor like jumping jelly beans. Meanwhile, Linda dumps all the cash on the ground, too. And just like that, Linda and I surround ourselves with hundreds of wrinkled bills and sticky coins that smell like stale alcohol.

"This is a lot of money, Linda . . ." I've never seen these many bills in my entire life. We could've been rich!

"Pos, let's count it." Linda and I separate the bills and begin stacking them like building blocks, but they sure don't go as high as I wish they would.

"Here's a twenty . . . here's a hundred," I say, making sure the bills are organized together.

"Let's wrap them quickly." Linda hands me coin wraps, just like we used to back when I would help her out with her snow cone business. She'd even pay me minimum wage. That was four years ago.

"Remember, put your thumb under," she reminds me as I insert one quarter after another, until the coins fill to the top of the wrapper.

I ask Linda how much money she's counted so far.

"¿Cuanto?"

"Eighteen thousand dollars."

No. It can't be. We're short twenty-two thousand dollars? "Wait. Wait . . ." I double, triple, and quadruple check her math.

She's right.

"What are we gonna do?" I panic. We're running out of time.

"Why don't you call your mom's family?" Linda suggests.

"Nah, they don't have money," I reply as if she doesn't know they rely on welfare, and Ma helps *them* out financially.

But even so, I still need to give it a try. I punch in Tía's number.

When she answers, I ask, "Tía? The kidnappers want forty thousand dollars. Can you lend us money?"

"¿No tienes todo el dinero?" Tía asks, as if we just have that sort of cash lying around.

I turn to Linda, and then answer Tía, "We're short by a lot." Crossing my fingers, I hope she miraculously says yes.

"Ay, I wish we could, but we have nothing." I try giving her a few ideas on how to get money. "Maybe you can borrow cash? Ask your friends? Ask anyone."

"¿Quién?" Tía asks.

"Anybody!" I shout, and hang up the phone.

Linda shakes her head. "Don't cry. Forget them. We're gonna figure it out."

"But she could've just tried. Ma always found a way to help her kids and never asked for that money back," I protest. "Even my friends asked their neighbors. How will I ever forgive them if Ma doesn't make it back?" If Ma dies, I'll hate them forever. I swear.

"Don't think like that." Linda says it's bad to think these types of things.

"But," I contradict her, and say, "what if she actually doesn't come back? My brother and I will be alone. Forever." The ugly thought brings more tears. "We won't have a family." I cover my eyes.

Linda taps my shoulder softly. "Un día, you'll learn to forgive them."

"Okay." I struggle to comprehend it.

"You learn as you get older," Linda says with a matter-of-fact tone that probably comes from experience.

I stop to think about what she is saying. Maybe it's like the forgiveness Linda has shown for her biological father. She went to great lengths to find him. Ever since they were reunited, they've grown closer, and they love each other. She's forgiven him for abandoning her. Suddenly, all of it makes a little more sense, and I begin to understand what she means. *Maybe it just takes time.*

"Thanks, Linda," I reply, feeling comforted for the first time in this whole ordeal and I drift off to sleep.

"Kristolla, levántate. I think it's your mom calling!" Linda wakes me up. I've somehow managed to doze off for a few hours and it's now 4:00 a.m. I watch Linda pick up the voice recorder and click the speaker button to answer the private call.

She motions me to speak. "Ma?"

"Por favor, no hagas nada que ponga en peligra el trato. Sin policia. Nada."

*No police. Nothing.* I look at Linda and wonder if they actually know that the agents were here.

"No. We haven't done anything. We're just trying to get the money, I promise," I lie to Ma again. I gotta.

"¿Tienes la mayor parte del dinero ya?" Ma asks about the ransom we've collected so far.

I'd like to tell her the truth, but what if the truth sends Ma to hopelessness?

"Umm." I glance over my shoulder, to the center of the living room, where the stacks of money mount as if we just robbed the bank. "We almost have like half the money."

"¿Eso es todo?"

"Yes, that's it, but I promise we're gonna get it all." There's something about Ma's voice that tells me she's doubting I'll be able to bring her back home. "Ma?" I wanna tell her that I'm sorry about everything in the past, just in case this is it. Our final goodbye. But she interrupts me.

"Por favor, ayúdame. No me quiero morir, amor," Ma cries. She is desperate to make it out alive.

"I'm gonna, Amá! I promise," I reassure her.

Each of her gasping breaths feels like bullets hitting my body. I've been shot. There's blood oozing out of my freaking gut. Somehow, I'm supposed to save Ma's life, even though I feel like I'm slowly dying inside. I just gotta keep on running to the finish line like death, too, is hot on my heels.

In that moment when I feel like I'm about to faint, Ma's

kidnapper says something to Ma in the background. He offers us a deal. We hand over Ma's Honda CR-V and he will accept half of the ransom instead. He wants the title, too.

The call drops. I tell Linda, "We only need two thousand and we're good. I got no idea where my mom stored the title, though."

Linda checks inside the CR-V, but nothing turns up. "It's probably in your mom's storage unit," she says, remembering when she helped me and Ma store some of our things about a year ago after moving out of our dream house.

Just a few minutes after Ma called, we show up at the self-storage unit before it opens, hoping someone is there. But no one is around, and we don't have the passcode to get inside the unit. We wait and wait.

It's 6:30 a.m.

Finally, we notice a worker walking into the office.

"Excuse me, sir!" Linda gets his attention, and we explain the situation, trying not to scare him. Either cuz we sound like two crazy chicks or cuz there are rules set in place, he tells us, "No. Sorry. I can't open it. These are the rules."

He says Ma must be present or she needs to place a call to give us authorization. And that's so not gonna happen right this second.

"Linda?" I look at her, feeling my heart pounding with every second that passes. I can't let Ma die cuz of this rule. "What are we gonna do?"

Linda stares out the window. Her nose crinkles; she's deep in thought. "No sé. Let me think . . . This isn't good."

I wonder if she's thinking what I'm thinking. *We can grab the keys from the office and make a run for it.* But there must be an easier way.

We sit there in silence, waiting for one of us to come up with an idea, but all I can hear now is Ma's voice when she used to say at my birthday parties during the giveaway prizes that required speed and quick thinking, "Kris, you gotta let other kids win prizes. You already have a ton of gifts." Ma didn't think it was fair that I won every game at my own birthday party. But it wasn't just me in the game, being so competitive. It was Linda, too.

I turn to look at Linda again, thinking back to all my parties as a kid, and how great a team we always made.

"Kristolla! Let's win this thing," she would often say as Clown Bolitas yelled the countdown. Once, we won while she danced to Cumbia music wearing a mariachi outfit covered in balloons; I popped them with the tip of a dart in under ten seconds. We won the game where she had to cradle me like a baby, feeding me a nursing bottle filled with red liquid that I managed to chug in two gulps. Or the time she mummified my entire body with toilet paper faster than the rest of the other teams. I just knew, whatever game it was, Linda and I were going for the win.

I hold back on the idea of confronting the manager, but instead I ask Linda, "Can you just tell him it's an emergency, please? We can't give up now." This obstacle can't stop us from saving Ma together.

Linda talks to him again. He gives in.

"Ay gracias a dios," Linda sighs, swiping the storage unit door up.

"You take the left y I take the right," Linda orders me, and we dive like we're treasure hunters looking for a golden ticket. Except it's just a piece of paper that says Ma legally owns her vehicle.

"Okay. Let's do this rápido," I remind her.

We begin ripping apart shoe boxes that Ma has used to store papers and photos. I come across a collection of photographs, images of when I was as young as Rafael.

I pick one of the photos up, quickly taking a glance. There's Ma with her natural curly dark brown hair, cradling me in her arms. And then there's my father, looking at me. My sparkling eyes gazing up at Ma. We looked like a happy family.

"Find something?" Linda asks, cutting open a sealed box with the sharp edges of her car keys.

"Nah! It's nothing. Just some random photo." I jam the photograph back in the shoebox and toss it to the side. The longer I stared at it, the more it made me wish everything could go back to how it used to be.

We keep on searching. Ma has a ton of stuff, but halfway through a giant cardboard box, about forty papers deep, I read the letters H-O-N-D-A in bold.

"Linda!!!" I jump up, waving a document in the air. "This is it!"

I found the golden ticket.

# RIP, FOURTEEN

**It's nine o'clock in the morning. We're back on the road again,** heading home from the storage unit.

"We still need to find more money. How are we gonna get the rest?" I ask Linda, wishing the last two thousand dollars would magically appear. We've run out of lifelines, like the show *Who Wants to Be A Millionaire. What I'd do to just be a contestant on that TV show right now* . . .

"I don't know yet," Linda's replies over the noise of the wind whooshing in the rolled-down windows.

There's a car honking in front of us as we pass by my skate park. Just a day ago, I was there laughing, having fun, and living carefree. It feels like a lifetime ago. I sink into the passenger seat. I don't want to look at the skate park or else I'll be reminded that I should've just gone with Ma to the wedding. Maybe none of this would've happened. As I look away, I notice a giant sign that's hard to miss but somehow, I never read before.

NEED MONEY FAST? COME IN. WE BUY. WE SELL.

I stare at Linda's gold necklace around her neck. *I got an idea.* We could potentially sell everything we own to the pawn shop and raise the rest of the ransom.

When we arrive back at the apartment, I sprint to Ma's room, searching for a box of jewelry that belongs to me. It's a collection of gold necklaces that my father has gifted me over the years. Ma stores them somewhere out of reach. She doesn't trust me with these types of expensive things. Rightfully so. According to Ma, they are worth a lot of money, and I always tend to lose things.

It's not that difficult to find them. They're under her bed, exposed. I grab the clear plastic bag filled with my jewelry, run to my room, and toss it on my bed.

Then I turn my attention to the rest of my room. I see dollar signs on every item in sight. Two guitars. Amplifier. Microphone. Drum set. All the things that once were on my wish lists for the past several years so that I could start my punk band. Bet they're probably worth some money.

I think about how I was just starting to learn how to play guitar on my own, singing songs I'd written myself and uploaded on MySpace. I guess I won't be a singer-songwriter anytime soon. I drag my soon-to-be-gone instruments to one side of my bedroom. Then I open a couple of drawers filled with over thirty porcelain dolls that are still in their original boxes with a certification of authenticity.

"Mija, someday these dolls will be worth money, a lot more than Mami could ever make in a lifetime," Ma whispered at the convention center in Corpus Christi, Texas. I was seven and in awe, staring at the different types of beautiful ornate Victorian dresses on the white porcelain dolls.

I promised Ma I'd buy us a house with the money I'd make selling the dolls when I'm older. I guess it's not gonna happen anymore. I'm gonna buy her life back instead.

"Pos ¿qué haces, Kristolla?" Linda walks into my bedroom wondering what the commotion is all the about.

I point to the gold necklaces and the pile of items in the corner of my bedroom. "I'm pawning them. It's gotta make the rest of the ransom."

Linda shakes her head. "I can't let you do that. Estás loca . . ."

"But why not," I protest. I'm not crazy. This is our best shot. Our real final lifeline.

"'Ay nambe, your mom wouldn't want you to do that. She worked super hard for those things," Linda explains.

I beg Linda, "Please!" and try to convince her. "We gotta! We don't have a choice anymore."

"No," Linda argues back, clutching onto the black bag that has the ransom money we've managed to collect.

"I don't want them, anyway! Swear to God!" I answer back, gazing at the things I'm pawning, attempting to convince myself I don't need them. They aren't mine anymore. My dreams are dying. Everything I ever wanted to be will soon disappear.

Linda calls her snow cone business and says she's gonna check how much money the store has brought in this week.

"I'll get the rest of the money from Tropical Snow," Linda reassures me. "You don't need to sell your things. But you do need to go to your cheerleading show today."

"Umm, no. I can't. What are you talking about?" There's no way I'm gonna go with the deadline this close. In less than three hours, all of this will come to an end.

"It's your mom's big dream. You know that. Do it for her."

Behind Linda, there's Ma's calendar with the words written in bold:

## KRISTY'S 1ST CHEERLEADING HIGH SCHOOL PERFORMANCE

She's right. Ma's dream has always been to see me perform as a high school cheerleader. Maybe it's cuz it was her dream, which was cut short when she became pregnant with me at seventeen. She was forced to quit and drop out of school.

As much as I hate my new high school team, Linda's right. I gotta do it for Ma.

"Promise you'll get the money, deliver the car and the ransom?" I lift my pinkie and make her promise me.

Linda looks me straight in the eye, exhausted. She pinkie promises.

"Fine," I relent, picking up my pom-poms and uniform, which have already been carefully laid out for me. Ma had prepared everything the night she left.

I put on my uniform and fix my hair, attempting to slick my hair tight just like Ma does it. Then I circle my ponytail in a bun and attach a curly ponytail wig. Next is makeup. Ugh, I dread this part. Two layers of red lipstick. Bright black and blue eyes, smoky eye. Eyeliner. Fake eyelashes. Sparkly gold bronzer.

I look at myself in the mirror and think, *How am I going to manage to look normal?* I fake a smile and practice a few times in the mirror. *Lift your top up just a little. No, not like that. More teeth, less lips. No, don't you cry. Your mascara will drip. You will look like a circus clown. Not a teenager.*

RIP, fourteen.

"I'm ready."

Linda drives me to my performance at the high school where

I'll start attending in a few weeks and pulls up to the entrance of the auditorium.

"Good luck, Kristolla."

I try practicing a fake smile, but it's hard to accomplish when I'm scared that the next few hours will change my life forever.

"Thanks," I say, not as enthusiastic as I wish I could be.

Linda unlocks the doors. "Your mom is coming back," she says.

There's nothing else I can do, except to focus on acing my performance, somehow. I've entrusted Linda with Ma's life.

When I arrive, I try to blend in with my teammates, even though everyone knows I stand out. I have a subtle accent. I'm the new chick from the south. The morena skater who wears black. The outcast. A few days ago, I was wishing I hadn't tried out for the cheer team at this new school, but today, all I can think about is Ma. I'm here for her.

Miss Roxanne, our cheer sponsor, grabs our attention with her deep Texas twang. "Girlies, come back to the stage. We gotta pray before our performance."

We gather in a huddle. I stand in the back, eyes wide open, peeking from left to right. I'm wishing I could make a run for home. But that would forever follow me in the halls of Anderson High School. I'd be the freak who quit the cheer team just seconds before a big performance. But I'm not running away. I'm staying right here. Besides, where would I run to? Nobody is home. And Ma wouldn't want me to quit, anyway.

"God, please protect all of these girlies as they perform for the first time," Miss Roxanne closes prayer, but then says, "and Kristy's mom."

Suddenly, I feel dizzy, exposed. How does she even know? Does everyone know? I start to look around, paranoid that everyone knows about my life. But everyone's eyes are shut.

Without any further details about Ma, she adds, "We got a full house today. Let's get going."

My mind is full of questions. *What if I can't handle it? What if I mess up? What if everyone figures out what happened to Ma and says that's what happens to ghetto people from the south?*

"Get in your positions, girls," our head cheerleader, Carly, orders.

I stand in my spot trying not to fidget or I'll get in trouble. I'm right smack center at the beginning of our routine. *It's just a four-minute routine. And then it's over. Ma will be here soon.*

Slowly, the curtains split open, and I fake a giant smile. I search the packed room. It's difficult not to look for Ma out there in the crowd where she would normally be, even though I know she's not there. Our song comes on, and it gives me the adrenaline boost I need to get in the zone. Thank god for muscle memory. Somehow, I'm doing it. I stick my tumbling passes and hit every beat, even the part of the dance routine where I feel uncomfortable cuz our choreography is provocative.

The curtain closes. Finally, the show is over. I wait for Linda for over half an hour outside the auditorium. I'm nervous while I wait. Has something happened? I'm in between two opposite emotions: happy and sad cuz I don't know what lies ahead.

Linda finally picks me up.

"Did she make it back?" I blurt out, hopping into her truck.

There's a pause.

"Just tell me!" I beg her to answer.

"Not yet," Linda replies, and I start to think the worst.

"You didn't get the money?"

"No, I got it."

"So then?"

Sometimes, kidnappers will arrange pickup of the money from the families, and then, nothing. No one hears back from the kidnappers or the victims ever again. It was doomed from the start.

"I got it all and spoke to the kidnappers. They're behind schedule."

"Oh my god, Linda!" I say loudly. "Thank you so much!"

Linda takes me to Rafael—he's at Ma's boyfriend's parents' house—parks outside and then turns to me in her seat and says that Ma should arrive here soon.

"You're leaving me?"

"I gotta go check in with work now."

I sit in the car and eye the house. I don't understand why she's gotta leave me here by myself. I don't know these people very well. I just met them a few months ago.

"Sure that you can't stay?"

"I just borrowed all the money from store. I gotta figure something out now."

"Okay." I don't like it, but I gotta come to terms with it. She's already done more than anyone has. She's truly Ma's best friend.

"Kristolla," Linda says, looking deep into my eyes. "You are super strong. No te olvides."

It makes me think about what Ma said earlier—be strong.

I smile, wishing I could say more. About how much she means to me. About how much she loves Ma. About how I want to be able to repay her, someday.

"See you soon," she says.

"Thanks for everything," I manage to say as she pulls out of the driveway, waving me goodbye. I try not to cry cuz it's not like I won't see her again, but now I really hate goodbyes.

I stand outside the house, and I dread knocking on their front door like some stranger. *Hi, I'm your son's girlfriend's fourteen-year-old daughter. Is it cool if I come inside and wait for my mom to be released by her kidnappers?*

Thankfully, the door is open, and I don't say anything. I just sneak in between prayers during a vigil. They're reciting the Rosario, the Hail Mary prayer. I'm standing here, waiting for someone or something to notice me. "Rafael . . . ," I whisper, spotting my baby brother. He's asleep, probably dreaming of Mami. I wish babies could speak so he could tell me what this prayer means.

A piercing fear shoots through my heart: Maybe Ma is dead and they just found out. Maybe that's why they're praying. My heart sinks. *If Ma dies, I'll live in grief forever.* I look back at the vigil and wonder if this could really be our new home. I hardly know these people.

*Please, if God is real, then bring her home. Right now.* I pretend to grab some water from their kitchen, but all I can do is stare out the window. The clock reads two o'clock. It's the afternoon. And they're still praying. Each time louder and harder than the last, making me feel nauseous.

"C'mon, Ma. Come, please." I hope she can hear me. With each passing car, my heart speeds up, only to be let down again, and again.

Suddenly, someone shouts, "¡Ya llegó!" I look out on the street. There's a black Escalade pulling up. I hold my breath in. Then jump, rushing toward Rafael.

"Mami's here," I gasp into his tiny ear. Grabbing his fragile body, I wrap him around my chest and run out the door.

Ma stumbles out of the vehicle, wearing her little black dress, which is tattered from the side seam, exposing her ribs. She's shoeless and her knees are covered in mud.

"¡Mis niños! Mis niños." Ma's sobs her way through the crowd outside, searching for us. When we finally lock eyes, I freeze. I can't smile. My lips are glued together. "Ma?" I hesitate to say. I know I should be happy. I should be jumping up and down in joy. I should be feeling like I won the lottery. I should be thanking God. I should be relieved, but I don't feel a thing.

"Kris!" Ma shouts, grabbing my body, squeezing us hard, as if she's trying to convince herself that we really are real. That she is alive. That she is free.

All I can do is stand still. Frozen. I'm unable to move or say a word. *Is something wrong with me?* I have a bad feeling that if God is real, I'm gonna go to hell for not crying like I should.

Ma shakes me as if I've done something wrong. "Look at me!"

I pull away like I'm being smothered. Something about Ma is different. Something has changed. *You're not Ma. Where's my mother?* The kidnappers released the wrong woman.

"Why won't you look at me? I'm your mother!"

I try looking into her eyes, but every time I do, they haunt me.

**By Taryn T. Walters**
LAREDO MORNING TIMES

A woman awaiting trial for charges related to a 2006 kidnapping was granted a continuance in federal court last week after attorneys announced evidence in the case recently became available.

Ruth Sarahi Lopez-Espinoza was indicted in April 2007 on one count of conspiracy to com-

mit hostage-taking and two counts of hostage-taking.

A warrant for her arrest remained outstanding until 2015 when she was arrested in Mexico. Records state Lopez-Espinoza was held in Mexico City for a year before being escorted to the U.S. on June 27 to face the pending charges.

After her ex____ do, Lopez-Espi___ er of arraignm___

guilty to the charges, court records state.

Lopez-Espinoza's case was granted a continuance in November after her attorney, Oscar O. Peña, informed the court of a potential co-defendant awaiting extradition from Mexico. It was Lopez-Espinoza's belief that the ___

Espinoza informed the cou___ she no longer wished to av___ the individual's extradition ___ opting to move her case for ___ to trial.

Peña requested a continu____ ance, stating he was inform____ by Assistant U.S. District A____

---

Dear Diary,

Well, it really ___
I feel today. ___
it and mostly ___
it with my friend ___
___ of Ma ___

---

5PM
Goal: 475
finish
finish strong

---

# PART III
# THE AFTERMATH

---

**Department of Justice**
U.S. Attorney's Office
Southern District of Texas

___ATE RELEASE                                    Tuesday, February 27

### ___a Sentenced for Participating in Kidnapping of Two U___ Citizens in Mexico

___xas – A 31-year-old Mexican woman has been ordered to federal prison for her role in ___ hold two U.S. nationals hostage in Nuevo Laredo, Tamaulipas, Mexico, announced U.___ ___n K. Patrick. Ruth Sarahi Lopez-Espinoza, of Nuevo Laredo, pleaded guilty Feb. 15, 20___

___ng U.S. District Judge Keith P. Ellison handed Lopez-Espinoza a total sentence of 153___ ___rison. At the hearing, two kidnapping victims spoke of the pain and destruction this eve___ ___ them and their families. In handing down the sentence, the court noted that this was o___ ___ases he has seen during his time on the bench. Lopez-Espinoza was ordered to pay $25,___ ___ to the two victims. Not a U.S. citizen, Lopez-Espinoza is expected to face deportation ___ ___s following the sentence.

___ 2006, four men wearing masks and brandishing pistols kidnapped two U.S. nationals ___ ___g a wedding reception of a co-worker from a Laredo restaurant. The masked captors ___ ___o the victims' vehicle and to wear hoods. They were taken to an unknown residence in ___ ___d detained for two days until the ransom demands were met. The captors demanded ___ ___tims' two vehicles.

___eir confinement, the captors told the victims there was an employee at the restaurant ___ ___ them with current information about what actions were being taken to secure their re___ ___rs also said they knew about the wedding reception and that they were targeted becau___ ___ a Chrysler 300.

---

opened my eye brow. B___
outside the door from ___
whining and started ___
She seemed worried a___
recognized my tears and ___
and she always ___
her love for me was ___
In the summer of 19___
day ever happened. B___
she died painfully, ___
down in the dumps all ___
days and nights for mom___
best friend, she never told me ___
and I never would tell he___
our first photograph ___

---

Dear Diary,

Today I was super nervous cuz ___
knew when Ma was giving birth ___
got a text message from my step dad ___
was gonna be a sister in a few ___
he picked me up and off I went ___
hospital. I named my bro Nathen.
beautiful. I'm gonna write letters ___
everyday and send him the ones ___
been writing when he was in Ma ___
like how good it is going to be, ___

---

aftermate
~~aftermth~~. I didn't take it
serious. But maybe it
do, I can ~~get~~ be o___
of the best in la___
This is my cha___
for freedom. I can ___
create my own pa___
And never end up h___
again. Cuz in o___
year I'm an a___
and ___ cold end u___

# NEW LIFE

**Life-or-death situations should bring families closer together** than ever. Right?

Not.

What a big, fat lie.

Well . . . maybe it was an unrealistic expectation.

I imagined a scenario where Ma would ask me what I went through, and I would tell her. How scary the whole thing was for me. How begging for money was humiliating. How people I thought I could depend on let me down. Then realizing not everyone will be there for you when you need them. Now I can't trust people.

Despite all of this, I didn't let fear take over me. I didn't run from the problem. I faced it head on and harnessed the strength inside me that I had no freaking idea I had. And I did it cuz I thought saving her life would make her love me more, and we'd live happily ever after.

Except Ma never asked me how I felt or what I went through. The reality is that even though I helped save Ma's life from kidnappers twenty days ago, a part of her has died, and I think a part of me has died, too.

"Get on the floor right now. Are you listening?"

She's been forcing me to sleep on the ground every night, double-checking if the windows are locked. I think she's worried someone might sneak in through the window. Or is she worried about a drive-by? Thing is, I don't wanna lie on the floor mattress with Ma and Rafael. I can't sleep. It's uncomfortable. I miss my bed. I miss my sheets. I miss my blanket. I miss my privacy.

"Fineeee," I say, trying not to look at her bloodshot eyes. It's not easy looking into a pair of eyes that look like they got stabbed and red dye exploded.

Ever since Ma returned, it looks like she's got the eyes of the devil.

"Do it!" Ma urges me, and I lie on my back next to Ma and Rafael in silence.

Ma is being cold and distant, so I turn on my side, away from her, and count the days until I get outta here. We haven't returned to our apartment since Ma's hostage situation came to an end. We've been living at Ma's boyfriend's parents' house, and I gotta pretend like they're my family now even though I wonder if they secretly hate us. Maybe they hate Ma for getting pregnant with Rafael, or for her going across to the wedding celebration, or for taking over their bedroom.

I don't feel comfortable. I need another pillow, so I get up to find one.

"What did I say?" asks Ma, and I don't even attempt to explain why I'm on my feet. I lie back down. I think Ma is afraid of returning to the apartment since the kidnappers know our address. They knew what I was wearing that day. They knew about Rafael. They knew about our lives.

How am I supposed to know anything when Ma doesn't tell me

what's going on? She's never explained exactly what happened that night. But me, I'm not scared of the thieves who stole our lives. My greatest fear is the possibility that this could be our new lives forever, and I really don't think I can live inside a turtle's shell for the rest of my life.

I'm different than Ma. I hate pretending I'm okay. I hate being inside a room all day and literally keeping all the lights turned off. Ma finds comfort in darkness, and mostly comes out of the room whenever Rafael needs to take a bath. Which is a lot less than she used to bathe him before she got kidnapped.

I wanna be me.

I wanna start high school in a few days like it's a new chapter.

I wanna make new friends.

I wanna get good grades.

I wanna help my cheer team win another national title.

I wanna join the track team under the coach who recruited me after my race two years ago.

Adults always say that high school is the best experience in your life, but it won't be for me with Ma not allowing me to go anywhere, not even the skate park. I'm worried I won't ever have a normal high school experience. I only have one life.

"Ma, when are we gonna go home? I can't sleep." I dare to ask her, even though it's bedtime. It's not like she sleeps either these days anyway.

"No sé, stop asking me."

I pissed her off again before bedtime. It's not how it used to be before. Back when we slept together on the same bed in our old casita in Ghost Town. On nights when I couldn't sleep, I would wait for Ma to come home from the bar. I'd lie on Ma's arms while she rubbed my lips, caressed my cheeks, grazed my eyelashes, applying invisible makeup to soothe me. The touch of her fingertips, light as a feather, hypnotized me and I would drift off to sleep.

These days I only seem to make her angry and I think it's best I live in my thoughts or write it in my journal. It's safer in these places.

"Okay." *Don't ask any questions.*

Even Rafael seems to hate our new life. He cries more than before, and I never imagined that a little body like his could cry so much. Ma says it's cuz she can't produce breast milk anymore, and he misses it, but I think he just misses our old life, too. Sometimes, I just want to scream like my lungs are on fire and destroy every single thing inside the house just so that someone will notice me burning alive.

# SET UP

*Dear Diary, good morning from another trapped life.*

I write in my journal entry today, then quickly sneak into the kitchen for a snack. There are a few people visiting today, checking up on Ma and Rafael. I sit at the dining table, noticing a copy of a Mexican newspaper from across. I glance over it. The front-page headline captures my eyes.

A BALAZOS DE RESCATES

I quickly flip the page to the main article and read two pages, side by side.

A couple of men arrested at the top right side of the page, and on the left, a photograph of two vehicles in a parking lot. The article is about the capture of Mexican kidnappers. They got caught when a young woman managed to escape from the vehicle she had been forced into. The woman jumped out of the moving car and ran for her life in the middle of a busy intersection in broad daylight. She flagged down nearby police, and a shoot-out ensued between the alleged kidnappers and law enforcement.

Four men apprehended. Hundreds of thousands of dollars discovered. A parking lot full of stolen vehicles and numerous driver licenses of American and Mexican citizens were found when they searched their property.

"If anyone suspects they were kidnapped by these men, please come forward," the article states, and it makes my heart stop.

Closely, I inspect the photograph with the two vehicles and focus in on the car used in the attempted kidnapping. It's a silver Honda CR-V and it looks exactly like the one we gave to the kidnappers as part of the ransom. *Oh my god.*

I run to show Ma the newspaper. She's preparing Rafael's bottle with baby formula.

"Ma, I'm pretty sure this is your car. Just look. Read what it says." I bring the newspaper closer to her face cuz she often complains about her vision going blurry.

She wraps her hands around the warm plastic bottle and scopes out the article.

"¿Verdad? It's identical," I tell her.

Ma's face grows pale like she's seen a ghost, but I know she must know. It's *them*. The thieves who stoles our lives.

I nudge her—"Ma?"—and look at her face. Her mouth isn't moving. It's frozen. Still. Shut. "You're gonna say something, right? You gotta. Call the number, right now," I encourage her. Ma must speak up, but I have a feeling she might not.

She walks back into the bedroom and shuts the door behind her. I stay back, taking a closer look at the photographs of the men in a lineup, and I begin to feel this hatred growing inside of my belly. *I can't let them get away with what they did to us.*

I examine their faces. All four men look nervous. They got the same hair and skin color as me—we're morenos with dark, brown hair. They could easily pass for one of my tíos.

Suddenly, I feel like I'm spinning, confused. These men don't look like the monsters I imagined they would be, big and scary. *But how could they steal our lives?*

Ma really needs to call this number. Explain to the detectives what happened to her that night. And have these men prosecuted for the crime they committed, give us our only car back and return the ransom to pay everyone back.

Then maybe I'll confront them someday and ask them questions.

*How could you do this to us? Do you have kids, too? Do they sleep okay at night? Why did you threaten me and my brother's life, too? What did we ever do to you? What made you turn to kidnapping? Why was the ransom more important than letting Ma go in peace? Can you please give my life back? And the ransom?*

I wish justice could deliver my old life back to me like a gift exchange, but reality has sunk in. This IS my new life.

"Get dressed. We need to go somewhere." Ma returns in a hurry.

I get dressed as fast as I can cuz I'm dying to leave this house.

Ma doesn't answer my questions about where we're going, she only replies, "...Yeah, that Honda is ours." Her tone monotonous. Flat. Dead.

"I knew it! It's over, Ma," I say out loud, feeling a small sense of relief that soon Ma won't be afraid anymore. No more sleeping on the floor mattress.

"Get in the car, Kris." Ma hurries me up to a borrowed car.

Finally, Ma fills me in on where we are going. The detectives want us to visit them at their office. The Mexican police retrieved the Honda CR-V from the kidnappers and ran the license plate. It traced right back to Ma. It didn't take long for Mexican authorities to contact law enforcement on this side of the border after the article in the newspaper was published.

"We're almost there," Ma says before going quiet, fixing the mirrors and fidgeting with her hair. She doesn't seem as thrilled as I am to learn the truth.

Thirty minutes later, we arrive at the Federal Bureau of Investigation building in one piece. The five-story building is right off Interstate 35, the highway that leads straight into Mexico.

Ma and I make our way into the lobby, and I'm in awe with all the high-tech security inside. I never knew a place like this existed.

"Please remove everything that's inside your pockets," the security guard orders us.

I dig deep inside my jean short pockets. I come out empty-handed. "What you think they're gonna tell us?" I whisper to Ma.

"No sé. Probably gonna be asked some questions," Ma replies, and I think back to the way the detectives interrogated me the night Ma went missing. I get this weird feeling in my gut that makes me hold on to my stomach.

"Clear!" The security guard gives us the green light, and we're escorted to an elevator.

Still holding on to my tummy, I follow behind Ma, reminding myself that it's different this time. We're on the other side. It's all over. I'm safe. Ma is alive.

But she's also kinda dead.

"Sit afuera, Kris." Ma motions me to sit outside on a hard black plastic chair. She won't invite me inside this private room, but I wish she would. Can't she see that I'm a part of this, too?

I sit outside thinking about all the things that could possibly be happening inside that room, and why Ma didn't let me go in with her. *What if Ma was actually involved in something illegal and doesn't want me to know? What if she gets arrested? Is that why she didn't wanna call the number? What if they tell Ma that I lied to her about the detectives not being involved from the beginning?*

I sit there, biting my nails as if they will grow back just as fast as I chew them. Looking left to right. Holding my breath that cops won't take Ma away in cuffs or that Ma won't come out yelling at me, disappointed that I lied to her.

About an hour later, Ma finally leaves the room and says, "Let's go."

"What they say?" I ask her.

"I'll tell you in the car."

I'm nervous about what she will tell me, but at least Ma hasn't been arrested and she doesn't appear angry.

When Ma and I hop in the car, she adjusts her rearview mirror again, looking around our surroundings carefully. "Kris . . ." Ma pauses, staring off into the monte.

"Uh, huh?" I stare at her, wondering what's on her mind.

"Remember this . . . Be careful who you trust. Do you hear me?" Ma says, emotionlessly. Like she's repeating it from someone else.

I nod, uncertain what she means.

"When's the last time you saw Claudia?" asks Ma, turning on the engine and beginning the drive back to the south side.

"Umm . . ." I remember seeing Claudia in the parking lot at Coyote Cantina, after Ma's coworkers gave me some money. "I saw her the day you were . . . ," I answer, trying to find a synonym for the word *kidnapped* that won't trigger Ma.

"The day you were gone," I decide to say instead, then tell Ma that Claudia gave me twenty dollars toward the ransom.

"Claudia and her sister Sandra are suspects."

"What?! Are you freakin' serious? That's so messed up!"

"Sandra's boyfriend was the ringleader," Ma says matter-of-factly, and continues to relay what the detectives told her.

Ma says Sandra's boyfriend is a cartel member who turned to kidnapping people for ransom cuz it's faster to make money from desperate family members.

So I guess Ma wasn't involved in anything shady. *Thank god.*

"But Ma, didn't we just see them together recently?" I recall Sandra and Claudia hanging out at our apartment a few months ago and even participating in Ma's baby shower.

"I don't get it . . ." Ma talks to herself. "But how could they do this? To me?" Ma's voice breaks. It's the first emotion I've seen from her in days.

I sit here uncomfortably, wishing I could turn to Ma and console her. I know what it's like to feel let down by the people who you thought were always going to be on your side. But I don't know how or what to say. It's easier for me not to say anything. What if I say something wrong?

I keep my mouth shut while Ma is probably dying inside.

Things just makes sense now. Claudia popping up out of nowhere, asking way too many questions. That should've been suspicious to me and Linda. That's how the kidnappers must have known what I was wearing. We were set up.

I turn to Ma, still avoiding her eyes but really wishing I could say something to her right now. *Just say it. Do it. No. I can't.* My body is hunched forward; she's trying to keep her hands on the steering wheel, but her hands keep shaking.

I feel terrible for her. Her own friends betrayed her. I wish I had the courage to give her a hug, but I'm scared she might push me away.

"Amá . . . they're gonna be caught real soon. Screw them," I say, instead, and hope Ma feels less afraid after today.

# 911

**Here we go, again.**

Ma and I are angry. We're screaming. We're throwing things. She hates me. I hate her. Fight. Fight. Fight. Fighting has become our sport. Ma typically wins. That's what we do every single day since we moved out of her boyfriend's family's house at the beginning of my freshman year. I'm a junior in high school now and we live in a different apartment, just a mile away from our old one.

Ma is yelling, "Give me that!" We wrestle for the house phone.

I yank it back from her and make my great escape—the bathroom. "Leave me alone! You've gone crazy," I scream.

"And you're a bad daughter!" Ma starts shooting word-bullets, but I feel dead already. Ever since Ma came home, her life is like walking through a minefield, and I'm being dragged into it, too.

Ma sees and hears things that aren't there. She screams in her sleep. She throws things. She's on edge and snaps way more than before. I think she's gone past the point of no return.

Whenever things get bad between us, she asks, "Why the hell

did you save me?" As if saving her life was a piece of cake and I came out of that situation unscathed.

"Thank you for your gratitude, Mother!" I usually reply sarcastically, wishing she could acknowledge what I had to go through.

Now Ma is banging on the door, telling me, "You better not call anyone, niña." As if I care what she thinks anymore.

*Who can I call?* I try to think of anyone I can reach out to before Ma breaks open the door and takes out the chancla and corners me, but my hands are shaking. I can't breathe. I can't think. I'm scared.

How did I get here this time? About ten minutes ago, I finally had the courage to tell Ma my dark, embarrassing secret—I think I'm suicidal. Like, how could someone like me ever feel this way? I'm supposed to be stronger than this.

"You're being so dramatic, if you wanted to die you'd just do it," Ma responded.

Knowing her, there's no way she would make an appointment for me to see a therapist or counselor if I ever mention it to her again. Ma believes therapy is only meant for crazy people.

"Yeah? Well, we seem like the perfect candidates," I'd said to Ma one too many times before.

People are afraid to ask for help, but I'm more afraid of spiraling into a deeper, darker hole. I'm worried there won't be any hope for me to crawl out of this alive.

"I need help!" I plead with Ma, resting my back against the bathroom door in the darkness and feeling my chest rising and falling with each shallow breath.

After Ma said those awful words to me, I ran to the kitchen and popped open a bottle of pills from the pantry. They were pain relievers, and I wasn't sure if they would actually kill me, but I opened my trembling mouth and swallowed them anyway.

Almost as soon as I'd done it, I stuck my fingers down my throat until I puked everything out. I got scared. The truth is, I don't literally wanna die. My skater friend Tommy died by suicide a few months ago, and I know that once it's done, I can't undo it. And knowing me, I'd miss my friends way too much just like I miss Tommy, too. Dying isn't exactly what I want. I just want to get rid of this pain that hurts too much, and I think if I stay here with Ma, I may end up doing something I'll regret.

"If you don't open this door, I'm gonna have to break it. Do you hear me, niña?" Ma is warning me con mucho coraje.

"Please, stop! I'm gonna go away, just leave me alone!" I warn Ma, yet I don't know how I'll be able to just leave home cuz I'm sixteen. I got no money. I got no place to go.

"Do you hear me?" Ma yells again.

"I can't . . . ," I whisper, gripping the phone tighter. I need to forget this mess I'm in. I need to start a new life. I need to get out of this endless loop before it kills me. I need a reason to live.

I dial three numbers.

"Nine, one, one. What's your emergency?" a woman says on the other line.

Five minutes later, the police arrive, and I come out of the bathroom, feeling relief that I had the courage to ask for help.

"Can you come with me?" the officer asks Ma. She's attempting to look relaxed, but I can see through her. She's furious.

They walk outside in the dark, while I remain inside.

When the cop is done chatting with Ma, he comes back and tells me he would like to talk to me outside now. Ma and I pass each other, and the air around her feels frightening. She doesn't dare to look at me.

"Tell me what's going on?" the police officer asks.

"I just wanna get away from her," I admit, without going into the details of our constant fights. I don't want Ma to get into trouble and potentially risk Rafael being taken away from her.

The cop sighs and says, "Your mom told me you were fighting with her." Before I can say anything, he asks me to turn my body, facing the wall. Maybe he's gonna inspect me for bruises.

"Okay, sir." I turn around, hiding the self-inflicted cuts on my wrists.

"You're under arrest for family violence." He handcuffs my wrists.

"What?" I freeze, not moving a single body part.

"Come with me." He motions me to make my way down the stairwell.

"No, sir. Please, this is a big mistake."

*How can Ma do this to me?*

"MA!" I scream.

The cop radios in, "Hispanic, sixteen-year-old female," and starts walking downstairs, gently pushing me to walk in front of him. It's hard to walk down with my hands tied behind my back.

"No. No. No. Stop, please!" I panic. My legs become Jell-O. Swear I'm gonna fall on my knees and face-plant. I drag the heel of my shoes into a dry patch of grass.

"Let me go!"

"No, let's go. I'm taking you in."

I'm in the back seat now. She really did it. She snitched on me. Through the glass window that separates me and the officer, I can hear someone radioing back, "¡Ándale! Take her to juvie." My heart is pounding like never before. The sound is inside of my ears.

BEEP. BEEP. BEEP. It's becoming louder and louder. I can't breathe again. I'm scared. Where am I going?

"Sir, please. Listen to me," I tell the officer calmly even though I'm struggling to breathe. "I made a mistake, I promise, I won't call again."

I shake my head no. I'm regretting all of this like Ma said I would.

"I don't wanna go to juvie." I keep talking to the cop even though I know he's not listening to me. No one is. I'm invisible.

"PLEASE!!!"

The cop isn't gonna let me go. We're pulling out of the parking lot of the apartment building. *I'm trapped.* I face out the window and try not to pass out.

*Why isn't anyone listening to me?* The red flashing lights bounce off the glass where my face is reflected. There it is. My ugly, crying face again just like it was at Tía's house two years ago. I thought saving Ma would make things better, but it's only gotten worse. Here I am now.

"Kid, we hear this all the time," the officer finally says in response, but he's gotta know, I'm not like those kids that go to jail.

I'm different.

"Just take me to an orphanage instead. My mom doesn't want me anyway," I admit to the officer, then I divulge everything as a last resort to persuade him to release me. I talk about Ma's childhood. Ghost Town. My dream house. The kidnapping. The ransom. Saving Ma. Her friends betraying her. The trial is happening sometime next week to prosecute the kidnappers. How everything has gone down the drain cuz of our past and how desperate I am to get help.

The cop says nothing. *Shoot. He probably thinks I'm crazy.*

"I'm serious! I'm not crazy. I know it sounds fake, but it's literally not." I try to get him to believe me, but I know my story sounds made up.

The officer glances at the rearview mirror, not to look at me, but to go around the traffic. It's Sunday night, and he has to avoid vatos driving home in their custom low-rider vehicles that they probably showed off at the La Sanber cruise, Laredo's unofficial weekend parade for adults.

We stop at a red light, and I try to hunch down as low as possible. *I can't let anyone see me like this. A bad reputation will follow me to my grave in this town.*

One of those vatos in a low-rider pulls up beside us. He's got a tattoo running along his temple, like mascara dripping down his brown face melted by the Texas heat. Narcorrido music blasts from the radio. The vato is trying not to flinch next to the chota.

Green light. *Clear.* I stare out the window at a dark, flat horizon. There isn't much to see—mostly yard shrines of La Virgin de Guadalupe, seedy motels, and women walking the streets down La Sanber.

We arrive at the juvenile detention center, enclosed by barbed wire, and I still can't believe what's happening to my life. *I'm not going to jail. I'm fine. It's all in my head. Man, I'm really going insane if I'm seeing things that aren't here.* I attempt to convince myself that I'm dreaming, but when a male security guard walks out of the juvenile building and yanks open the back seat door, he snaps me back to reality.

"Move it!" he says forcing me out of the vehicle by the arm.

I refuse—"No, déjame"—and give him the mal de ojo for pulling my arms like I'm a rag doll. I wiggle around in hopes the handcuffs will slip off my skinny arms so I can run free. But I'm too weak to fight back.

Inside, a woman named Lupe who's got a square face and bushy eyebrows barks at the security guard, "Get her to stand still," but now my chest is heaving, and I can't just stand still.

I'm gazing at the exit door. *If only I could escape.* The officer eyes my every move, guarding between me and the exit door like a linebacker. He would squash my body if he really wanted to.

"¿Cómo te llamas?" Lupe asks for my name, and I mumble, "Elvira," then shrug to explain, "but my friends call me Kristy. It's short for my middle name."

"Stand there," Lupe says, pointing at the ground. There's an outline of a square in red tape. I step inside the box, and ask, "Here?"

"Yup. I'm gonna take a photo of you," she says, and no this isn't the time to smile. I always smile in photos and stick out my tongue. Not that I can smile anyway now, cuz my lips feel glued together.

Before I can speak a word and confirm if this is a mug shot, Lupe counts, "Uno, dos y tres."

*Great.* Now my ugly crying face will leak out to the public someday and ruin my life even more.

Lupe liberates my shackled hands and takes my right hand up to the counter. "Press down." One by one, my fingers are rolled from side to side on a blank ink pad, and pressed to a notecard dated:

November 23, 2008

"Fill out these forms." Lupe hands me a sheet and a green crayon.

*Please, answer the following. In the past few days, have you felt . . . ?*
*Depressed?*

*Suicidal?*

*Wanting to hurt anyone?*

I check yes to all the questions. If I'm honest about how I feel, maybe these people will help me feel better. For the first time ever, I admit my secret to a stranger, and it makes me feel exposed and yucky. Like my skin is inside out. It hurts. My hidden life at home is being revealed to the public.

"Ma'am?" I fidget. She's focused on filing the paperwork. I interrupt her. "Is this gonna be on my record, forever? Like if I wanna go to a university someday, can this affect my chances getting in?" Not that I know anyone that's ever been to a university and gotten a degree, but what IF someday I wanna be the first person in my family to do it?

I worry that my life could really be over now that I'll be considered a criminal for life.

"We're gonna wait and see what they do with you."

"Who?" she makes me sound like I'm just an object.

"The judge." Lupe doesn't explain any further. Instead, she tells me to follow her into a brightly lit white room behind the front desk.

She shuts the door behind us. "Abre la boca," she orders me.

My jaw drops like a nutcracker doll and Lupe pulls out one of those wooden Popsicle sticks that restrain your tongue at the doctor's office. I don't know what she's looking for, but "There's nothing in there," I tell her as she examines underneath my tongue.

Then she says to empty my pockets while holding on to a clear plastic bag. I got nothing on me.

"Now take off your clothes."

I show her the side of my underwear and ask, "Even this?"

"Sí. Pos ¿qué esperas?" She doesn't know what's taking me so long, but the truth is, I don't feel comfortable getting naked in front of a stranger.

"Can I just change like in the bathroom?"

She shakes her head no and says she's gotta make sure I'm not hiding anything.

"Like drugs?"

"Yup," she replies.

"I don't do drugs, though." In fact, I promised myself years ago I'd never touch a single illegal drug. How can I support the very thing that has ripped apart so many families on both sides of the border? I'd never. Hell no.

"It's procedural. We have to." Lupe darts her eyes. She's annoyed at my hesitation. "Everything comes off. *Rápido*." I have no other option, I guess.

I take a deep breath and close my eyes. *Okay, just do it. Nothing bad will happen.* I undress completely naked from head to toe. Then Lupe slips on a pair of latex gloves. She bends down on one knee and nudges the back of my knees, "Spread 'em."

"Ma'am, do I really have to?"

Lupe gives me a side-glance and sighs.

I widen my stance, shoulder-width apart. *She's not gonna hurt me. It's procedural.* Shielding my breasts with my hands and anticipating the strip search, I focus on the decaying beige ceiling, counting the lines connecting each grey, dull block. Noticing how run-down this building is.

*Mmmmm.mmmmmm . . . mmmmmm.* I hum.

All sorts of questions begin to pop up in my head like, *Will she notice I'm not a virgin? Will she ask me when I first did it?* Then Ma will find out more secrets and when I tell her what happened, she won't believe me.

When it's all over, Lupe gives me an orange suit, sports bra, and long gray socks that perhaps at some point were crisp, white socks. She also hands me granny-looking underwear that might as well fit like diapers. Then, at last, my first white pair of shoes that have Velcro straps instead of shoelaces, shoes two sizes too big for my size four feet. My new clothes reek like an old vintage shop. I put them on, and then I stash the clothes I arrived with inside a plastic bag. Lupe takes my things from me and throws them in a locker.

"Ven," says Lupe, and I'm led down a dark hallway that comes to a dead end in front of a metal door.

I get the creeps, so I follow Lupe on the edge of her heels inside.

"Number three," Lupe says to me.

I step into a dark room. It's a cell block.

"This is you."

I can hardly see my hands in front of me, so I use my sense of touch to feel what's inside of this place. There isn't much room for me to move around, but I come up the side of a flimsy mattress that sits on top of a metal platform. I launch myself on top of it and cover my body with a thin blanket that feels more like sandpaper.

"Wake-up call is six in the morning. A punto, okay?"

"Mmm-hmm," I reply, feeling tempted to tell her that this place feels like a closet, and I'm scared of the dark. I wish she could stay, or turn the lights on, but then she will discover my fear of the dark. I doubt she'd care, anyway.

Lupe closes the door in front of me. Keys clasp against one another. The dead bolt lock clangs shut.

# JUVIE

**A loud, blaring noise outside my cell pierces my eardrums.**

I dab the inner part of my tired eyes with the cuffs on my orange jumpsuit. It's smeared in black from my mascara. I was crying all night long.

Above my sleep-deprived body, a fluorescent light flickers off and on, exposing the depressing beige concrete walls that entrap me. There's a stainless-steel combination toilet and sink in the corner that looks as gross as the cement floor. It's covered in smudged, dark patches as if someone spilled gasoline and allowed it to dry out. There's no window in my cell or glimmer of sunlight to illuminate this soulless place.

I blink a few times just in case this is just a dream. But these days, nightmares could be a real-life thing. This is it. I'm locked up in a prison cell. Waking up inside this tiny room makes me wonder about other girls who ended up in this situation. Did they feel hopeless, too? Did they feel scared, too? Did they try to get help, too? Before I can wonder how they eventually made it out of here, the metal door in my room unlocks.

"Wake up!" a woman's voice echoes just outside the door, and it gets me on my feet.

Suddenly, the door swings wide open, inviting a ray of light.

*FREEDOMMMMMMMM!*

This must mean I'll be released now. I tippy toe toward the door and lean my head out. There's a central area surrounded by cells numbered one through seven. A few feet from my cell stands a big, scary woman with puffy hair. She's pointing at a red bucket filled with water while five other chicks in orange jumpsuits stand around it. I notice how each chick takes turns pulling out a sponge from the bucket and taking it inside their cells.

The scary woman walks up to me and barks in my face. "Numero tres, whatcha waiting for? Ándale."

My back snaps straight. "Huh?" I reply, unsure what I'm supposed to do. I thought I was leaving.

The woman grabs my skinny arm and brings me to the center of the room. She introduces herself as Ms. Morales, but tells me to call her "La Jefa." She's the boss. "Niñas, this is Elvira," she tells the chicks in orange jumpsuits, who don't seem to care who I am.

"Hi," I say anyway and tilt my head down. My chin rubs against my chest. I'm way too embarrassed for anyone to see me like this. *I don't belong here.*

"Tómalo." La Jefa tosses a wet sponge and motions me to observe what the other chicks are doing. "Mira. Asina."

Sponge in hand, the chicks scrub their cell walls. Repetitive, circular motions. Eyes half open and half closed. They're sleepy. They're like robots. *What's the point of this?* I wanna ask but say nothing. It doesn't seem like I have a choice.

"Scrub. Scrub. Scrub, let's go." La Jefa orders me back into my cell like I've done something bad and need to go to time-out.

"Okay." I obey, but it feels pointless.

I'm back inside my dim cell with a wet sponge, looking around to check for areas that need to be cleaned. I start off by scrubbing the toilet seat like a hundred times until it feels clean.

"Keep scrubbing!" La Jefa orders all of us.

I keep scrubbing, harder, deeper, and longer. Now I can't feel my wrists. They're going sorta numb. I'm tired.

"Okay, stop," La Jefa finally calls it quits, after about sixty minutes of labor.

I attempt to sit on my flimsy bed to take a breather, but La Jefa invades my cell and says, "No, no."

So I stand on my feet.

"Here, take this," she says when she takes out a white toothbrush with rough bristles from a pouch and squirts toothpaste on it for me.

"Thanks," I say, and turn on the faucet in the toilet sink and begin to brush my teeth while La Jefa watches over me. She eyes the motion of my tired wrist as if she were a dentist inspecting me for cavities.

When I'm finished, she snatches the brush from me and says, "We hold them."

I nod and say, "Okay."

"Now, go shower."

"Where?" I ask, and La Jefa walks out of the room and points toward a corner. There's a shower head. No curtain. No stall.

"The girls here take turns."

The chicks line up for a shower, and La Jefa turns on the water. One by one, the others undress in front of me. I look away and try not to look at them. I don't wanna make them feel uncomfortable.

La Jefa takes out a timer like the ones officials at my track meets use and says, "Remember. Ninety seconds." We have less than two minutes to rinse from head to toe. I'm fifth in line, and I desperately wish the timer could slow down. By the time I'm next, I tell myself I'll probably be released from this place, and I don't gotta get naked in front of random chicks and feel exposed.

A raspy voice from behind me says, "Cáele. You're up, ruca." I look back and it's a chick with a pixie haircut with cheeks as puffy as a chipmunk. She calls herself Cha-Cha.

"Apúrate." La Jefa says to hurry, and I undress.

I detach the Velcro strip from the front of my orange jumpsuit and launch the clothes on a table that's next to the shower. I quickly wrap my hands around my chest and take one step forward under the shower head. The timer begins, and the cold water splashes over my tangled hair. It makes me shiver. My knees buckle a little. I hate cold showers.

When my time ends, I realize that everyone else has put on the same jumpsuit they were wearing before they showered.

Afterward, everyone sits at a round plastic table, and we're fed breakfast on a food tray with little squares. Breakfast consists of a tiny pile of scrambled eggs, one pathetic sausage link, and a carton of strawberry milk.

I eat my breakfast before the rest of the girls do, and I hope we get seconds. I'm starving still.

La Jefa steps out of the room.

"You drinking that?" Cha-Cha points at my milk carton.

"Ummm." I look at my milk and slide the carton toward her and say, "You can have it." I only give it to her cuz I know I'm gonna leave soon, and I overheard her say that she has been locked up in juvie for months. She's a veteran.

In one giant gulp, Cha-Cha chugs it. "Yummm." She rolls her eyes and busts out a little dance with her shoulders. She jokes about how many cartons of dairy she's drank in one sitting.

"Ten, rucas! You wanna compete against me. Pos dale . . . ," she challenges the others. Everyone but me joins the banter. I remain silent and observe. The other chicks in orange jumpsuits look much younger than me.

There's La Güera, a light-haired chick with hazel eyes and blond highlights. She has a scar that runs across her right cheek. Then, there's Chaparra, a short morena with straight brown hair. The other chicks don't speak as much as Cha-Cha, La Güera, or Chaparra do, but they laugh at Cha-Cha whenever she gets excited about something. She moves her hands, shoulders, and hips from side to side like a Cuban dancer. I think that's why she's nicknamed Cha-Cha.

"Puro Santo Niño," Cha-Cha says throwing a hand sign, and jokes how tough people are in her barrio.

Cha-Cha is from a neighborhood that is like Ghost Town, a place with Mexican American families who don't make much money, live in aging trailer homes or small, colorful houses that might be condemned in other areas.

I sit on my seat, just listening and regretting giving Cha-Cha my milk cuz I'm still hungry, and now I'm dreaming about having an unlimited amount of Big Red and Whataburger.

La Jefa returns and sits down with us. Everyone goes silent. She motions us somewhere, to another room, wherever they have us going next after breakfast. *Can she give me an itinerary? A rundown?* I don't like not knowing what's next.

Out of nowhere, a voice is heard over her walkie-talkie. "CODE RED. CODE RED."

She hops on her feet and runs out to the hall, instantly alert, leaving the door open behind her. There's some commotion just outside our hall. The only thing separating our area and the boys' is a long hallway partitioned with glass. We try to see what's happening. My heart is pounding a little.

Cha-Cha's dark brown eyes bulge wide open as she rushes toward the glass windows. I stand frozen, unsure what to do.

La Güera screams, "Over there!" She points at the far end corner, and that's when I see him. A young boy, not older than eleven, is strapped in a white jacket or something. His upper body is constrained tightly like he's been mummified, and he's running toward the glass.

"La neta, go help him!" La Güera begs Cha-Cha. The boy is now banging his forehead against the glass, and I start to think his head is made of steel cuz it hasn't cracked open and bled yet.

"Párale!" Some of the other chicks start yelling for him to stop, but he's not listening. I don't think he's here.

His eyes are shallow. Dark. Empty. He's a zombie. Cha-Cha sprints toward the door that La Jefa left open. For a split second, I contemplate making an escape, but where would I run to if Ma doesn't want me? I don't have a plan, so I just stay.

"Nambe, sir! Leave him alone!" Cha-Cha pleads as two guards press the boy's body against the wall. He's screaming and kicking, but they get a hold of him and drag his body away, into the unknown.

Cha-Cha is back. She's pacing back and forth, mumbling something. I don't know what.

"Cálmala. He's gonna be good. Al chile, güey." Chaparra attempts to calm Cha-Cha down.

"Nah! Pos sobres. That's my carnal's lil bro," she says, slamming her fist against the dull walls.

Chaparra asks, "Osea you don't think he's gonna like kill himself o qué?"

"No mames, güey. He just misses his brother. That's all he had," Cha-Cha replies in frustration.

*What happened to his brother?* Maybe he ran away. Maybe he's in jail. Maybe he died. I wanna ask, but it's none of my business, and anyway, I'll be leaving here soon and forget everything and everyone. But I can't keep my mouth shut. "Why was he wearing that?" I've never seen a piece of clothing like that before in my life.

"It's called a straitjacket, ruca," Cha-Cha says, and explains that they put it on you if you're suicidal.

*A straitjacket? I don't want that on me.*

When the situation is under control, and other staff members come to help, La Jefa returns.

"Show's over ladies, back to your cells. Vamos," she barks.

"Ms. Morales?" I call La Jefa by her real name and ask her, "Do you know when I'll get out? I wanna leave already."

Her thick bushy eyebrows slant as she says, "No sé. You're supposed to meet with a judge, y el te dice when you can leave."

"Pero when?"

La Jefa shrugs her shoulders and points at number three. My cell. "Get in there."

I walk back to my cell without an answer. Without a departure date. Without any certainty. I'm standing within the frame of my cell, looking out into the main hall. One by one, La Jefa does her rounds. The sound of doors shutting and locking makes me feel alone. Soon, I'll be next.

I can hear Cha-Cha's voice. She's cussing at La Jefa.

When I'm next, I walk to the back of my cell and prepare to

be caged in again. I desperately wish La Jefa could see that I don't belong here. *Set me free!*

My cell door shuts, and the lock clicks. I crawl on my uncomfortable bed, itching my body. Then I bury my face down in the mattress and cry. I know even quiet sounds will echo throughout our main hall, and everyone will know—I'm weak. *Stay quiet.*

I curl up, hugging my stomach. I'm hungry. Cold. Tired. Worried. What if I end up here for as long as Cha-Cha? What if I don't ever get to sleep in a real bed? Shower in private or eat pancakes and orange juice? What if I end up in a straitjacket, too, for writing down my feelings on that stupid paper they made me fill out?

I wanna get out of juvie, but if I'm freed, where will I live? I don't know what's worse, dealing with Ma's wrath or being locked up in juvie. If I end up back where I came from, who's gonna rescue me if the police won't help me? There's nothing in here for me. But I'm not sure if there's anything out there for me, either.

# LA SMART RUCA

**I've been in juvie for five days and it feels like I've been here** *forever*. Every day is the same . . .

The schedule:
6:00 a.m. Wake-Up Call / Scrub Walls
7:00 a.m. Eat Breakfast
7:30 a.m. Shower / Change / Brush Teeth
8:00 a.m. Study Hall
12:00 p.m. Lunch
1:30 p.m. Wash Dishes
2:00 p.m. Study Hall
5:30 p.m. Dinner
6:00 p.m. Back in the Cell

"Wake up!" La Jefa's callous voice catches me off guard, again. I don't think I will ever get used to it. It frazzles me.

La Jefa bangs on my door. "Number three, let's go!"

I wish I could sleep for two more minutes. But that's not an option around here. I get out of bed, fix my sheets, and make my way out into the open room. Half asleep and disoriented, I take the last sponge from the bucket, squeezing out the murky water. *Yuck.* I walk back toward my cell block, peering into each cell, taking count of everybody. Everyone is still here.

I've been told people can be released while we sleep. You wake up the next day. And BAM! They're gone. Around here, there are no farewells. No going-away parties. No way to stay in touch.

This feeling kinda reminds me of waiting for Ma after practice when I was a kid, wondering if I'd be the last one to get picked up again, but around here, I'm not alone.

There are five of us who are still here, and lately we've gotten close, even though La Jefa keeps reminding us, "NO TALKING TO EACH OTHER." We're not supposed to be friends, but we break the rules. I wonder if I'll ever see them again when we get out. I don't even know anyone's real name.

When we get to the classroom for our "Study Hall" session, La Jefa has reorganized our desks today, probably cuz she caught Cha-Cha and La Güera chismeando yesterday. Those two won't stop gossiping. La Jefa has nicknamed the duo Chiclets. They're like bubble gum, stuck together.

Now I'm sitting in between them. *Trouble.* I take a purple crayon cuz we're not allowed to write with pen or pencil, and I grab a new schoolwork booklet. It's about one inch thick and consists of multiple sections. Math. Reading. Writing.

"Remember to turn in your work todo completo by the end of the day," La Jefa reminds us, and I tackle the work head-on. It helps time go by faster.

I flip through the fifty plus pages and try to get a rundown on the type of questions. I notice how similar the math equations are to the rest of the math work I've completed in the last few booklets. They always begin with basic math questions, like the ones taught in elementary school.

How many candies are left if . . . divide these two numbers . . . if x=n, then . . .

*Easy.*

I get started on the work, while Cha-Cha complains. "Ma'am. Why we gotta do this? It's so boring." She's drawing funny faces on the booklet instead.

La Jefa snaps her fingers twice and says, "Put your feet down. Ándale ya, finish your work."

But how can she? Cha-Cha dropped out in the fifth grade just like my abuela Myra.

I put my head down and try to focus even though Cha-Cha and La Güera are communicating in some type of sign language and I'm stuck in the middle.

I plan to finish my work before lunchtime. I got less than four hours left. Then I can daydream about what I'll eat and do when I'm free.

It's 10:00 a.m. and I raise my hand. "I'm done," I tell La Jefa, and hand her my booklet. She scans the pages, pretending like she's checking my answers.

"Todo bien." She gives me the thumbs-up.

I let out a deep sigh. Then wrap my arms around my chest and slump over the desk. I'm off to La La Land, where I can imagine a better life. Sometimes, I can faintly taste Hot Cheetos at the back of my tongue. It makes my mouth water, and other times, like now, I imagine my body jumping over a hurdle. I'm flying.

I tap my feet quietly. I'm counting my steps in between hurdles. I gravitated to the hurdles cuz they felt like a challenge, like something a girl like me isn't supposed to do or be good at cuz I'm barely five foot tall. I just wish I could get out right now and focus on hurdling. Prove to everyone that nothing can stand in my way. Perhaps I could be as good as those girls at the state championships. Tall. Strong. Fierce. Or not. I got nothing in common with them.

*Daydreaming . . .*

I guess that's what you do when you're in juvie and have no idea when you'll ever leave. But I promise myself, when I'm out, I'll savor everything I eat. I'll not miss a single practice. I'll appreciate sleeping in a little longer.

I jump when I get hit in the arm with a crumbled piece of paper.

"Eyy, shh, shh." I hear a whisper.

I pretend not to hear it. La Jefa is in the room on her phone, but knowing her, she can still hear everything.

"No talking," she reminds us, her eyes glued to her phone. Minutes later, La Jefa steps out of the classroom to speak to Lupe.

Cha-Cha taps my shoulder, and says, "Attention. Attention." All eyes fall on her. With her small palms facing up like she's presenting a grand masterpiece at an art gallery, she reveals, "This is La Smart Ruca."

I've been given a new name: the Smart Chick. I give her a dubious look. If only she knew I'm not as smart as she thinks I am. Well, at least not at my high school. According to Cha-Cha, I'm officially the first ruca to have finished a booklet in less than two hours. It's a new juvie record.

"Pásemelas answers." Cha-Cha wants my booklet.

I don't hesitate. "Here." I grab it from La Jefa's desk and say, "Hurry, before she comes." She copies as many answers as she can, and then passes them to the others. Now I feel like I belong here. They think I'm smart. When the clock turns noon, La Jefa returns, and Cha-Cha shows some of her signature dance moves.

"I finished it, ma'am!" she announces, waving the booklet in the air.

La Jefa snatches it, rolling her eyes. "You guys want the good or bad news first?"

*Bad news, first. ALWAYS.* Everyone gives different answers.

"Okay, ladies, the good news es que you're going outside. And the bad news is that you girls have to wash all the dishes mañana."

"Y también de los boys?" La Güera asks if we need to wash the boys' dishes, too.

"Sí, all of them."

Cha-Cha gets angry and replies, "Nambe, Ma'am! ¡Qué chafo!" *Not fair.*

"No recess, entonces," La Jefa threatens us.

*Objection. Objection.* I wish Cha-Cha could read my eyes cuz I'll do anything to breathe fresh air. To feel the sun. To run.

I interrupt. "What if I wash them all by myself?" I hate doing the dishes, but I'll do them if I gotta. All the chicks turn to Cha-Cha. They wait for her approval, then turn to look at me. Cha-Cha doesn't say a word.

"I promise, I'll do it," I say.

"No manches, if you leave antes de los dishes, I'm gonna find you. ¿Entiendes, ruca?" Cha-Cha warns me, but she's only twelve. She doesn't scare me.

Anyway, I don't even know when I'm getting out of juvie. I haven't talked to this so-called judge. Neither has Ma checked up on me.

"Sobres," Cha-Cha accepts my offer.

All of us get in a line. I'm third to last, and we make our way to recess. On our way past the boys' section, they blow us kisses behind the glass window.

Cha-Cha flicks them off, and says, "¿Qué onda, homitos?" She seems to know everyone here.

"Keep walking," La Jefa orders. As we get closer to what seems to be the exit door to planet earth, I feel my heart pumping hard. *Can't they walk a little faster?* Finally. La Jefa unlocks a metal door, and when she pops it open, I feel the dry, hot air rushing deep into my lungs.

For the first time in my life, I appreciate being able to breathe. I appreciate the sounds of the howling wind. I appreciate the dust that twists and turns like a tornado. I appreciate the way the sunlight casts shadows on the ground. I appreciate the way the birds chirp. I appreciate being able to walk more than four steps forward without hitting a cement wall.

We're out here on a basketball court enclosed by barbed wire. I look up to see the clear blue skies blurred by the wire fence that hovers above us.

La Jefa brings out a cart full of basketballs and looks at her watch. "Tienen twenty minutes and that's it."

She moves to the corner of the yard and buries her face in her flip phone, again.

I grab a ball. Try to bounce it, but I can't. The balls are deflated. *Ugh.*

I take one anyway cuz I wanna play basketball like Ma, Linda, and Las Machas used to back at Three-Points, a park near Ghost Town, but recess isn't anything like that here.

Doesn't seem like anyone but me is excited to play.

Instead, the chicks mark their territory at the far end of the court, away from La Jefa and the security guard, whose belly reminds me of a perfectly rounded bowling ball.

They sit with their backs against the wall, and chat.

I grab a ball and shoot a three, then a free throw. I miss each time and almost stumble cuz my pants are so big the bottoms drag on the cement, reminding me of Pelon.

"¡Tienes manos y patas chuecas!" Cha-Cha yells across the court, walking with her wrists dangling like a T. rex and her feet tilted inward. For the first time in a long time, all of us laugh so hard that my stomach hurts.

Maybe it's the way the sunrays bounce off our faces that makes us feel less trapped. More relaxed. More open. I smack my lips and say, "Nada que ver," back. *I'll show her that I don't.* I roll the bottom of my pants up to my knees. Slap my thighs—*wake up*—and shake it out.

I'm in a running stance, inhaling deeply. *On your marks. Get set. Go.* Exhale. My arms swing forward, and my feet follow. I sprint from one side of the court and back. One. Two. Three. Four times.

The warm, dry wind sucks the cool air out of my lungs. My breath turns shallow. The hot weather makes me feel like I'm roasting inside an oven. My eyes burn. There's sweat beading down my temples, my armpits, my legs, down my entire body, and soon I'll soak this reused orange piece of clothing that was never meant for one-hundred-degree weather.

I feel liberated. I'm in control. No one can tell me to give up running. Only me. Not even the pain that I feel creeping up my thighs can stop me right now.

"Run fast, Smart Ruca!"

"¡Córrale!"

"Track star!"

The chicks are clapping and stomping their feet against the cement like they are spectators at a track-and-field meet, and I keep running faster and faster. The chicks chant, and it reminds me of Ma, Isela, Miss Marissa, and the cholos yelling at me to run faster. *Run faster from the other competitors in the race. Run faster from la chota. Run faster from the man in the car. Run faster from stray dogs.*

"Ladies!" La Jefa blows her whistle, forcing me to come to a complete stop. My legs wiggle, and I hunch over my knees. I can barely manage to look up at La Jefa to see what she wants.

"This is Karina," she says over my loud breathing. I try to say hello to the new girl, but I don't have the strength.

"You're freakin' fast!" Cha-Cha ignores La Jefa and the new girl, raising her hand to give a high five. I lie on the ground to catch my breath, staring at the puffy clouds floating above me. When I'm finally able to inhale, I notice the chicks surrounding Karina.

She's not speaking a single word, but she doesn't need to. Her eyes say more than a thousand words could.

"Hi." I wave, trying not to stare at her face for too long and make her feel uncomfortable.

"What happened there?" Cha-Cha points at Karina's face and grimaces at her bloody eyeball. She has no filter.

La Güera chimes in and asks, "You got hit?"

"No hablo inglés," Karina answers.

There's another chick named Galleta who has a birthmark the size of a round cookie on her arm. She makes a punching motion toward her face, "¿Asína?" she says to Karina.

Karina nods and admits, "Pos me saltaron." She got jumped.

"¿Quién?" Cha-Cha inquires who did it, and all of us chicks listen closely.

She makes some sign with her fingers, and Cha-Cha nods her head, saying, "Te tiro esquina. I'll hit up mi carnal if you want. They can protect you," Cha-Cha offers to help.

Karina smiles, without saying yes or no.

I grin. Then chuckle even though it's probably not appropriate. It's just that for the first time, I feel like we are all connected. Like we can talk freely without having to hide from La Jefa.

I just listen to everybody talking and notice how the sun gets brighter, illuminating our brown skin like golden bronzer. La Güera's scar is more vivid than ever when the sun hits her face.

Cha-Cha catches me staring at it and explains, "They got her gacho bad, too."

"Al chile. It was gacho," La Güera adds.

"¿Y tú?" Galleta dares to ask me about the scar that runs underneath my left eyebrow. I don't wanna reveal what exactly happened cuz it's hard to explain how a baseball bat whacked me in the face and knocked me unconscious.

"I hit myself by accident," I lie, and before anyone can say anything to that, Cha-Cha jokes, "Somos Club Scar Face or what?" turning the conversation away from me. Now we're laughing hard again. With every conversation, all my worries of feeling unwanted dissipate. I'm learning that we're no different than each other.

Cha-Cha opens up about her life. She's living with her grandma. She's never met her dad, and her mom is in prison. She landed back in juvie after attempting to steal a car. "Sometimes it's better being in here than out there. We're firme here." Cha-Cha likes the tight-knit family she's cultivated inside juvie.

"Sí, güey. Pura raza," Galleta says.

But . . . I don't think I could ever get used to being locked up in here, it's like a closet and I don't wanna live in one. Whenever I'm out of this place, I'm gonna go back to school and convince whoever the new hurdles coach is that I deserve to compete at the big track-and-field meets.

Screw what Coach T. said to me before he quit his job as the hurdles coach. Track meets outside of Laredo aren't just for boys, but for girls, too. Girls can be as mentally tough as boys regardless if they may be faster. If I can survive this place, I can pull through over the hurdles. I'll show them. *I just need to get out of here first.*

"Don't you guys think there's more out there? Like a better life?" I ask the chicks, looking at them seriously but also nervous they're gonna think I'm weird.

Cha-Cha grunts and says, "You're coming back, Smart Ruca," and adds that once you're registered in the "system," you'll just come back for another reason.

"Nah, I don't wanna." I envision a life outside of these barbed wire fences. Even if Ma doesn't want me, I'll leave. I'll go somewhere else and make a life of my own someday. Maybe I'll be the first to get into a university and get a degree.

"I think I'ma study after I graduate from high school," I tell them confidently even though I have no idea how I'll get into a university. This could end up on my record. Lupe never gave me a straight answer about that, and I haven't talked to a judge yet. What types of degrees are there, anyway?

Cha-Cha bursts into laughter, then La Güera and Galleta follow.

I nod my head and say, "I swear." I feel angry cuz La Jefa often says we're all delinquents, which annoys me. Maybe she's brainwashed them. *No. This isn't right. They gotta see what I see!*

"Nada que ver," Galleta adds. She doesn't think I'm serious.

Instantly in that moment, I think of this incredible woman named Gerda Weissmann Klein, a Holocaust survivor who spoke at my middle school when I was in eighth grade. Most students didn't care to listen to her. But everything about her story made me cry as I sat in the last row of the bleachers. She told us about her experiences during World War II at the hands of the Nazis. By the end of the war, Gerda had lost almost everything—all but her life. Despite enduring so much pain and suffering, she held on to hope that someday she would be liberated.

I googled her later that day and found out she published a book. The only books I ever read were the ones assigned to me in class. But listening to her story motivated me to figure out where I could find Gerda's book. It's incredible how the whole freakin' world could read it and learn how her will to survive overpowered darkness.

*Whoa.* Things begin to click in my head. Maybe hope isn't lost. Beyond all the darkness, there is light. Like Gerda, I could take on the mission to hold on to hope and overcome everything I've gone through. Immediately, I feel grateful for the opportunity to be alive. *I can change my life. If Gerda did it, I can, too.*

"Dude, I'm gonna write a book and talk about us," I blurt out to Cha-Cha without thinking twice. Maybe I can share my story with the world so that kids like us don't feel alone and the adults know we don't belong here. Prison isn't for kids. We're meant for bigger and better things. I feel it!

"Whatever, Smart Ruca from Anderson High School." Cha-Cha pushes her nose up, mocking me. It makes me wanna shake her. Wake her. Even though I go to a "better" school, whatever that means, I'm just like everyone here.

"I promise. I will." Not that I know how. *How do I write a book?* Okay, maybe it's like writing in my journal entries. *How do I get it out into the world like Gerda?* Okay, I know I gotta leave my hometown cuz I don't know anyone around here who has written a book. *How do I leave and with what money?* Okay, maybe I need to get an athletic scholarship from a university cuz we can't afford tuition. *How do I get a scholarship?* I should focus on the hurdles and become one of the best in the state. *How do I become the best hurdler?* I need to do anything I can do to get better, give it everything I got.

Maybe the track coach at Union High School was right. *"You could be the best hurdler Laredo has ever seen."* I hold onto the memory from last track season after finishing third place at the Regional Track Meet.

I jump on my feet and say, "And I know how! First, I'm gonna get out of here and get a scholarship for running."

La Jefa blows her whistle, and screams, "Recess is over! No talking."

# PART IV
# THE HURDLES

**2009 Goals**
- District Cha___
- Regional Qu___
- Top 3 @ Re___
- STATE!

# HURDLES IN THE DARK

**It's been two weeks since I got out of juvie but I'm still waking up** to the sound of an early alarm. At least I'm not sleeping on a lumpy, concrete bed made for humans without a spine.

Still, I wake in a haze, wide-eyed and bleary. 5:00 a.m. *Dammit.* I bury my face into my pillow. I know I gotta get up for practice, but I'm also trying to figure out this intense dream I was having. In the dream I was sprinting around endlessly on a dark, empty track that had no finish line. But something told me the race is supposed to lead me somewhere. Where? I'm exhausted from chasing nothing but the darkness. *Run. Kristy, run,* I heard voices calling from the stands.

Then I woke up and I'm realizing, it's not the sounds or sights that bother me the most about nightmares like this one. Or the others, like the police handcuffing me. Me begging them to release me. Not dreams of the girls in juvie locked up in a dark closet, waiting for someone to set them free. Not even the kidnappers chasing me on foot, in front of people that could help rescue me. Not even Ma screaming. Shouting she's unhappy I saved her life. *Nope.* It's not the images or the sounds or the memories. It's feeling powerless. Like I'm not in control of any of the outcomes in my life. I'm just a passenger in my own journey.

For once in my life, I wanna feel like I can control something. Anything to make me feel like I can steer my path, my future.

*It's just bad dreams. Not real,* I remind myself as I lie there, frustrated that my dreams could feel so real. I'm worried someday, I won't be able to tell the difference between nightmares and reality. I suppose that's what happens to your brain when nightmarish things keep happening to you in the real world. It's all too confusing sometimes.

I get out of bed, yawning and stretching. I drag my feet to the closet and slip on a black hoodie over my tank top and jump in a pair of gray sweatpants. I make sure I double knot my shoelaces. *It'll be worth it. First day of many practices.* Sometimes I need to remind myself of my new goals. *A scholarship. Leave this city. Get an education.* Swear to God, I'll find a way.

I walk to Ma's room. "Ma, where's the keys to the Honda?" I whisper into her ear, trying not to make too much noise and piss her off. There's still a weird vibe between us. Like Ma and I pretend like nothing went down the night we fought, and I was sent to juvie.

"Maaa?" She's knocked out cold, so I nudge her gently.

"*¡Ay! ¡Me asustaste! ¿Qué* quieres?" Ma throws the blankets over her head. She's startled.

Most people might find her reaction a bit exaggerated, but I know it's a natural reaction when you go through something traumatizing and develop PTSD.

Post-traumatic stress disorder . . . That's probably the only thing Ma and I have in common. But whenever I bring up it up, she's like, "It's not like it happened to you!"

She has a point, though. I wasn't there. I wasn't held at gun-point, blindfolded, and taken away to be held captive for thirty-six hours. But I do carry my own baggage from it, even if she won't acknowledge it. This pretend-like-nothing-is-wrong game we play has turned into a habit, but maybe it's for the best. If I stay out of her way, try to do everything she says, and ignore my feelings as much as I can, then things may just go smoothly around here for me.

Ma turns the clock toward her. "For what? It's bien temprano."

Damn. I knew it. I knew she would ask questions. Back when we lived in Ghost Town, I hardly had any rules. Like, I could go outside to play canicas with the cholos and come back after midnight. No questions were asked. Then again Ma was always at work. She didn't always know what I was doing.

Now she's paranoid about everything I'm doing. Even though I'm sixteen, nearly an adult, and able to make my own life decisions.

"Umm . . ." I fight between telling a lie or telling the truth. She's gonna think I'm making this shit up.

*Ma, I need to practice for the upcoming track season cuz we don't have an actual hurdles coach, and the only time I can train without a coach is when no one is awake.* I should 100 percent leave out the part where I'll be sneaking in and trespassing.

Instead of all of that, I just answer, "Riverbank Track."

Ma may go all detective mode if I told her the whole truth. She takes my probation way too seriously. I'm supposed to follow the rules for six months:

7:00 p.m. Daily Curfew
Attend and Pass Monthly Drug Tests
Pass Random Check-In Calls from Probation Officer

"For what?" Ma is asking now.

I answer, "Practice."

"With?"

"Sola." I can train myself.

I think back to how I stumbled upon hurdles in the first place during freshman year. Gina, my best friend, who dreads taking any risks, couldn't figure out what track-and-field event to try out for. She desperately wanted to make the varsity team.

I looked over the track, and there it was . . . a lone hurdle.

"Go jump that," I encouraged her.

"You go first." Gina dared me, and without thinking twice, I took the leap.

Next thing I knew, the boys' head varsity track-and-field coach walked up to me. "I'm Coach Miranda. Come with me." We walked over to another coach training a group of boys practicing hurdles. "Coach T., I got someone for your girls' hurdles events."

Coach T. looked at me and scoffed. "Are you sure you want to hurdle? Hurdles is a tough event. You need to have balls."

I ignored his machismo comment. I had heard it a hundred times before. That only motivated me to prove his ass wrong.

Now Coach T. is gone, and the school says it's a liability to practice the hurdles without supervision.

Hence, the trespassing to train secretly at 5:30 a.m.

Ma looks over her shoulder. Checks the time. "Kris . . . it's five in the morning. How are you gonna practice? It's dark . . ." Ma starts to act suspicious.

"I just am." It's the truth. I need to practice every morning cuz I only have two spring track-and-field seasons left.

"Ah-huh . . ." Ma doubts me. She doesn't trust me. She knows I've lied to her a million times before.

"I'm just gonna practice. I swear . . ."

If I tell her the part where I'm hopping the fence, she'd give me a hard no.

"Okay. Vete. Take my keys." Ma gives me permission, finally.

I drive in silence on my way to the track. The roads are empty. When it's this quiet and I'm driving Ma's Honda, I wonder if the woman who was kidnapped in this car ever has nightmares. Occasionally, I inspect the back, and make sure no one is there. It's just weird to be driving it after everything that happened, but Ma says it's a good vehicle to keep. The engine runs strong.

Six minutes later, I arrive at Riverbank Track.

I park underneath a mesquite tree fifty meters from the stadium and pull the hood on my sweatshirt up over my head. I take a flashlight and make way to the track like a fugitive on the run. I'm ducking, trying to hide from the cameras.

NO TRESPASSING

There's a sign in bold letters screwed on the fence. I ignore it. I gotta train.

I check out my surroundings. The coast is clear. I shove the flashlight inside the cuff of my sleeves. *Let's do this.* My fingers grip the metal fence tightly. I lift one knee up like I do into the hurdles and begin to climb the ten-foot fence. With each pull upward, the cold winds of winter thrust down on my chest, making my elbows buckle a little.

I look up at the night sky. The stars twinkle. They're the only witnesses around to greet me. *Hi. All of this will be worth it, right?* I think they can hear me. *Just stick to the plan. Don't you want to see what's on the other side?*

I continue to ascend, higher and higher. My fingertips reach the top of the metal gate. The prickling, sharp metal presses against my skin like a needle, but not deep enough to stop me from reaching the other side. I swing my legs around and perch at the top of the gate. Taking a deep breath, I make the jump from above and land with knees bent. This is exactly how you land safely. Learned this trick when I first started skateboarding.

There are no lights on the field. That's alright. I'll work with what I got.

I walk away from the warm glow of the parking lot and onto the dark track. It's like walking into nothingness, just like in my dream, but it's my only way forward.

I place the barriers on the 300-meter hurdle marks labeled on the track.

My first workout of the season will be running the 300-meter race three times with the hurdles set up and a full recovery rest of about three minutes in between each time.

I do a quick warm-up around the track, feeling a sense of peace come over me as I jog all alone. All the problems in my life have vanished in the night. After several laps, I switch to agility drills. Once the sleep has been shaken from my body and my muscles feel loose, I move on to practicing the hurdles. I get in a three-point stance like a lineman in a football game. I get a countdown in my head. *Ready. Get set. Go.*

Beginning with my left foot, I push off first, and the rest of my body drives forward in motion and into the first phase of the hurdles. From the starting line to the first hurdles in the 300-meter hurdles, it's

45 meters long. Enough distance to push hard and transition into an upright body position like a sprinter, accelerating to maximum speed. My goal is to attack the first hurdle quick and smooth. It's way easier to achieve a smooth hurdle clearance when my legs are fresh.

As I'm rolling through the straightaway, I anticipate the barrier. I've never actually hurdled when it's dark. I didn't think about how difficult it would be to see on the track, but it's really all about focusing on just one hurdle at a time anyway. Not becoming distracted by anything on the sidelines, the rubber track, or the girls running against you.

I suppose hurdling in the dark could help me focus on just staring down the crossbar since it's the only damn thing I can really see now as I approach the first hurdle. The crossbar looks like it's floating in the air since it's white and the rest of the hurdle is dark gray.

But I keep sprinting. If this is what it takes to be able to train without a coach, then so be it.

Hurdle one approaches. I attack the hurdle fast, trying to shake off the dust. It's been six months since I last hurdled. Now on the second phase: the backstretch. Hurdle two. My eyes adjust to the next white crossbar. I'm running up fast. I clear it.

Third phase: Hurdles three, four, and five. This is my favorite section of the race even though technically hurdling on the curve is the most difficult part of the event. When a hurdle is on the curve, the crossbar doesn't bend into the direction I'm running. It's straight.

To be most effective, I need to lean forward, with my midair body position on the same angle as the crossbar. I can't be leaning sideways toward the inside of the track or I'll be thrown off-balance. Once I clear the hurdle and my trail leg touches the ground, I move like a sprinter and then I'm able to lean on the curve between hurdles.

Something about running this section makes my turnover feel fast. I'm not a fan of straightaways, anyway.

One after the other, I attack hurdles three, four, and five without clipping them, but now I'm definitely feeling out of shape. My brain is still trying to remember how to step over a hurdle when I'm tired. I come out of the curve and into the fourth phase: the homestretch. But I call this section the DEATH ZONE.

Once I enter the homestretch, my legs begin to feel like they're dragging weights. The longer I keep pushing through this painful zone, the more I gotta battle my doubts. I worry I will slow down. I worry my legs will collapse. I worry I won't have the power to lift my body off the ground and clear the hurdle without clipping the crossbar and face-planting.

Truthfully, this part of the 300-meter-hurdles race is what keeps me up the night before a track meet. I sometimes hyperventilate just thinking about it.

I've never known a greater physical pain than running this section of the race. My body is on fire, burning up my lungs and legs. But if I give in to the pain and quit, I'll never get stronger.

As I fight through the death zone, my mind battles mental barriers. And I start imagining lots of things. Suddenly, the hurdles in front of me become more than just an object made of plastic and metal. They turn into things of my past or present. Things I wanna fight and overcome.

They're kidnappers. They're the police. They're juvie. They're bullies. They're the coaches telling me I'm not good enough to be a hurdler. They're all trying to get in my path on my way out, testing my inner strength and my desire to reach my goals.

Here comes hurdle six, and I wonder if I'll chicken out as I begin to feel dread mixed with physical pain. I'm angry, but I'm also hurting. My muscles feel like they're tearing apart. But I know this is part of training. I can't give in. It's just lactic acid building up within the layers of muscle fibers inside my body. I gotta keep pushing. I need to prove I can do it.

*Just run faster. Attack them. They can't hurt me.* I stutter-step behind the hurdle. Then wobble over hurdle seven, barely making it. *Are you gonna give up?* I can't feel my legs now. My form breaks and my hips sink as the eighth and final hurdle appears in the dark, looking way taller than thirty inches. Coaches say, "Pain is weakness leaving the body," but it sure as hell feels like it's only entering my body and never leaving until I stop running.

I push off the ground with the little energy I have left, attempting to remain on a seventeen step stride pattern in between hurdles. Quickly, I swing my arms up and down cuz the faster they pump, the faster my legs will move. But as I approach the hurdle, I give in to the pain. To the doubt. To the fears. And I go from sprinting on the balls of my feet to jumping like an exhausted horse trying to break free from being wrangled.

*Damn!* I clip the plastic crossbar with the front part of my trail foot and tumble down with the hurdle. My left shoulder hits the rubber track, which is meant to be spongy, not stiff like a wooden board.

*Owwww.*

I lie on my back, feeling dizzy and seeing stars in my vision. I blink twice and see the real ones up in the sky. My silent accomplices looking down upon me. Feeling like I suck, I wonder if my dreams of getting a scholarship for the hurdles are unrealistic. But if that's so, then why do I gravitate toward the hurdles?

Maybe what's on the other side could one day save my life.

# DREAMS AND PROMISES

**Rudy and I are sitting at the edge of his bed. He's a year older** than me, and we've been kinda dating for a few months. I feel comfortable around him and feel like I can talk to him about anything.

"I don't even know if I'm getting any better," I say to him, feeling frustrated about training without a coach. Lately, I've been relying solely on my extensive online research on hurdling technique and applying it during practice. It's been challenging considering that I can't watch myself hurdle. How am I supposed to know if I'm positioned in the most effective way?

Apparently, it's all about physics.

"Don't give up. Nomas dale. Keep going," Rudy says, like it's that easy.

I discovered hurdling is more than just running and "jumping" over a metal barrier. Hurdles is a sprint event. Not a jump event. Hurdling is a continuous action. Mastering the hurdles in track and field requires a deep understanding of biomechanics through Newton's third law: "For every action there is an equal and opposite reaction."

The first principle is momentum, and it makes or breaks the

race. A hurdler must gain momentum at the start of the race to set up their rhythm between the hurdles. They must maintain that momentum in order to finish strong.

The second principle is the pair of force and motion. They work together like yin and yang and enable hurdlers to successfully clear a hurdle.

The third principle is *center of gravity*. This will move according to the position of hurdler's body frame and limbs. When going over the hurdle, the athlete's center of gravity should stay low to the hurdle so they can maintain speed, rhythm, and timing.

So what I need to do is accelerate off the starting line, get over the hurdle enough to clear the crossbar, and maintain speed between the hurdles, all while maintaining proper form, even when I'm tired. Even though I understand all of this, it doesn't mean it's easy to do.

"I just feel like I'm never gonna get a scholarship if I don't have a coach."

"Pero, why can't you just train with your coach at school?"

"We don't have a hurdles coach for the girls' team."

There's Coach Miranda, who occasionally coaches us, but he's the boys' head coach. He doesn't coach physics. He's the type of coach who says, "Do it like this," without explaining why.

I've already attended a few practices after school this season, in addition to hurdling by myself every morning. There have been a few times that I've jumped in with the boys hurdling group and gone head-to-head against them, but Miranda won't let me ask questions. Well, what's the point of being a student of the sport if we're not allowed to ask questions?

The best thing about school practices though is running against the football team during sprint workouts and outrunning all but two

or three of them. Despite what Miranda may think about my enthu-
siasm for the hurdles, I wanna do something no track-and-field
athlete born in my hometown has ever done in the hurdles. I wanna
go all the way to the state championships and catch the attention of
college recruiters.

I think if something's never been done before, why can't I be the
first to achieve it?

I sigh and say, "Sometimes things in life seem way too hard."

Rudy gets flustered by my negativity.

"Why are you being so emo?" asks Rudy, and it makes us chuckle
a little. I'm being way too hard on myself.

But sometimes, I don't wanna feel like I gotta be so strong.

"*Es que ...*" I start to explain as Rudy is holding my hand, exam-
ining the dark creases on my skin. "I'm tired of trying to get my high
school coaches to help me." I snap my hands back and hide them
between my legs. "I want things to be easy," I say, dragging my words.

Rudy replies, "Kristy, you got everything you need to make your
life easy one day. Can't you see?"

"But I don't! How?"

No, I can't see it. All I can see is that I want these nightmares to
end. I want a coach who cares. I want to be the fastest hurdler in this
town. I want an athletic scholarship. I want to leave this city. I want
to be the first person in my family to get a bachelor's degree. I want to
write a book and publish it to help other girls feel less alone.

"Ay, nambe. You're the one that has more than me," I say.

I look around his room and I wish I had grown up in an actual
house with my own bedroom. I wish both of my parents were married. I wish I had family that has each other's back. I'd give everything to just have a family like Rudy's.

Maybe I'm just *envidiosa*, jealous my home was nowhere as spacious as his.

"Yeah, hmm-mm." Rudy acts weird.

I give him a little push and say, "What? I'm serious."

"I wish," Rudy says in a low voice, fidgeting with his hands.

"What's wrong?"

"Dude, you can't tell anyone. Okay?"

"What?" I pinkie-promise him as we sit side by side on his bed.

"I couldn't even apply for the job."

For weeks, Rudy wouldn't stop talking about working at HEB, our local grocery store.

"Why?"

"It's cuz I wasn't born here," explains Rudy.

"Okay?" I don't understand.

"You know what I'm saying?"

"No?"

"I don't have papers." Rudy whispers cuz his parents are next door watching a novela, and they probably made him swear not to tell anybody.

"Shut up! Your English is better than mine," I reply.

"I'm serious. My parents just told me."

Rudy tells me he asked his parents for his birth certificate, cuz he needed to first apply for a Texas ID in order to apply for the grocery store position. That's how he found out he's undocumented.

"Whoaaaaa." I'm lost for words.

"It's so messed up."

"Can't believe they knew your whole life that you were . . . ," I add, attempting to find the right words to say.

"A *mojado*," Rudy fills in the rest.

I shake my head. "Nah, don't say it like that," I reply, knowing that some light-skinned folks from the north side laugh at the expense of people who look like us.

"I'm screwed for the rest of my life, verdad?" Rudy asks me, his eyes looking as if he's wishing he was talking to a fortune teller.

"You're not!" I say, trying to offer some sense of hope, but I don't know if it's true. I know what it's like to fear what lies ahead in the unknown.

"How am I ever gonna make money? I can't get a job. How am I gonna go to school? I need a social security number." He sucks in a breath. "What if I get deported?"

I shake my head. I don't have the answers, just like he didn't for me.

"How am I gonna survive if I have to live across . . . ?"

"You won't have to," I say to offer some reassurance. I can't imagine moving across and moving away from your home and everything you've ever known.

"My whole life has been a lie," he says, looking defeated. "Don't tell anyone!" Rudy begs me not to say a single word.

"Okay. Okay. I won't," I promise him again, and hold his hand firm.

"Kristy"—Rudy's teary eyes look into mine—"do me a favor, okay?"

"Yeah, for sure anything."

"You needa get the scholarship. Go to college y lo haces for the both of us, por favor. Do it . . ."

"But . . . ," I reply, pausing and thinking about all of the real obstacles standing in my way. "What if I'm not good enough?"

Maybe I'm in way over my head.

"Nah, don't even go there. I know you. You don't give up."

"I guess." I shrug my shoulders and think, *But sometimes, I really do wanna give up.* Still, I say, "Okay, I will."

"What happened to that coach who congratulated you last year at regionals?"

"The coach who told me I could be really good?"

"Yeah, that güey!"

He's talking about Coach A., the best track-and-field coach in town. He coaches the girls' team at Union High School. His team has won six back-to-back district championships. They even shattered most city records across multiple events. I wish I'd known all of this before I started at Anderson, but Ma became dead set I attend the school after Coach Richard recruited me during a middle school track meet.

"Nahhh, I'm so sure! Like he's gonna help me. Anderson and Union are rival schools."

"Maybe he will nunca sabes." Rudy thinks I should just tell him what's happening.

"Dude, I don't know him like that." I've only met him twice.

Rudy hands me his phone and says, "If you don't contact him, then I will. Just do it." He's serious.

"Fineee." I take his phone and log into my Facebook account. "But he's gonna think I'm a weirdo."

I search for Coach A.'s profile and easily find him.

"Oh my god, mira . . ."

He's wearing a white wifebeater shirt tucked in. Khaki, baggy pants. His arms are crossed around his chest. Thumbs up. Chin up. He's drinking a beer with another guy who's dressed in a green plaid shirt.

"He's all cholo-ed out." Rudy takes the words out of my mouth.

Maybe he's from the barrios, too.

"That's so interesting . . ." Something about Coach A.'s profile picture resonates with me and my childhood.

I write him a message:

Hi Coach. Do you remember me? It's Kristy Gonzalez, the hurdler who runs for Anderson High School. This is probably weirdddd but you talked to me after a race last year and just wanted ur advice on something if that's cool? Okey. Talk soon. Thanx.

"Ugh . . . He's gonna think I'm crazy now."

"He's not!" Rudy reassures me. "He probably gets a lot of messages like that anyway. It's not a big deal."

Ten minutes later, I receive a notification. He replied!

"Rudy, o-m-g. He answered!" I jump up in excitement, but I'm also feeling nervous about his response.

How can I not be freaking out? He's the best track-and-field coach in our town.

"You're good. Chillax." Rudy laughs at the way I'm acting.

I hand the phone to Rudy and say, "You read it first."

"No, you do it."

I smack my lips with my tongue. "Ughhh. What if it's bad?"

Rudy checks it out first. I wait, anxiously preparing for Coach A. to say something along the lines of, *No, sorry, I can't communicate with athletes from Anderson High School.*

Rudy breaks the suspense, "He sent his number. He said to call him. SEE! You're good."

"When?"

"Call him right now," Rudy encourages me.

I dial. Coach A. answers.

"Hey, Kristy. It's real nice to hear from you. How are you?"

"Umm . . . So . . . I . . ." My tongue won't move with what I wanna say.

Rudy mouths silently "T-e-ll . . . him."

"I just wanna call and wish your team good luck this season." I hold back the truth.

"That's very thoughtful of you. Thank you," Coach A. replies, and asks if we already started training at my school for the upcoming spring season.

"Kinda. I mean, I've been mostly training myself."

"What do you mean? You guys don't have a hurdles coach this year?"

"Nah, not really. Coach T. resigned."

"That's not good. I'm sorry to hear that."

"Uh, hmm. It sucks. But I'm still practicing really hard, hopefully I can get a scholarship next year."

"Well, I said this once to you before, but I'll say it otra vez. Out of all the years I've been coaching in this town, you're the most talented I've seen. You got a big chance to landing an athletic scholarship. I'll even bet my money you can do it. You just need to focus and train hard. It seems like you're doing just that already."

I feel my heart flutter. "Awww . . . that's very kind of you to say."

"I mean it, kid."

"But I might move to just the sprints if we don't get a coach soon. Do you think I can get a scholarship in the open sprints?"

"Hmm . . ." He pauses.

"Or no?"

"Well, in my honest opinion. I think you are super-duper fast. But personally, I think your bread and butter is in the hurdles."

"Hmm-hmm."

I think he's right. But I desperately need a hurdles coach, then.

"What if . . ." I start to think about crazy things. Like what if I convince Ma to move us apartments, within the Union High School zoning, then I can just be a member of Coach A.'s girls' track-and-field team.

"What if I transfer to your school and I can train with you guys?"

Coach A. says, "That would've been fantastic!"

I interrupt, "Would've?"

"Yup. Between you and me"—he pauses between words as I press the phone speaker deeper into my ear—"I just resigned from Union."

"For reals?" I don't ask him why. "That's crazy," I say, feeling my initial excitement fizzle.

"But tell ya what . . . ," he starts to say. "I can probably help you with your hurdling for two weeks. Should give you enough time to get your bearings before the first meet of the season, right?"

I feel my heart drop to my feet, like I can't comprehend what's happening. *Holy sh*—"Shut up!" I shout into the phone, then apologize. "Oh my god, sorry, I didn't mean like *be quiet*. Just like, I can't believe it. This is so cool."

"Oh, I understand. I'm not that old," Coach A. responds flatly. Whoops. I shouldn't have explained myself and make him feel like an old fart.

"Thank you, Coach A. That would mean the world to me. I swear."

"Let me just make sure that we're good to go. Gimme a day or two to sort it out."

"Sounds good!" I say, giving Rudy the thumbs-up.

We get off the phone, and immediately, I run around in baby circles in Rudy's room, screaming. "Yes! Yes! Yes!"

I feel like I just won the lottery.

# BECOMING THE RHYTHM

**5:29 a.m.**

**I park outside of Riverbank Track.**

Rolling up the window manually, I yell, "Coming!" I'm on my fourth day of hurdle training in the dark with Coach A. and can't be late.

Panicking, I grab my spikes, which are so thin, you can practically stick a pen underneath and rip them apart. But they're my lucky spikes. I love them!

*Hurryyyy.*

I'm not late. Well, almost. Got less than sixty seconds left.

I'm still struggling with anything to do with time and deadlines. Makes my heart beat wild. It's like my body wants to intentionally be late and see if nothing bad happens if I miss the deadline.

"Give me ten seconds!" I shout from the parking lot. I'm scared to death of disappointing Coach A. He's strict when it comes to time. If I'm late by one millisecond, he might think I'm not the serious athlete he thought I was and potentially stop training me. "Sorry, Coach A!" I'm barely able to say out of breath as I approach the locked fence surrounding the track.

Coach A. unlocks the fence. Thankfully, cuz he's a PE teacher at the elementary school next to Riverbank Track, he's got access to the track. "You're right on time, kid," he says, glancing at his watch, hinting there will consequences if I'm ever late. "I expect all my athletes to be on time, plain and simple. And moving forward, just call me Coach."

"Okay."

The more we work together, the more I agree with all the rumors about him. Former athletes say he's strict. Intimidating. Tough on punctuality. His workouts are so hard it makes people throw up.

"Kristy, did you sleep well?" he asks with such curiosity that it makes me feel like he cares about me.

I pause to think. Even though it should be a simple yes or no answer, with him I think before I speak. Ever since he agreed to coach me, I've been too nervous to sleep at night.

I stay up late obsessively imagining running through the hurdles, making sure I don't look like a total beginner, so I watch YouTube hurdling videos on repeat.

"Umm . . ." I clear my throat.

*Just act cool. Be normal. Don't sound overly enthusiastic.*

"Yeah, think I did," I reply in a high pitch tone.

*Ugh, embarrassing.*

"Good. Good. So, check this out, I already set the hurdles up for you," Coach says, pointing his flashlight out to the far corner of the track, illuminating the exposed cracked pavement and the worn-out, synthetic rubber surface. Conditions here aren't ideal for hurdling.

I sigh, relieved he didn't notice how weird I sounded.

"Thanks, Coach," I tell him.

I ask, "Coach, what's the workout for today?"

"Tell you later. Right now you just got to focus one step at a time."

He never reveals the workouts until it's time to line up and do it. I hate it. It makes me feel nervous. I begin my typical warm-up jog—a slow one mile run.

"Run it slowwwwwly," he reminds me since I always run it way too fast.

"You got it, Coach."

I pop my headphones over my ears, turn on my iPod Shuffle and listen to Alanis Morrissette. I begin my run and stare up at the still-dark sky.

As I look up at the stars, I feel light as a feather. I feel so damn lucky to finally meet someone who believes in me and wants to be my private coach.

Two days after I spoke to Coach at Rudy's house, I had an in-person meeting with him. I made Ma and Linda come with me. That's when Coach discussed our potential two-week training plan after receiving the green light from the UIL, the high school sport association in Texas. Ma handed Coach an envelope with a couple of twenty-dollar bills for the training. That's how it became official.

*Stars, thank you for watching over me. I promise, I will do my best and not disappoint my coach.*

When I finish my warm-up jog, Coach claps loudly. "Okay. Let's go. Time to put in some work!"

"Yes, sir."

Coach bunches up ten hurdles, leaving no distance between them.

After doing a warm-up jog, hurdle drills, and stretches, Coach has me doing basic hurdle walk overs, gradually moving to quicker rhythmic drills, half hurdling, and then later, hurdles at full speed.

"Good job. Keep those arms nice and square. Try not to twist," Coach calls out to me. "Remember, the midpoint. Don't cross it."

I imagine there's a line going down the center of my chest. *Keep my right arm on the right-side area of the midpoint line and keep my left arm on the left-side area of the midpoint line.* Crossing the midpoint line will cause my body to compensate and lose balance.

"You don't want to twist your upper body at the top or coming down the hurdle," he reminds me. Twisting my upper body is a bad habit of mine.

Once I'm done with these drills, Coach separates the hurdles two feet apart and I begin the trail-and-lead leg drills to help me become more explosive and quicker off the ground as I work on clearing the hurdle.

In hurdling, you have a lead and trail leg. The lead leg is the driving knee that comes up toward the hurdle first. The trail leg is the leg that trails behind the lead leg, and it's the last body part to clear the hurdle.

"PA-PA." He claps to a beat and says, "I need to hear that rhythm louder."

I stay on the balls of my feet, driving my knee up toward the top of the hurdle. Opposite arm, opposite leg action over the top.

Aggressively, I snap my left lead leg down and whip my trail leg over the hurdle. Both of my legs almost contact the ground at the same time. The quicker I do both of those movements, the less time I'm in the air and the more time I'm on the ground running.

"Good, Kristy."

*Yay, I did it!*

Fifteen minutes later, we wrap up with the drills and I make my way to another area of the track where there are six hurdles spread five feet apart on lane number four. I do more skipping drill variations in between and over the hurdles, but this time I pick up some speed.

"I want you to really work hard on maintaining the same rhythm throughout these drills."

"Okay, Coach."

Coach reminds me that a hurdler's rhythmic stride pattern is their signature beat.

*TAP-TAP, TAP-TAP, TAP-TAP, TAP-TAP*

Coach claps to the beat of the rhythm of each of my foot strikes.

*Muscle memory.*

Slowly, I start to get a feel for it. It's like music to my ears and I love music. I suppose that's one aspect that attracts me to the hurdles. Focusing on a hurdler's rhythm tells you a lot about that person. It tells you if they're speeding up. It tells you if they're offbeat. It tells you if they're fatigued when their rhythm sounds heavy, flat-footed or on their heels, instead of staying on the balls of their feet.

Hurdlers can tell if they're slowing down or speeding up based on the cadence of their rhythm, which is crucial when they gotta determine what actions to take during a race.

"Let's hear that breath work now," Coach says.

*Phew. Phew. Phew.*

My breaths are on beat. They synchronize with my hurdling beat.

"Hip to pocket arms, Kris."

My arms move up and down with a slight bend at the elbow. I mimic my hurdling arms.

"Now put everything together."

Cadence + breaths + arm action. I sync everything together. It's a beautiful harmony. Something about this combo makes me feel like I'm a flamenco dancer.

"I need you to whip your trail leg over the hurdle faster, let's go."

The faster I can bring my trail leg over the hurdle, the faster I'll land on the ground and get back into my sprinting running mechanics. It's only when my feet are on the ground that I can accelerate ahead, faster and faster.

The goal: less time over the hurdle and more time on the ground. Except, this part of hurdling is one of my weaknesses.

"You're too high over the hurdle," Coach says for the tenth time.

*Ugh.* I'm usually about five to six inches over the white, plastic crossbar. *Not good.* One of my many wishes is to grow a couple of inches. Then I won't be afraid of the hurdle's height and jump too high to make sure I clear it.

*But that's not gonna happen . . .*

The thing is, having a center of gravity just above the hurdle requires less effort to clear the hurdle and less chances of clipping and falling over. For a shorter person like me, I gotta exert more force off the ground and get into a deeper lean when splitting over the hurdle to clear it.

"Kris, you ready for the workout?" Coach asks nonchalantly, as if whatever he says isn't gonna make me collapse on the floor. I've already jumped over six hundred hurdles during our sixty-minute warm-up.

"Ummm . . . okayyy . . ." I elongate my words, fearing for the worst as I put on my spikes, pushing down on the rubber on the track to see how much sponge is left.

There's hardly any traction. The sole purpose for using spikes is to provide grip so that I can push off the ground as hard as possible, improving my stride turnover.

"Yup. The track's beat up a bit, but we have to work with what we got," Coach answers before revealing my workout.

# THE WORKOUT OF THE DAY

100mH

2 rounds:

H1x1, H2x1, H4x1, H6x1, H8x1

Today, we're practicing my least favorite hurdle race, the 100-meter hurdles, aka: the high hurdles.

It's hard not to become discouraged when there is a slight disadvantage in the high hurdles if you're really short. The margin of error is tiny when the race is short. There are ten hurdles at thirty-three inches in height. The crossbar reaches all the way up to my belly button.

There are eight hurdles in the 300-meter race that are thirty inches tall. There's more room to recover from mistakes in a longer race.

Coach says, "Running the high hurdles will only help you become a stronger hurdler."

I'm determined to master this race, then.

I walk to lane number three. Coach has prepared the lane with eight hurdles at the thirty-inch height, instead of the normal height during a race: thirty-three inches. He's also jammed the hurdles in about three feet from the regular hurdle marks. Although my legs are tired as heck, I believe in Coach's training plan.

I get on my running blocks and look up. In the distance, the sun begins to peek in and out of the gray clouds. Finally, there's some light. I look toward the hurdles up ahead. Now they're all I see.

"Ready?"

"Yup. I'm ready."

"Get set," Coach commands. My hips move forward and rise. "Go!"

I swing my arms and push off the ground with all force. My first eight steps to hurdle one are powerful.

"PA-PA." He claps, reminding me of my hurdle rhythm. I drive my left knee slightly bent into the hurdle, my body midway over the top. Snapping my lead leg down, I bring my trail leg over the hurdle. Coach's cues help me stay in sync with my three-step cadence. As soon as both of my feet contact the ground, I push forward and sprint.

"One . . . Two . . . Three," Coach yells.

That's how many steps I need to take between hurdles. The spacing is fixed for everybody with 13 meters to the first hurdle, 8.5 meters between every hurdle that follows, and 10.5 meters from the last hurdle to the finish line. Taking a three-step cadence isn't all that easy for me. I tend to overstride between hurdles to make sure I cover the distance instead of shuffling through quicker, more powerful strides. I'm worried I won't reach the hurdle.

The first season I tried the hurdles, I did a five-step. I felt like there was no way I could even four-step. My right hamstring is too tight to be able to alternate lead legs. That season, I was the only hurdler with a five-step during my first high school varsity track season. That's probably why I ended up placing second to last at most meets. But then, I realized if I wanted to get better, I needed to master three-stepping even though my fear of not clearing the hurdle is always there.

I finish my runs, and my legs are D-E-A-D.

"Okay, here's the thing, Kristy." Coach's words make me worry. *Please, don't say another one.*

"Yes?"

"I'm gonna throw in a 150 with the hurdles and see what you got in the tank." He wants me to do half of the distance of my stronger race, the 300-meter-hurdles. "You're kidding, right?"

He's serious.

"Oh . . ." I sigh, and try to remember why I'm here. "Okay, how fast do you want that?"

"Sub twenty-one seconds." Coach is out of his mind.

"On your marks," Coach yells, and I'm in a haze. I fear the pain that's coming soon, but *I really need to believe in his training plan.*

As soon as he claps his hands, it's like something inside of me ignites and my brain is hijacked by my competitiveness. My nostrils flare and I clench my fists.

I dig in deep. Somehow, I'm reminded of why I wanna leave here so badly.

"Tackle the hurdle." Coach's faint voice echoes around the track, and it pushes me to run faster and faster past the thoughts in my head.

When I'm finished, Coach yells, "Twenty seconds flat!" I collapse on the ground, trying to catch my breath.

"Get up, kid." He tries to help me off the ground, but my legs feel detached from my body.

"You have some major things you got to work on, kid." Coach lists the bad habits I've picked up from poor coaching and self-coaching.

"Do you think it's too late for me to, like, unlearn them?" I ask while I attempt to catch my breath.

"No, not at all," he says, causing the knot in my stomach to loosen a little.

"But . . . ," he adds, "you don't have that much time to train. You're a junior now, right?"

"Yeah?" I nod my head. "Why?"

"Most junior track-and-field athletes who plan to run at the collegiate level have already begun the recruiting process. Some have even unofficially committed with a school already. You got to pick this up faster or you won't have a chance."

*Reality check.* I can feel myself panicking. I hate feeling like there's no time left. It sorta makes me go into a frenzy. It's like something bad is looming in the future. What if I don't meet it? Is my life over?

Coach has a valid point, though. I'm running out of time to make an impression on the track and to college coaches. I need to make it to the state championship and run a fast time if I want a scholarship. I need to go head-to-head with the fastest girls in the state.

"I'll do whatever it takes, Coach. I mean it," I tell him. I'm ready to give it my best. I'm on a mission.

"Well, c'mon, kid. Let's get after it!" Coach claps. "Actually . . . let's do that run one more time. Show me what you're made of."

I can barely feel my legs, but his words of encouragement make me feel like I can accomplish anything.

# STAY HUMBLE

I open the second meet of the season with two wins and a silver at the 77th Annual Border Olympics, a local meet that brings in more than forty teams from different parts of Texas.

"Let's take a photo, guys!" my friend Amanda squeals. She's mesmerized by the plaque I was awarded for being the highest scoring local athlete. I giggle, feeling ecstatic about my performances and seeing my friends supporting me at the track meet. Unfortunately, Ma couldn't make it this year.

"Smile, y'all . . . ," Gina says to the girls huddling around me.

We take more photos with the plaque than we probably should, posing in all types of ways. Each of us taking turns holding the plaque while making a serious face. Funny face. Normal face. We're just acting silly. It's been a few weeks since I got to hang with them. Ever since I started training twice a day, it's been almost impossible hanging out with anyone outside of school.

"Gotta go talk to my coach! See you guys." I wave at my girlfriends, and ping Coach over text.

**Me:** Hey, Coach! Where r u? Don't c u at the bleachers.
**Coach:** Meet me at my truck

I walk to the parking lot, searching for Coach's truck. The medals around my neck clink and clang. "Hey, look!" I say as I walk up to his truck and pop in, showing off my medals and plaque to Coach.

"Great job, kid," he says, looking in each direction.

"I broke the city record in the hundred hurdles and would've probably run faster if I didn't run the open hundred but that's fine, right?" I say, remembering how difficult it was to run back to the start of the 100-meter dash right after I won the high hurdles race in a final.

"Running them back-to-back will make you stronger once district comes around. You got a chance in winning the district title in the sprints, too. Just keep that in mind."

"Ah, okay." I nod. "Just thought we'd focus on the hurdles."

"Trust me and the process," Coach says. I didn't mean to question him.

"Oh, yes. Sorry. I agree. It's a good idea," I say even though a bunch of times other coaches in the past have told me and my teammates that Mexicans don't make it to state in the 100-meter dash. They told us to focus on another event.

"Do you need a ride home?" Coach offers. Of course I take it, or else I'd have to ask one of my friends to give me a lift, and then they might ask why Ma didn't make it. I'd rather avoid that question.

Coach starts the drive to my apartment. He turns on the stereo, playing a burned CD. "Is that your jam?" I chuckle. It reminds me of the music the cholos used to play back in Ghost Town. Didn't expect my private coach to listen to hip-hop music. Then again, he dresses between a mix of a basketball coach and a cholo.

"Chopped and screwed. Houston music."

"Oh yeah! You said you're from Houston."

"I am . . . ," he says, slouched in his seat, one hand on the steering wheel. "From the hood," he says in a way that reminds me of growing up in the barrio.

Kinda makes me miss it.

"Coach?" I change the subject.

"Do you think I can win the next race?" I ask him, already anticipating the next meet. Still got four more meets before district.

"Kris, I'ma tell you one thing, okay?"

I look at Coach as I always do. Ears tuned in. You never know; he might give me some really good advice.

"Do me a favor and don't let winning get to your head. Stay humble," he advises me. But I like hanging my medals and displaying them on my wall in my room so that Rafael will be proud of his big sister when he's older.

"Okay, Coach."

"We're not here to win. Winning is a plus. Your job is to drop your times each meet, do your best. That's how you'll know you're improving and I'm doing my job."

I get it, but I didn't join track and field for the gold medals. For me, running has always been about survival. Sprinting is in my bones as a barrio girl. I mean, it does feel amazing to be good at something and get noticed for my hard work. Coach is right, though. To qualify for state, I gotta run PR's, personal records. I would feel gacho bad if I let him down.

"And Kris . . ." Coach lowers the music. "I can train you for the rest of the season. What do you think about that?"

"Oh my god! Really?" I say, jumping in my seat.

"But . . ." I think about Ma and how worried she was about not being able to afford paying for more coaching.

"I . . . umm." I wanna tell him the truth but instead ask, "How much money are you charging?"

"Don't worry about it," he answers without hesitation.

"I mean, I can pay you back when I grow up?"

"No . . . That's nice of you to offer, but no. I mean it. I see the potential in you and I want to help. Just work hard and don't be late to practice. That's how you can pay me back," he replies.

All I can think about is how I'm the luckiest girl in the whole wide world. I get to have a private coach for free. Someone who believes in me. And wants to see me succeed.

"Thanks, Coach. You're the best!"

Finally, things are falling into place.

# CAFETERIA

**"Can't believe we have to wear this."** My best friend, Steven, slumps in his seat, covering his belly with his book bag. He hates how his tucked-in polo shirt makes his body look.

"Same. This is so not cool," I complain.

A few weeks before the beginning of this school year, our school district implemented a school "uniform" policy. All students are barred from wearing open-toed shoes, tank tops, dresses, skirts, sweaters, heels, facial jewelry, and most colors. Everything basically. Unless it's khaki pants and a polo shirt in one of our three school colors: Navy blue. White. Mustard yellow, which is the closest to gold, somehow? According to rumors, the dress code is supposed to be a way to ward off students from being recruited to gangs.

I sigh. "I miss wearing my skate shirts." Gone are the days we could express ourselves freely with our clothes. Now if you're not wearing top designer brands, those polos with crocodile or horse logos, you're not cool for school. *Whatever.*

"Now, we're on a Narco polo trend . . ." Steven chuckles, making a reference to La Barbie, a local cartel kingpin who is partially responsible for the violence spilling into our barrios. And now his style has influenced fashion across Northern Mexico and along the Texas border. I find his analysis both amusing and ironic, considering our school is trying to curb gangs while accidentally adopting a fad that glorifies drug traffickers.

"No manches, güey. I wear whatever I want," Karla chimes in from behind us.

She's standing up, showing off her baggy blue polo. "Look . . ."

If you ask me, her polo shirt is more like baby blue, not even close to navy, and soon she might end up at Mrs. B.'s office for not following the dress code to a T.

I laugh. "Guess we'll see you next month after detention, then."

"I'm leaving early como sea," Karla says. She's skipping lunch and sneaking out of school with her older sister's ID. You're not allowed to leave campus for any reason unless you're a senior. It's almost impossible to sneak out with all the cameras, metal detectors, security guards, and barbed wire fences.

On her way out, Steven says, "Karla, call the Taki dealer. I need a bag. No, wait . . ." He pauses, looking at me, "Want one también?"

"Ay! Steven . . . ," I groan. "I can't eat those anymore." We used to eat a bag of spicy chips during every lunch period, but now I'm focused on eating healthy.

"Just eat 'em. You're not going to dieeee," Steven pushes me.

I think about Coach and training and why I can't eat processed foods anymore. Coach says I'll earn one cheat meal after each meet I set a new PR.

"Nah, I'm good," I say.

Karla goes out to find the Taki dealer, who keeps a low profile. It's illegal to sell snacks on campus. But Taki dealers have been around for two years now. They're in high demand. They're like Waldo, pretty tricky to find cuz all of the students dress up the same and the salesman is different each time.

A few minutes go by, and the Taki dealer slides in between me and Steven. "¿Cuántos, carnales?" He parts his green backpack open just enough for me to take a quick glimpse. He's got over fifty bags stuffed in there.

Steven answers, "Dos."

"Steven!" I say out loud, smacking him on the arm.

He asks, "How much?"

"Three dollars." Prices have skyrocketed, but I suppose the rich kids on campus can afford them.

"How about two?" Steven haggles, and then whispers, asking me, "Have a dollar?"

I check my book bag pockets and find four quarters. I would normally use the change to pay for lunch, but now since Ma doesn't really work, I qualify for free lunch just like Steven does. Not that Steven eats cafeteria food, anyway.

Steven attempts to stuff the Takis in my book bag. "Just take it."

"Alright . . . fineeeee."

"Anywayyyy . . ." Steven changes the subject. "Are you taking the SATs next month?"

"Hell no," I answer, thinking about what happened last year. "Are you?"

Steven cracks up. "Definitely not."

Last year, Steven and I, along with our entire sophomore class of 690 students had to take the ACT exam. We had no idea what the exam was for, all we knew was that it was mandatory.

I think back to opening the first section of the exam, feeling dumb. Like how in the world am I supposed to answer anything if I don't even understand the question? Words and symbols my eyes have never laid eyes on were popping out of the page like a horror movie. My heart was beating loud inside my ears. Then, halfway through the exam, letters and numbers began to look blurry. Now, thinking about it, what would other students at a university think of me when I speak in Spanglish, and they realize my English sucks?

"Had to do process of elimination on each question and close my eyes to choose one answer and shit." I admit to selecting my answers like my abuela chooses her lotería cards.

"Yeah, girl, you definitely need a track scholarship," Steven says, laughing.

"Soon, I hope." I cross my fingers.

"Yo, I can't wait for graduation, though." I can hear the day-dreaming in Steven's voice. He reminds me of graduation day on a weekly basis, I swear.

I look around the cafeteria, imagining the last day of our senior school year and my last meal right here. This is the same place where I had the cheerleading showcase when Ma was kidnapped.

"I wish that day would come sooner," I groan.

For years, we were told that high school is supposed to be the highlight of our young lives. But that didn't happen for us. Quite the opposite. I wish I could go back in time, beg Ma to stay back in Ghost Town and South Middle. I miss being in a place where I feel like I belong.

"Dude just imagine when we leave this place . . ." I smile at Steven and picture it. "We'll end up at a university. Meet new people. Travel the world."

Both of us could be the first people in our families to earn a degree and fly on an airplane.

"Until then," Steven says, "we just need to fake it until we make it."

That's Steven's motto lately, now that he's starting to get folded into the popular group. He joined the yearbook committee, many of whom are members of Las Marthas. Both clubs are filled with popular kids.

The kids that are known to bully other students, including me.

"Less than two years and we'll be outta here," he adds.

"If you say so." I peel my eyes away from Steven.

I know this may sound crazy, but I'm not even mad at him for hanging out with the popular group and pretending he doesn't know me at times. He probably would be disqualified if they found out he hangs out with a freak.

The truth is, I *want* Steven to feel like he belongs.

I just hope someday he could feel comfortable enough to be himself cuz no matter the width of his pants or the environment he was born into, he's still my best friend.

I get it, though. I used to lie to my friends at South Middle, thinking they would judge me for living in a run-down house, our yard so litter-strewn that it resembled the American Red Cross donation drop-off location. Even though back at that school there was hardly any bullying.

The jocks. The nerds. The freaks. The cholos. The caga palos. The outcasts. We all mingled together. We were all from the barrios and our families struggled to survive. A student became popular only if they were nice to everybody. Not mean. Not like it is here.

Nowadays, I refuse to change who I am just to become "popular." I think it's cool to not be pressured into being something you're not—or putting other people down to impress others. I'd rather be authentic and true to myself.

I mean, it does get lonely sometimes without Steven, especially when the few close friends I do have at Anderson are in different lunch periods. I often end up eating inside the bathroom stall to avoid the bullies.

Anyway, I trust Steven. Even if he can't let the popular kids know it. Plus, he tells me every time they mention my name and what they say.

*Her mom got kidnapped cuz she's a drug dealer.*
*Alicia intentionally broke her nose.*
*What a slut and freak.*
*She's black, that's why she runs fast.*

I try to ignore these rumors about me. Most of their bad-mouthing just comes from what I call social-hatred mob mentality. Peer pressure can make people say and do things that hurt others, and that's something I want no part of.

What I can't understand is why anyone at our school would demonize my skin color. Something about those of us with darker colored skin automatically makes some people think we are "indios," natives from the mountains in rural areas in Mexico, or "nacos" who crossed the border and should be sent back across.

I guess it doesn't matter to them that nearly all of us in our border town descend from a mix of people and cultures.

We're all raza. Even if we're not, what's the big deal?

Moving to the north side only made me realize there's a caste system and being a morena means you're at the bottom at Anderson High School. At the beginning of high school, there were times where I dreamed of waking up with light skin, the dark creases on my hands no longer a part of my body.

I look at Steven. He's finishing his Takis and licking his fingers clean of the red chili powder. Suddenly, out of the corner of our eyes, we see the bullies walk across the cafeteria. It makes Steven pop up from his seat, his empty bag of Takis falling to the ground.

"Gotta go! Chat later." Steven struggles to get up.

"You really don't have to hang with them, though." I give him my two cents, but he probably doesn't feel like he has a choice.

"Don't you worry, girl," he says as he speeds away, clutching his backpack against his chest.

*Twelve more months. And this will all be over soon.*

# IN THE SHADOWS

"Hey, Kristy!" Coach Richard, my former cross-country coach calls out. He's now the head coach of the girls' basketball team. "Can I talk to you?"

*Oh crap. He saw me.* In between class periods, I usually take a detour outside of the school building to avoid the bustling hallways and his classroom. But not today cuz I'm running late.

"Hi, Coach. I can't be late to class." I try jogging along, but he says, "It's okay, I'll write you a pass, come."

I stare ahead in the distance. My next class is just thirty meters away. So close, yet so far. I squeeze the straps of my backpack like they'll protect me from whatever comes out of his mouth cuz I can't seem to find another excuse to escape at the top of my head.

"What's up, Coach?" I reply, faking a smile. I notice the students in his computer science class watching us. They're probably wondering why I'm here. So am I.

"I haven't seen you around. How have you been?" he asks, like he cares how I've really been. No way he cares after what he put Gina and me through during our freshman year on the cross-country team. Aside from that, I kinda blame him for ending up at this school. After all, he was the one who recruited me and made Ma see shining stars.

"I'm fine, thanks," I answer, even though I'm not. I don't wanna talk to him cuz he used to ask me and Gina about our sexual history whenever no one else was around after practice. It made me feel uncomfortable and suspicious. So I googled his name and discovered he's got a history of sexual harassment. He was accused of doing similar things at the previous high school where he coached and was forced to resign.

I almost reported his behavior during my freshman year. Even rehearsed how I would present the evidence to our principal, Mrs. B. But then I found out he's buddy-buddy with her. I already thought Mrs. B. was scary, and the idea of talking bad about her friend made me second-guess myself. Plus, other students think he's cool. So I kept quiet.

I thought, *what would really happen if I reported him?* Mrs. B. must already know about his past and probably doesn't care. Cuz if she did, she wouldn't allow him near girls ever again. It makes me upset thinking about potentially getting into trouble for saying something about one of the school's most well-liked coaches and teachers. Like, why the heck would I wanna deal with more drama at this school than I already have? *No thank you.* I just try to hide or run past him whenever I spot him, but today isn't one of those days.

"Kristy, sit right here." He orders me to sit next to his desk like I have any other choice. I give in cuz it feels awkward not to.

"Okay . . ." I sit down, wondering what will happen next, and say, "but I really need to leave soon. If not, my teacher will mark me late and get super mad." I'm already on the verge of flunking English cuz

I don't get grammar and I haven't gotten anything higher than a C on my essays. Now I don't think I've ever wanted to be in my English class this badly.

Richard sits down, waving a newspaper at my face. *Yup, that's me, again.* One would think I'd find it cool to land on the front page of the sports section of the newspaper, but I don't. It only attracts attention I don't want. *Like this.*

"I just wanted to say congratulations," says Richard with a slick, too-friendly voice, making the hairs on the back of my neck stand up. I bob my head, studying his moves. His eyes watch like a hawk even while his voice is smooth.

"Thanks," I reply.

"You and I both know who noticed you first."

*Of course I do.* It was Miss Marissa, my pre-K teacher, who advised my mom to get me to try out for the track team after she noticed me outrunning all the boys at the playground.

"Yup, you did." I just give him what he wants to hear.

"This school should be praising your name. We're lucky to have you."

*As if.* The less my name is spoken at this school, the better it is for me.

"The announcer didn't even congratulate you over the intercom this morning!" he complains. Although it does sting a bit, it's for the best. I need to be invisible. Be nobody here, or I'll attract drama.

Competing in track and field at this school is about getting the job done with or without cameras and local sport reporters. *Stay humble.* Running is a personal thing.

"It's all good. Doesn't bother me." Not getting noticed also keeps me out of trouble, keeps secrets safe, away from others like Coach

Miranda. If he suspects I'm training with a personal coach, he might throw a fit.

"Well, I gotta go now." I stumble over my words, barely audible over the conversations of his students in the classroom behind me.

"Ay, nambe. Don't go," he says, and I look around, wondering if any of his students will ask why I'm there.

"Stay."

I stand up anyway and try to leave.

"You do know that Miranda knows what you're up to, verdad?"

He stops me in my tracks. "Huh?" I let out, and say, "Knows what?" I feel this tightness around my throat. *I hope it's not what I'm thinking.*

"That you're training with Coach A."

"What?" I deflect. *How does he know?*

Richard says he overheard a couple of sports coaches talking about how someone had seen me training with Coach at Riverbank Track early in the morning.

"He feels insulted."

"That's ridiculous," I dare to say back. Then I ask, "Would a teacher feel insulted if one of their students hired a tutor outside of school?"

After all, our school limits practice for in-season sports activities to a maximum of eight hours per school week, per activity. To master hurdling before the end of my high school track season, that isn't enough time. Anyway, I make him look good. I show up at all our after-school practices, win race after race, and break both school and city records under his name. And *he's* upset?

"Kristy, of course not," Richard replies. Then he admits, "Mira, I like Coach A. He's a great coach. You're in good hands."

"Yeah, he is super cool." I finally let out a big smile. I feel very lucky.

Richard leans forward and says, "I'm on your side. No te preocupes. You know Miranda hates Coach A., verdad?"

"No, why?" This is the first I hear of this.

"Just think about the past district championships and records. You'll know why. Coach A. is just a better coach. Everyone knows that."

Miranda used to be a track-and-field coach at another school for many years. His team used to be on a district champion–winning streak, up until Coach got hired as a head coach at Union High School. Since then, it's been all Union High.

"Just be vigilant. He might figure out a way to kick you off the team," Richard says, giving me a serious look.

"What? It's not like I committed a crime," I quickly say, knowing that the UIL organization gave Coach and I the greenlight to work together.

"I'll tell you if he's planning to do it and give you updates." His voice is low, like he's now my own private detective.

I nod my head yes, and say, "Okay, sounds good. Thanks." I can't pass this up. My future depends on it.

"But first, come and help me with something."

I follow Richard as he walks to the far end of the classroom and into a large dark closet where he stores snacks. I get a little bit uncomfortable. I hate closets. They remind me of juvie.

He pretends like he's grabbing a plastic container filled with pretzels high up on a shelf, while using his right foot to close the door behind us.

*Oh no.*

Richard whispers things into my ear. And I can't shut out the words. He's telling me about inappropriate things he did to my teammates. I had my suspicion two years ago. It wasn't all in my head.

"Mmm-hmm," I manage to let out, trying hard not to imagine these things happening.

"This stays between you and me. Don't go talking about this, okay?" he says in the nearly pitch-black room.

"I won't," I say, attempting to conceal my disgust. If I could, I'd wiggle my shoulders to get this feeling off me.

We exit the closet, looking like nothing happened. Well, except for me helping him bring out some snacks for his students.

"Gotta go! Bye." I speed up to the door.

"Let's talk again later," he calls after me.

I hustle to my classroom with a hall pass Richard gave me. I hand it over to my English teacher and sit at my desk at the back of the classroom, thinking about what just happened.

A wave of panic rises up and crashes down upon me. I feel nauseous. Suddenly, I realize I can't tell this to anybody. If I open my mouth and Richard finds out, he might join Miranda's militia and kick me off the team. I can't afford to lose everything I worked hard for.

Unable to bottle everything in, I take out my journal from my backpack and write out what Richard told me to get it out of my head. *Dear Diary* . . . Then, to distract myself, I draw a track and place eight hurdles. My pencil quickly moves to each hurdle. I envision my 300-meter-hurdle race as I draw a line to each hurdle.

"Kristy, pay attention!" my teacher calls on me.

I slam my journal shut.

# EXTERNAL BARRIERS

**"He found out, Coach."**

Miranda's given me an ultimatum—stop training with Coach A. or be kicked off the team. Then, at the next meet, he pulled me out of the hurdles event and told the entire team on the bus that I don't have what it takes to get a scholarship cuz I'm too chiquita to be a hurdler and cuz sometimes I run to the bathroom crying after a big race. But he doesn't understand these horrible cramps in my pelvis cuz he's a guy.

I lean my body forward, my legs on a pike position, stretching my hamstrings.

"Keep those feet dorsiflexed." Coach presses my spine forward. "If a sports reporter asks about your training regimen, don't mention my name. I don't need the recognition. He wants it. Give him what he wants," Coach continues.

I shake my head. "That's not fair, though. So you want me to say he's been training me?" I start thinking about all the times I've read newspaper articles with athletes thanking their coaches for all their support off and on the field. I wish I still had that type of support like I did back at South Middle.

*Why does Miranda get the credit, though?* According to some of my girlfriends on the team, most of our male coaches at school have big egos. We're not allowed to challenge their knowledge or question them. You just do as they say cuz they're supposed to know more than any of us combined. We're just kids.

Just last week, I attempted to explain to Miranda about the biomechanics of hurdling so he could focus on my technique and know what to look for in my form, but he barked, "Okay, if you know everything, pos then train yourself."

I hope I'm never like him. I wanna learn as much as possible about everything and anything, no matter who it comes from, especially if it means getting a free education with an athletic scholarship.

"That's just the way things are done here." Coach snaps me out of my thoughts.

I stomp my feet and raise my voice. "Yeah, maybe it's small-town mentality. I hate it! I wish he could just leave me alone."

I mean, maybe it would've been better if I told Miranda about my first conversation with Coach, instead of going behind his back, but he'd barely even let me hurdle before. And why should I ask him for permission? I didn't do anything wrong. It was approved by UIL. I suppose I got myself into this trouble.

I shield my face. "I'm sorry that I'm crying."

"No, no. Don't be sorry," he says, patting my back. I try to stretch and touch my toes again, but I'm actually just masking my face. My knees rub against my forehead.

"Hey, Kristy—look at me for a second."

I come up for some air, wiping my tears with the back of my hand. He stares at me with his hazel eyes. I feel nervous.

"I need you to know something, okay?" he says.

I nod way too many times, anticipating his response. "Yeah, Coach?"

He flicks my chin slightly up with his index finger, and says confidently, "You're a true hurdler and you will persevere through anything."

*Does he really see that in me?* These days, I feel like I'm losing who I used to be, a strong and courageous person. "Thanks, Coach. That means a lot to me." I smile, feeling like maybe he might know me better than I know myself.

Maybe it's not just the hurdles on the track that I need to overcome, but the real ones, too. I wish I had the courage to confront Miranda and yell, *I'm a teenager. Leave me alone!* And accept the consequences for standing up to him. I wish I had the courage to confront Richard and scream, *You're a sick bastard!* And accept the consequences for standing up to him, too. But speaking the truth feels like it could be a big mistake.

Richard could just call me a liar and convince Miranda to kick me off the track team. I don't want to risk losing my only way to leave this place. I hate feeling trapped. I look at Coach, just like Rudy once looked at me, wanting some comfort that everything will be just fine.

"So you promise I'll make it? I'll get a scholarship?"

"Yes, kid. You just keep doing what you're doing. All this hard work will pay off. I see it. Trust me, Kristy." I feel a thousand times better. *He sees it!*

Waking up at five fifteen in the morning, doing two-day practices, pushing my body and accepting the external barriers is all gonna be worth it, someday. *Just keep pushing.*

I add, "But Richard said that Miranda is coming up with a legit reason to consider me ineligible to compete if we keep training together. He's serious. And I'm in trouble if he keeps pulling me out of the hurdles at the meets."

For some reason, I feel guilty for relaying this information to Coach. Like I gotta keep everything Richard tells me a secret.

"No, he's not going to kick you off," Coach says as he taps my arms, reminding me to stretch them.

I cross my right arm over my chest, and with my left hand, I pull my elbow toward my body.

"But I think he can, even though he's the boys' head coach. How am I gonna compete if that happens?" I feel panic bubbling up inside me.

"No, he won't. He needs you for the district title. You score most of the points at track meets."

"*He* needs *me?*"

I think on this. *Everyone needs something.* Richard "needs" me to listen to his horrible stories. I need him to tell me what Miranda is up to. And Miranda needs me winning to make him look good. But maybe that's the thing. Maybe me working with a personal coach makes him look bad. But at least Coach doesn't need anything from me, except for my best.

"I guess," I say, unconvinced.

Coach adds, "It's just a threat."

*It's not just a threat, though.* Anxiety chews at my insides again, and I bite my nails, looking around Riverbank Track. I flashback to the sound of Ma's sobbing and pleading me for help, and the voice of the kidnapper.

"Are you okay?" Coach asks.

I hesitate.

"You can tell me anything," he says.

Before the next wave of panic comes over me, I start to talk. "Coach, I don't know if you know, but my mom got kidnapped across two years ago and the guys threatened to kill her, my lil brother, and me." As soon as I say it, I regret it. Coach is gonna think I'm weak or dramatic. I should just shut up.

Instead, Coach leans in, shocked. "Are you serious?"

"Yeah. So . . . I don't do well with threats," I admit.

"Kristy, I'm so sorry that happened to you and your family. That's horrible."

"It messed up my mom, and I think it kinda messed me up, too. That's prolly why I ended up in juvie."

I tell him more, about my personal life. How I saved Ma. How I ended up in juvie. Why I train hard. Why I wanna leave this city and be the first one in my family to reach for the stars. Coach walks closer to me, and I stand there frozen, wondering if I said too much.

But he surprises me again. "You're one hell of a strong kid. That's probably how you got that fire in you." He hugs me and it feels warm. I don't push him away. This is the first time I ever told an adult how I feel. And this is the first time anyone has said it's okay. "This means a lot to me." I let a tear out.

Coach pulls back and looks at me. "Go out there and kill these motherfuckers with kindness."

*Kindness.* I chuckle and say, "Okay. I think I can do that." I didn't expect him to say "kindness." Coach is what I wish I could have in a father: protective, caring, and supportive. Ma used to have some of those qualities back in the day, but now it's few and far between.

If I tell Ma about Richard, I worry about what she might say. Ma hardly ever says the things I need to hear these days. Not like this, right now. I mean, I'm certain she'd report Richard, but at the same time, she might make me feel guilty for being in that situation. I rather stay quiet than feel like I should hate myself for something I couldn't avoid. I guess I could call Linda. She was there for me when I needed her. But I already gave her enough trouble.

"You're done for the day, Kristy. You can head to school now," Coach interrupts my thoughts.

It's eight fifteen in the morning. I've got thirty minutes to get dressed and make it to school on time.

"Bye, Coach." I wave and walk away, feeling like I could trust him with my secrets. With my feelings. With my whole life.

*What if I tell him about Richard?*

"Hey, Coach?" I turn back to him.

"What's up?"

"I gotta tell you something, but no one else knows." I lower my voice and tell him, "Richard has been talking to me, like." I pause, afraid to say it. "Like, strange, ya know? He's a little bit weird. Says things he shouldn't say." I can't seem to say the words *sexual abuse*.

"I think I know what you're talking about," says Coach, and my shoulders roll back in surprise.

"Really, you do?"

"Yeah, he made an inappropriate comment about an athlete of mine years ago." I feel a sense of relief that Coach has noticed something off about Richard, too.

"Just stay away from him."

I know this. But to stay on the track team, I need to listen to him, and keep quiet while I keep my eyes on my goals.

# FIGHT, FLIGHT, OR FREEZE

"Come on in, Kristy." Coach lets me in through his front door. "Did you have a good day?" he asks as I'm checking out the interior of his home, from the beige carpets to the framed portraits, wallpaper, and antique wooden furniture. This is my first time visiting his house.

"Yeah, it's been so-so. I mean, aside from working on my vision board and umm . . . ," I admit. It's this new project I'm working on at home where I cut out images from magazines and create a collage of things I want to manifest in my life. ". . . That's it."

I wanna tell him about what happened at the principal's office earlier today. I was one step away from getting kicked off the team, thanks to Miranda. He falsely accused me of not showing up to practice. I protested, but no matter what I said, Mrs. B. believed him instead of me. She ended up giving me one more chance, which didn't sit well with Miranda.

"That's great, I wanna hear more about this vision board of yours." We walk into the kitchen. "Hey, Mom. This is Kristy, the girl I told you I'm coaching."

A woman with pale skin, round glasses, and soft eyes like Coach's is having dinner at the dining table.

"Hi, Mrs. A., your house is very cozy and beautiful," I say, trying to be polite.

"Hello, honey." His mom greets me warmly, and tells me, "Please, call me Laura. That's my ex-husband's last name."

"Oh, I'm so sorry," I apologize, not realizing Coach's parents are divorced.

"Ana!" Coach calls out loudly. "Come say hello, Kristy is here."

A lanky, tall young woman I recognize as Steven's art teacher at school walks into the kitchen and says, "Hi."

She disappears as quickly as she came. I didn't even have time to greet her. *Weird.*

"My sister is probably on the phone with her fiancé. He lives in another country."

"Oh, okay."

That explains her coldness, I suppose. I try to ignore the odd interaction, but something about Ana's demeanor makes me wonder what the hell was that all about. Maybe it's awkward that she's a teacher at my school, and a student is at her house.

"I'll check up on you later, okay, Mom?"

"Wait, son."

Laura gets up and walks into the kitchen. She opens a drawer, pulling out a stack of papers. "Look, honey, I've been collecting these. They're stunning."

I take a closer look, noticing they're photos and interview articles of me published in the local newspaper this season. Blushing a little and with a smile on my face, I reply, "Aww. That's very nice of you. Thank you so much." I wish Laura could be one of my abuelas. I mean, she could be.

Coach commented last week that he wished he had a daughter like me. He doesn't have children, and he's never been married. Well, maybe he could adopt me. Ma complains often that she can't wait for the day I graduate and move out.

"Okay, Mom. We really need to get to work. We got things to do," Coach cuts the conversation short.

"Bye, Laura," I say, and add, "Hope to meet you again soon."

"It's lovely meeting you, too. You're always welcome here. Anytime," she says.

Today we're supposed to watch videos of my last race and analyze my form before the district championships this upcoming weekend. I follow Coach to the backyard, where it's almost completely dark.

I whisper, "Coach, your mom is super nice." It makes me wish Ma was nice like that to me these days, but she keeps threatening to kick me out of the house if I don't do things the way she wants me to. That's sorta why I try to avoid her at all costs. I'm hardly at home. I spend my free time outside of school training and competing.

When I need something, Coach is there to help me. I don't even have to ask him. It's like he can read what I need. Like last week, he surprised me with a new pair of running spikes. The ones I'd been using had a hole on the left small toe.

"Thanks. She really likes you," Coach says, and I feel grateful for having someone like him in my life. Sometimes I just wish I had someone to call family, and I guess this is as close as it gets. Although not blood related, I could be Coach's long-lost daughter.

"Coach, how much do I owe you for real?" I ask him. I wanna make sure he knows how thankful I am for all the things he's bought me and for all the training.

Someday, when I grow up, I wanna pay him back, with interest.

"For what, kid?" He fidgets with a TV that's mounted outside, but it's not working right yet.

"For everything. The shoes. The sweatshirt. The food. The training." I list everything that comes to mind.

I mean, Ma paid for the first two weeks of practice, but after that, Coach said I didn't need to pay him anymore. All our trainings have been free. Not like Ma could afford a lot these days. It's hard enough raising Rafael, being in debt, and she hasn't returned to working at that bar.

"No, don't worry about anything. They're gifts from me to you."

"Wow! Seriously, Coach?" No one has done anything like this for me. Well, Ma did for a while, but she doesn't really anymore ever since that night.

"I want to help you reach your goal. You deserve it, Kristy." I get a warming feeling in my belly. He always knows what to say to make me feel good.

"Do you need help, Coach?" I ask him since I notice it's taking a little while to figure out this TV thing, and it's getting late.

I told Ma I'd be home before 9:00 p.m., which is two hours past my probation's 7:00 p.m. curfew, but that's fine. No one from juvie checks, anyway.

"Let's just skip this tonight." Coach stops messing with the TV and leans over to flip a switch.

A sound comes on, like a waterfall or a stream, and I ask, "What's that noise?"

"Follow me."

He turns on a flashlight, like the one we use at practice, and I notice a giant pool in the distance along with a freaking hot tub.

"Wow, that's so cool!"

I've never met anyone with a pool or a hot tub. I mean, back in Ghost Town we had one of those four-foot portable pools that Ma bought at Walmart, but it didn't last long because once all the cholos jumped in at the same time, and the entire thing exploded, flooding our backyard. I always wished that someday I could have the real deal.

"Instead of watching video tonight, let's loosen up those muscles," Coach suggests. He typically has me sit in a bucket of warm water and Epsom salt up to my calves after a practice or before a race.

I remove my pink chanclas, dip my toes in the hot tub, and sigh. "Ahh, it's so nice, Coach. So jealous your family has a hot tub."

The way the warm water feels on my skin, it soothes me, and somehow, makes me feel relaxed despite it being just under one hundred degrees outside.

"Well, what ya waiting for? Don't be shy. Get in."

"Oh, I'm not shy," I shoot back instantly.

Well, maybe I am shy, but I don't want him knowing that.

"Can I just go in like this?" I ask him, pulling at my T-shirt and shorts cuz this is all I got. Not like I have a bathing suit that fits me. It's been a while since I went to the local lake or a swimming pool at the Boys & Girls Club. I don't know how to swim, and Ma says being in the water is dangerous.

I sit on the edge of the hot tub, dipping my legs first. Then I pull my body inside the hot water, fully clothed. My T-shirt starts to float up. Now I'm wishing I had a bathing suit. Instead, I just tuck my shirt into my shorts.

I stretch my arms out wide and recline my back against the wall of the hot tub. I feel free. The sound of water trickling down from the hot tub's bedrock is soothing. All my worries slowly disappear like a ship sailing away from a storm. I don't even wanna bring up what happened at the principal's office. I feel invincible. Nothing can touch me right now.

I lean my head back. "Coach? Can we do this more often instead of the bucket?" My muscles feel loose and relaxed. This could really help speed up my recovery after all the intense workouts.

"Mind if I jump in with you?" Coach asks, jolting me back. He's right above me.

Another wave of panic. Something tells me I should leap out of the hot tub or say no. I feel uncomfortable, but instead I freeze.

"Umm . . . okay?" I squirm, trying to make room for him. *It's gonna be tight.*

"Coming in now," he says, placing the flashlight on the ground facing away from us. But it's still lit up enough that I can see him removing his T-shirt.

I see his bare, hairy chest and I quickly turn my head away. *Great. He probably thinks I'm rude.*

"Coach, I just wanna say thank you for everything again," I blurt out. I don't want him to think I'm not grateful. My life just isn't the same since we started training together. Now I'm faster, and physically stronger than I was before. I've been dominating on the track and crushing my previous PRs. I owe it all to him.

"You got it," he replies.

Coach makes me feel that I can excel at the hurdles, or like I could do and be anything I want. Something about Coach's presence has that effect on me. In fact, that's what a lot of his former athletes would say at track meets when I would run against them freshman and sophomore year. "He's strict, but with Coach A., we dominate at everything."

I suppose it's the way he believes in me more than I actually believe in myself.

Coach splashes water at my face, distracting me from ruminating. I chuckle, rubbing my eyes dry. When I open my eyelids faintly, he's suddenly one foot away from me. I'm cornered. I want to move away. But he's so close, I don't wanna upset him. I freeze again. Coach doesn't move. He's hovering over me.

I smile nervously, hoping he will say something, but all I can hear is the sound of the treading of water, chirping crickets, frogs croaking, and the howling noises of dry, summer air pushing into my ears.

He inches forward. I try to back away, but with nowhere to go, my skin presses deeper into the cement wall. I turn my gaze away from him. Stare up at the moon and stars to distract myself from what's happening.

"You're so beautiful," he says softly, grabbing my chin and pulling my face to his direction. For one moment, I feel almost normal. Like all the horrible memories from the past don't belong to me. Like I'm loved. Wanted. Free. *But why does this feel so wrong?*

My heart drops. My stomach turns into swirls of confusion. I gulp and think. *No, nothing inappropriate is about to happen. It's all in my head.* But something does happen. *Pause. Wait. Halftime. What if someone catches us? Can we get in trouble? Is this illegal even though I'm seventeen? How can you like me romantically? I thought you said I'm the daughter you wished you had.*

Then I think about what he's done for me.

*Just trust him.*

I convince myself that this is part of our training. Or maybe, just maybe I owe him big time for . . . the shoes . . . the sweatshirt . . . the food . . . the training.

FOR EVERYTHING.

# PRETENDING

**Practice comes too soon the next morning.**

My head is still trying to process what happened last night. Nothing like that was supposed to ever happen. We were just supposed to watch film. Analyze my form over the hurdles. Determine what could help me fix my hurdling technique this far into the season, but instead, I made another error. Our skin was never meant to touch. He was just supposed to be my coach and me, his athlete.

Now it's never gonna be the same. Well . . . not unless we could just be like me and Ma, pretending like nothing happened. Like we didn't do the three-letter word. Like I don't need to panic about pregnancy or catching an STD. Like I never semi-cheated on Rudy. Actually, he's not officially my boyfriend. Rudy will surely understand. *No, he will think I'm a horrible person.*

"Goooooooood morning, Kristy!" Coach says enthusiastically as he unlocks the gate to let me in.

"Hi," I say, wondering what will come next. Will we chat about last night?

I try reading him to see if anything is different about him. He's standing there expressionless, holding his hands behind his back like he always does. Meanwhile, my hands are crossing around my chest, my shoulders shrugged up. He makes me feel small.

I blink and start to panic.

"Good . . . good morning." I stall on my words. *Gosh, I suck at acting normal.*

"We're polishing your start off the blocks into the first hurdle today. Then it's go-time this weekend."

Nothing about his tone, his body language, or the way he looks at me has changed the slightest bit. From the outside looking in, he's just my personal track-and-field coach. *Nothing happened last night. It was all in our heads. Okay, you got it.*

"Yeah. Sounds good, Coach."

"Give me a slow six-lap warm-up, okay?" He starts to walk toward me.

One step forward. Two steps forward. Three steps forward.

His head turns from left to right, right to left. I look around, too. No one else in sight. Just me. Him. And the same stars that witnessed the event less than twelve hours ago.

His hand locks onto my forearm. I feel my heart skipping again. My shoulders sink. I freeze.

I'm standing on the track feeling nervous he might make a move on me, and someone might catch us.

*Please, don't. We'll get in trouble.*

He leans in, and whispers, "From now on, call me Carlos in private."

"Sounds good." My voice trembles. I try not to look into his eyes or I'll get nervous. *What am I supposed to say to an adult who had . . . who did that with me?*

"Let's get going now, we don't have all day," he says, turning away to unlock the hurdles behind us.

I run off to the empty infield and slip on my headphones. Ears are sealed. I block out the world with music.

*How can he act like nothing happened? Does he do this with other girls, too? Was it all in my head?*

With each guitar strum, I pick up my pace, feeling rejected.

My cadence aligns with the beats of the song, my breathing turning shallow. My lungs begin to fill up with air faster than I can breathe out. My hands clench. I'm not jogging anymore. I'm running. I just want what happened last night to go away.

Last lap.

I turn my head to look across the field. I only see his silhouette, but I feel Coach's eyes on me. Makes me feel exposed in the open turf field. I swing my arms to propel me forward to run faster so I can finish my lap, but I'm out of breath. I abruptly end my run short of the finish line.

*What the hell happened last night?*

I pull the headphones out of my ears and immediately, I hear Coach yell, "What was that?" His points his flashlight at my face. "I told you to jog. Not sprint."

I cover my eyes, and reply sharply, "What?" I can't think or see right now.

"Run back and finish through," he orders me.

I reply, "But it was just like three feet away."

"When did I ever teach you to finish short of anything?"

He's serious.

"Never," I answer.

*I know. I know.* As a runner, it's been ingrained in me to never stop or slow down before any finish line. It's the golden rule. But I'm frustrated. Not like I've ever come short of anything during our practices or races.

Surely, he will give me a pass.

"Go, now. Don't get used to cutting things short or we're shutting practice down. Is that clear?"

*Jeez.* I pissed him off. Well, if only he knew that he pissed me off, too.

I hate that I feel rejected. That I feel used. That I'm scared someone might find out and think I tricked him into doing it. Why would anyone believe someone like him would freely want to be with me?

I imagine everyone in town finding out. Me being forced to carry a SLUT name tag until I graduate and leave this town, if ever.

Back to eating lunch in stalls, hiding in shame forever.

This is what's been replaying in my head since I woke up. It's in an endless continuous loop of panic. I wish I could ask him why we did it, but I'm not allowed if we're playing quiet.

"What's the workout for today?" I ask instead, grabbing a hurdle and leaning it against the gate to swing my legs across the crossbar.

*Act natural. Don't fidget.* I'm tempted to bite my nails.

"Come over here," Coach says, dropping the running blocks on lane number four.

I walk over thinking he needs me to double-check that the blocks are placed at the right lengths for my feet and height.

"Listen, Kris," he says while I adjust the angle of the blocks. I pause and look up at him, but it's quite dark and I can't see his expression.

"Hmm-hmm," I'm listening.

"Whenever we're on the track, we work. We're here for business." He's assertive. Frightening.

He's told me this before, when he caught me yapping away with some of my teammates during a track meet. I'm here to seal the deal. Not talk. Make friends. Or think of anything other than my event. Hurdles. Hurdles. Hurdles. Hurdles.

"Our personal relationship. What we did last night. It stays off the track, okay?"

*Finally. He acknowledged it. As if it wasn't a big deal.*

"Okay, I understand . . . ," I answer, wanting to ask him why, but I don't want to question him. "I won't mention it."

He tugs at my chin and says, "I need you to focus."

"Okay," I answer, trying to forget the way his skin felt on my skin. *How can I focus?*

"Forget all of that when we're here."

*How can I separate the two?* "Okay." I can't mess this up. I awkwardly walk over to do a couple of drills cuz I'm trying to put on an act.

Nothing happened. Nothing happened. Nothing happened. Nothing happened. Everything is like before. Everything is just normal.

If normal is this constant twist in my stomach, if normal is questioning every decision I make since the summer of 2006, if normal is feeling confused about people's intentions. Then, yes. We're back to normal.

I get on with agility drills, but I'm clumsy today. I must have not slept enough.

"Need those drills nice and tight," Coach calls out.

Today is our last practice before the district track-and-field meet. It's in three days, and my mind is a wreck.

When I'm finished with all the agility and hurdle drills, Coach says, "Actually. Let's go one through four."

"You got it."

I walk over to my blocks, slapping my temples to wake up. I'm feeling off today. I get in my running blocks, and I take one look up ahead at the hurdles. I just gotta tap into my three-step rhythm and I'll be fine. I'm ready. My previous performance times prove it. I haven't lost a local hurdle race this season. I'm seeded at number one coming into the district meet.

I just gotta believe in the process. First is district, then regionals, and then state.

"Get set," Coach calls out.

I lift my hips upward, my body leaning forward. Both hands on the ground.

He blows his whistle. I burst out of the blocks and swing my arms frantically. My legs follow.

"Speed up! You gotta move faster!"

I push off the ground, running toward the first hurdle, lessons flashing in my mind about the starting blocks to the first hurdle being the most important section of a sprint hurdle race.

*You gotta be quick off the blocks.*

It'll help me transition into my signature hurdling rhythm. More important, having a strong, clean start builds confidence throughout the race.

Hurdle one: I clear it way too high.

*Focus.*

Hurdle two: I clear it with my arms crossing my midpoint.

A thought interrupts my focus. *What if everyone finds out about Coach and me?*

Hurdle three: My rhythm is off, I four-step between hurdles two and three. I switch lead legs. Awful.

Somewhere in the back of my thoughts, I can hear Coach's frustration. "C'mon. C'mon. What are you doing?"

There's absolutely no way I can switch back to three-stepping to the last hurdle. My legs aren't moving with my mental commands.

"Shiitttttt!" I yell loud and ram my stomach against the white crossbar of hurdle number four.

I shove the hurdle forward. "I can't ... I can't hurdle today," I moan. I'm pissed at myself for letting all these thoughts get in my way.

Coach stops his watch, and with a quick mutter, I apologize, "I'm sorry. I don't know what's wrong with me today." I've never had a run as bad as this one since we began training three months ago.

I must be nervous for the upcoming district meet. That's it.

"What did I say about the word *can't*?" Coach is next to me now.

"*Can't* is unacceptable. *Can't* is negative. *Can't* is not in our vocabulary, cuz I can achieve anything if I say I can." I repeat those words like I'm a soldier in his boot camp.

He pats me on the head twice, and says, "That's right."

"But Coach," I say, then stutter, "I mean Carlos." I gotta remember to call him by his real name when no one is around. "I feel like I have brain fog." That's the best way to describe it.

I watch his dark shadow lean up against the fence, saying nothing. Scratching his head and looking at his watch, he says, "We're shutting it down. Right now."

"But," I try to tell him I wanna try again. I will do better. I gotta train harder. I need to show him I got what it takes.

"No, I don't need you getting hurt right before district."

"I'm not."

"You got way too many things in that little head of yours, Kris."

"No, I don't. I'm fine." I mean, I'm not really, but I can be alright. If only I could outrun these intrusive thoughts the same way I've done it in the past. I can overcome my fear.

"Please," I beg him.

"Okay, but only if you're actually gonna do it right," he says.

"I will." I try to get into the zone while I walk back to the starting line.

*Nothing happened last night.* I want this so bad. I need to kill it at district. Make a statement and qualify to regionals.

"Get set . . . go!"

This time, off the blocks, I push harder for four strides before gradually reaching top speed like an airplane would.

"Good! Snap down! Let's keep moving," Coach says from the infield.

I snap my trail leg over hurdle number one quickly. I'm off to a great start.

Hurdle two: How bad do you want to escape everything? *Bad.*

Hurdle three: How bad do you want to make it to state? *Bad.*

Hurdle four: How bad do you want that scholarship? *Bad.*

I feel my feet as light as a feather, yet powerfully bouncing off the track over each hurdle. I finish strong, past the orange cone next to where hurdle number five would've been. Coach walks over to the finish line to show me my splits. I clock in a new personal record off the blocks and into the first hurdle at 2.11 seconds.

"Great job finishing strong, Kris!" He pounds my fist.

Maybe he and I will be fine after all.

Maybe we'll move on like nothing happened.

Maybe he will help me reach my goal.

Maybe everything will be alright . . . if I stay focused and quiet.

# SECRETS

**Coach and I are parked at the far end of the stadium.**

"I got you these sweatpants." He removes the tags off the gray pants and presses the elastic band against my waist. "They fit you, no? Looks like you lost all that baby fat you had on when we first started to train."

"Yeah, I think so!" I reply, noticing how much lighter I feel since January. It's probably from training twice a day and removing fast food from my diet. No more tacos. "Thank you so much!" I add, placing the sweatpants across my lap.

"Good. I knew you'd like them," he says, observing the cars passing by. It would be weird if people saw us hanging out in his truck for this long.

"Can I go now?"

"Yup! But warm up with them today," he orders me.

"Sure . . . ," I say, pulling the new sweatpants on over my blue track shorts, hoping he can't see the lump from my pad. But thank god I got my period, even though it's really painful and heavy.

I think back to him reminding me that a runner needs to have class and style on the track. Well, what's wrong with my style? Maybe he doesn't like the clothes and accessories I wear. But I make them, and it's a way I can express myself. Right now, I've got my handmade bright yellow headband. It's the only thing that helps keep my long, thick hair away from my face during a race.

"Where's the pink sweatshirt I got you last week?"

"Umm . . ." Oops. I forgot it. I hid the sweatshirt under my bed or else Ma would ask where I got it from.

"You forgot it, didn't you?" He knows me too well.

I pretend to search in my duffel bag that's sitting in between my feet on the floor. "I thought I brought it with me. Sorry."

He wanted me to wear it today. I think it's kind of him to buy me things, but I feel bad I can't repay him. I got no money. And weirdly, I worry that I'll end up developing funny feelings for him now that we *did it*. Usually if a boy likes me at school, and I like him back, we'd exchange handwritten notes and hang at the mall. Coach doesn't give me the impression that he's ever written a single love letter, just workout programs.

He sighs, frustrated. "I didn't buy that for you for nothing."

"Sorry," I apologize again, then promise him I'll bring it next time. *Don't forget it next time or he'll be pissed*, I remind myself.

Coach glances at his watch, and I know what that means. *It's race time.*

Instantly, it's like something snaps in his head and he begins coaching me. "Okay, go now, but remember when you go out there, you have to keep believing in yourself . . . Show everyone what you're made of . . . Tackle one hurdle at a time . . . And run with balls!"

Another one of his pep talks moments before I gotta walk straight into the stadium where I'll be competing for the district titles in the 100-meter dash, 100-meter hurdles, and 300-meter hurdles.

"Don't let people doubt you . . . You're the best this city will ever see . . ."

"Mm-hmm. Mm-hmm. Mm-hmm." I nod my head like he's drilling lines into my brain, forcing me to replay them a million times over and over again until I believe them.

"Remember what I'm saying," Coach reminds me. "Just give it your best."

"Mm-hmm," I reply quickly to his repetitive positive affirmations.

Out of nowhere, my phone vibrates. *Whoops.* I peek at my cell phone screen under my thigh, just enough so I'm able to read Linda's text.

**Linda:** Kristolla, your dad's here.

*Ugh. That's just great.*

This will be my dad's first time at any of my meets, and I haven't talked to him in years. The last time I saw him was *that* night.

Now I need to worry about my dad finding out that I slept with a man his age. *I'm dead.*

"Kris?" Coach notices I'm distracted. He doesn't like when I check my phone when I'm in front of him, especially the same day of a big meet.

I slip my cell underneath my shorts, and quickly reply, "Yup. I'm gonna do my best out there." I mean, that's really all I can do anyway, right?

On top of all these new fears, I'm gonna try not to think about the usual things that stress me out before a race. Things like clipping a hurdle and falling face-first, stuttering in the low hurdles, or not being able to beat even one single girl of the twenty-four I gotta race.

*Noooooo.* I'm gonna try not to think about all of that even though winning is never a guarantee, and neither is running a new PR.

"Just focus on yourself, you've done a great job so far," he says, and I can't help but grin, lifted by his compliment.

"And remember," he continues, lightly pressing on my forearm. "No matter what, I love you."

*Huh? He loves me?*

I don't remember the last time Ma told me she loved me, and she was the only one who ever did. I don't know exactly how to feel about it. All I know is how his words make me feel. He does make me feel special. That I'm good enough. That I'm wanted. That I'm capable of achieving greatness. That I deserve to get that scholarship. He injects me with confidence. It's like he knows I sometimes doubt myself. I guess it doesn't matter that I'm young enough to be his daughter, and he's old enough to be my father. For a moment, I wonder if he's like Coach Richard. But that thought quickly goes away. I'm confident I'm the exception. Things are different with me and Carlos.

Do I love him back? Maybe I do. How am I supposed to know what it's like to be in love with an adult? I just wish *we* didn't happen like it did. Now I worry about people finding out and me losing everything I worked hard for. People will blame me for this. Like, how could the best coach in town do something like that with someone like me? Maybe it is my fault.

We lock eyes. He's in the driver's seat and I'm in the passenger seat, and instead of replying with "I love you, too," I bump fists.

"Bring home a PR and a win," he says as I get out of his truck and make my way to the track.

An hour later, I'm on the starting line of the 100-meter-hurdles finals. My least favorite race of the two hurdle events. I'm on lane number four, waiting impatiently for the announcer to start us off. I look up at the bleachers to see crowds of people huddled in groups of three or more, wearing the colors of schools they came here to cheer for.

Despite coming into the 2009 District Championship Finals as the number one seed in all three events, I'm still a nervous wreck. As usual, I slept zero hours last night. The restlessness. The palpitations. The hyperventilating. The ruminating. Over. And. Over. Again. Like a broken record before a big race.

What if I bleed through my shorts in the middle of leaping over the hurdles? What if my secrets reveal themselves in the middle of a race to my teammates. To competitors. To other coaches. To parents. To the sports journalists. To the hundreds of people in the stands? I imagine being booed off the track and getting called all sorts of things. And I don't know which is worse, being labeled a *slut* or a *big, fat liar.*

My throat tightens up. The longer we wait behind our running blocks, the deeper I get lost in my thoughts. *Please, no one find out. Not right now or my life is over.*

"Kristy," someone whispers on the line. I turn my head. It's Alicia out of lane two. She's a hurdler from Union South High, the school I would've gone to had it not been for Richard convincing Ma that I belong at Anderson High School.

I whisper back, "Hey," while keeping my eyes on the hurdles ahead of us. If I don't, Coach will reprimand me when I'm done. I'm not allowed to talk to anyone on the line.

"Kick butt today. You got this," she says, and it helps get me out of my thoughts.

"Shut the hell up, bitches!" Lane five hisses at us. It's Celine. She used to be Coach's athlete before he started coaching me. *Great. She's right freaking next to me.*

I say nothing to Celine. Neither does Alicia.

At times I wonder if things would've been different if that conversation with Richard and Ma never happened. Maybe Alicia and I would be best friends, and we could build our own all-girls hurdle group and spread our views on positive sportsmanship before a race, instead of trash talk. *The real fight is on the track. Bring it on.*

I've actually never spoken to Celine. She's not approachable, and her attitude doesn't match her face. She looks nice. All the boys like her. But I'm pretty sure she doesn't like me. We've been competing against each other for three years, and not once has she beaten me. She's a senior now, and there's probably some pressure to claim the district title, especially since this is her team's first year without Coach. If she found out her former coach is now my coach, she'd probably hate me even more. I heard from one of her teammates she was the first to cry when Coach announced his resignation.

"Quiet on the bleachers," the announcer says over the loudspeaker, while I suddenly can't help but wonder whether Celine also had feelings for him.

"Runners, on your marks." The announcer finally makes the call, and immediately, I snap out of my head. I shake my legs and slap my tights. I disguise my nerves by fidgeting. *It's go time.*

Loosening up the muscles in my body before I get on the running blocks, I do a tuck jump, springing upward into the sky, bending my knees in front of my body. *Here I go.* I sit on my running blocks in a kneeling position. Arms locked in place and hands shoulder width apart. With my fingers perfectly in a straight line behind the starting line, I tilt my head up and stare blankly ahead.

I squint my eyes, crinkle my nose, and glance at my lane from start to finish. A total of ten hurdles are in my path, each standing at thirty-three inches tall. I've got tunnel vision. That's what I call it when I can't see anything except the hurdles that are in front of me.

Each obstacle on my lane represents something I desperately wanna overcome. A bad memory. A fear. A negative thing someone said to me. Something, someone I badly wanna run away from.

I take a deep breath, feeling my stomach sucking in. Slowly, my peripheral vision pulls my attention away. The symmetry and spacing of the hurdles create an optical illusion. My eyes are playing tricks on me. It appears as if there are a gazillion hurdles ahead of me. An endless sea of metal barriers.

*Focus on your lane or you'll get distracted.* Still in blocks, I tilt my head in a neutral position, away from the hurdles ahead, and twist my arms, elbow and palms face outward. Hands face inward. I'm hunched and locked in.

*They can't bring you down*, I repeat to myself, fueling my body and mind with adrenaline. My nerves recede like a wave that has come and gone.

"Get set."

I lean forward, my backside raised, all my body weight shifting to my fingertips. Eyes locked on the rubber track, I inhale in sharply.

*Freeze. Don't move. Don't try to gauge the starter gun or you'll false start.* I wait for the gun to pop. One second . . . two seconds . . . three seconds . . . four seconds . . . I'm still holding my position. *Why does it sometimes feel like forever?*

*BAMMMMMMMM!* Gunshot.

I exhale forcibly, letting a *whooshhh* sound out of my mouth, and I explode out of the blocks. I sprint down the track. My eyes quickly focus on hurdle number one.

*One, two, three—clear the hurdle.*

I apply more force into the ground with my feet and keep a natural three-stepping rhythm in between each hurdle.

I'm attacking each hurdle as if I'm plowing through a door.

*One, two, three—attack the hurdle.*

*One, two, three—attack the hurdle.*

*One, two, three—attack the hurdle.*

Halfway through the race, I can feel Celine one stride away. She's up on me. She's a right-lead hurdler and I'm a lefty, so I can feel her body. Hurdlers have exceptional spatial awareness. *She's too close.* Staying tall on the balls of my feet, I fight the dry wind blowing directly into us. It threatens my ability to maintain my rhythm. Somehow, as I'm pushing harder and harder, my contacts go blurry. Blinking and squinting my eyes, there's no way I'm gonna fix them during the race.

*Dammit.* I try to hold off a little longer, barely able to see, but I trust that training in the dark has prepared me for this moment. *Tune into my rhythm. Trust my cadence.*

One, two, three—takeoff.

I clear the final hurdle with one eye open and one eye closed, crossing the finish line strong. I win the district title in the 100-meter hurdles, set a new PR and a new city record.

Sixty seconds later, I'm back at the starting line, rubbing my eyes. I hardly have enough time to adjust my running blocks for the next race—the 100-meter-dash finals. My recovery time between each of these two races during finals is less than five minutes.

I'm competing in the open 100 event to help my team score points, but also cuz I have an opportunity to sweep gold in all three running events. That's if everything goes according to plan. A few seconds later, I sprint through the finish line. Again, I win the district title, set a new PR and a new city record.

After clinching two first-place victories, I get ready for the toughest event and my strongest event of the day—the 300-meter hurdles. The race that can land me my scholarship.

Truth be told, I'm soooo tired now. I can't feel my body. I'm in a haze. Being sleep-deprived for two days and on pure adrenaline is both physically and mentally exhausting. *I should be used to this by now.* Doesn't help that it's one hundred degrees, and my skin is sizzling. The dry air zaps out every single hydrated cell in my body. Even my contacts need to be replaced now.

I switch to a fresh pair, then walk over to the check-in tent, where event officials count attendance. They give me my hip number sticker, which is the lane number I'm running in, and I slap the number five on my hips. Then I make my way to the start of the 300-meter-hurdles race. *Last race. It's almost over.*

I talk to myself, fixing my running blocks on the staggered lanes, realizing that in a few minutes, I'll come out of the backstretch and be welcomed by the death zone around hurdle seven. I gulp just thinking about that part of the race.

That's when I'll know if all these practices have been helping. I'll have to push past the threshold, embrace the pain moving from my legs to my stomach. I gotta dig deep to finish the race. That's the only way I know how to run a PR.

"Go Kristyyy!" I hear teammates and friends chanting from the bleachers and around the track.

I stand behind my blocks, closing my eyes for a moment. I envision my race before the battle begins. *All the hurdles ahead can't bring me down. They will test me, but I will persevere.*

"Runners, on your marks."

I do my normal routine of taking a couple of tuck jumps, stare at the hurdles, get tunnel vision, and then get angry at what the hurdles represent to me. I get a boost of adrenaline.

"Get set."

*BAMMMMMM!*

I push out of the blocks. Forward explosion. Arms swing wide. I catch the girls on the outer lanes before going into the backstretch and feel confident that I'm in first place.

I'm on a seventeen-stride pattern between each hurdle, trying to maintain my rhythm. Any more strides between hurdles and I'm slowing down. I gotta try to hit all the hurdles with my left lead leg. I don't feel comfortable leading with my right knee. I'm not as flexible on that side.

I'm ahead of the competition coming out of hurdle four. I'm running alone. I'm running against time. Vaguely, I hear sounds around the track, but I tune them out.

Out of the curve, and into the straightaway, my hips begin to wobble.

*Swing the arms. They will follow your legs. Attack that next hurdle.*

My eyes zone in on the next obstacle. It seems far away and a lot taller than usual, but I know, soon I'll be confronting my fear.

*Don't stutter.*

There always comes a point late in the race where I second-guess myself. It happens when my body starts running out of fuel and my muscles are starving for oxygen, and the lactic acid is building up. I can feel it seeping into my muscles like crawling ants. Instead of charging toward the hurdle, I stutter-step.

I don't trust my cadence, nor my right lead leg. The thing about stuttering is that it slows down my momentum, and I gotta speed up again between the next hurdles. Which requires more energy to regain my rhythm.

And then I do it. I freaking stutter over the fifth hurdle, and stupidly, still lead with my right leg, my less dominant one. *Ugh.* Double negative.

It causes my fists to clench, which then makes me tighten up. Which then causes my form to break.

*Push harder! More power.* Need to get back to seventeen strides.

Digging deep from a place that hurts like hell, I know exactly where I'm at now—the death zone and into a strong headwind.

Running from hurdles six to seven is like running on hot coals. *Are you gonna give up?* I can hear voices in my head telling me to quit. Those damn hurdles wanna bring me down. *Never!*

Running from hurdles seven to eight is even tougher. The wind is trying to mess with my strides, feels like someone is pushing my shoulders back with every stride I make. I furrow my brow and push my body to places I've never been. My thighs are burning. There's that dull, sharp pain creeping in again toward my navel.

*I'm the queen of pain.* I zone into the last hurdle, gritting my teeth.

I'm ten feet away from the last hurdle, though it looks miles and miles away. Is it possible to not feel my body and still be able to take off into the hurdle?

*You can't make me fall. Not today. Not right now.*

I fight the urge to stutter before the hurdle and I manage to accelerate the last two strides. I'm able to have a quick lead action with my dominant lead leg. I snap it down as fast as I can.

The finish line is soooo close.

*RUNNNNN.*

I cross the white line feeling nothing, and I win with another PR. I also qualified for the regional championships in all three running events. I'm one step closer to the state championships! *Yay.* I wanna celebrate but I can't cuz I'm in so much pain.

Once I feel better, I hear someone calling out my name. It's my dad waving hello from outside the stadium gate, wearing a pair of jeans that's got oil stains at the knees.

"Hey, Dad. Thanks for coming," I say brightly, as if we talk often.

He says, "I was able to see you run from here," making me feel sorry that he probably doesn't feel comfortable coming inside.

I try to have a quick exchange with him, so I'm not coming off as unwelcoming, but the thing is, I don't want Coach running into us.

The last thing I need is for them to meet. *Hey, Dad. Meet my private coach, who is also like my dad, but I also slept with him. Hey, Carlos. Meet my absent dad, who could've been in my life, but I also don't need him anymore.*

Yeah . . . right. No thank you.

I say, "Awww," giving him a smile without teeth showing. "I appreciate it."

Worried about Coach, I gracefully look over my left shoulder, then my right. A crowd of people leaving surrounds us. *Please, don't run into us right now.*

With sparkles in his eyes, Dad asks excitedly, "How are you so superfast?" Well, it's probably part genetics and part me wanting to escape my own thoughts and this town. Maybe if he and Ma stayed together, I wouldn't be in this situation.

My mind flashes back to when I was younger. I think of all the time lost. Moments I wished he would randomly show up to my cheerleading competitions. The time I beat all but one boy at the local skate competition. The hundreds of races I pushed myself to the finish line. I'd always fantasized about my dad finally noticing me, making me feel like I had a normal family for once. I used to think maybe, just maybe, I could be one of the few lucky ones with two parents cheering from the bleachers.

*I know. I know. It's never too late.* But truth is, I don't think I need him to act like my dad anymore. Coach has my back.

"That's a good question," I answer, thinking I should probably thank him now for giving me my DNA and for paying Ma child support. At least.

Leaning into the gate and squeezing his light-skinned fingers on the metal fence, he reveals to me, "Pos I've been reading about you in the newspaper every week. Good job on winning all those races. I'm proud of you."

*Good Job. He's proud of me.* I repeat these words to myself.

For the first time in my life, my dad praises me for something that matters to me. *Wow.* This should be our father-and-daughter moment. A feeling of elation should come over me and sweep me off my feet. Instead of succumbing to the *right* feelings, I twirl the fake gold metals around my neck with my fingertips and end up with a familiar tug of guilt.

I'm not mad at my dad for taking this long to be what I've been wanting him to be for many years.

I'm just sad.

Sad that he's been replaced by my coach.

# KICKED OUT

"Where were you?" Ma isn't happy. I didn't answer her texts tonight and got home at 11:00 p.m. on a school night.

I roll my eyes and sigh, pretending like it's not a big deal even though my curfew is at 7:00 p.m. Not like my probation officer checks up on me, anyway. There's only been one time they made me go in for a drug test, and of course I passed it with flying colors.

"Somewhere," I answer. I can't tell her I was with Coach this late. Ma squints, inspecting my entire face.

"Stop!" I back away, moving closer to my bedroom. My back bumps into the doorframe.

"Chingada madre, you're drinking!" she accuses. I burst into laughter cuz I've never ever tasted alcohol in my life. Thanks to her and her coworkers at the bar who would constantly bring the party to our apartment, I swore to myself I'll never end up talking gibberish, throwing up on myself, or passing out on the floor.

Ma probably thinks I'm drunk cuz my hair is disheveled. I'm walking funny. My T-shirt is wrinkled. My mascara is smeared, and

I'm pretty sure my eyes have turned red from wearing contacts for longer than I should.

"Dime," Ma asks to tell her the truth.

I huff and puff. "What? I'm not. Just leave me alone."

Ma tries hard to believe I'm sober.

"Where were you, then?" She's persistent.

"Ma, I gotta go to sleep." I try to end this conversation, to squirm away, to ignore her question.

"You're not sleeping until I get an answer." But she won't let me go.

"What the heck, I got practice in a few hours."

"You're not going to practice."

"I have to!" I yell. "Coach is gonna be pissed if I don't show up."

"Coach this . . . Track that," Ma mimics me. My face scrunches up as she continues, "All you do is talk about track and your stupid coach."

She's right. Those two things are taking over my life right now.

"So what?" I snap.

"Ever since you started practicing with him, you're never home."

That's cuz around here, nothing is good enough for her.

"And you don't clean your room. I'm tired of finding all these papers underneath your bed."

She gets my attention. I interrupt her, "What did you do with them?" Those are journal entries about Carlos I tear out after writing them.

*I hope she didn't read them or I'm in deep trouble.*

"Están where they belong." She points at the trash bin. "I'm not your maid."

Relieved she hasn't read them, but not wanting her to know, I look at her and shrug. "Whatever."

"Mira, since you started training te crees mucho. You talk back to me. You think you're better."

I'm not better, I just don't wanna put up with her attitude anymore. Coach makes me feel like I can do anything. One more school year and I won't ever have to hear her complain about every little thing I do wrong.

"Oh my god." I slouch my shoulders and admit, "He's freaking helping me a lot, in ways you probably can't. What do you expect?"

"Entonces, why don't you depend on him?"

*Good question. Maybe cuz he's not my parent, but he sorta is becoming now.*

"You're soooo . . . ," I start saying, rolling my eyes, and finish with the greatest insult ever, "dumb."

She whacks me across the face. Hands closed. I take it.

*Don't fight back or you'll end up back in juvie.*

This is all her fault. She refuses to get help for her PTSD even though it's ruining our lives. She's the one who listened to Richard so that I ended up on a dead-end track team at Anderson. She left me in juvie when I admitted to feeling suicidal. Who else would I go to?

He cares about me more than she ever could ever these days.

These two last years, she's been too busy taking care of Rafael, complaining how I shouldn't have saved her life, how excited she is that soon I'll turn eighteen and I'll be on my own. She lives in the past when all I wanna do is leave all of this behind. Start a new life.

Holding on to my hot cheek, I try not to yell and wake up Rafael. But I can't hold back, after everything.

"You're just jealous of my coach, but he's the one saving me from all of this shit that's happened!"

Coach is everything I needed her and my dad to be.

Ma stomps on her way to her bedroom, screaming, "Then go ask him to support your living expenses. We don't even have money."

"He already does!"

"Oh really?" Ma comes back, following me into my bedroom. "Pack your things and leave my house, then. This isn't your home anymore. Go ask him to support you."

Without any hesitation, I open my drawers, shaking, pulling out a couple of things I need and then stuffing them inside my gray backpack.

*Polo for school. Sports bra. Running socks. My journal. Pen.*

From the bedroom door, Ma watches me coldly as I tell her while rustling through the drawers, "You're right . . ." I close the drawer. "I don't need you."

I needed her to support me with love, not money. Just listen to me and not judge me. Is it that hard for her to care how I feel? Love me even if I'm not perfect? Thank me for saving her life? Is it too much to ask for that in a mother?

I don't even remember what it's like to have parents anymore.

Ma slaps the door with an open hand and shouts, "Get out now! Time is up," cutting my packing short.

"Wait . . . I gotta . . ." I try to grab my running spikes, but she's shoving me out the door. She's a lot stronger than me.

"Nope," she says firmly.

Feeling sad and tired, I start crying. "Just stop," I plead while she manages to push me out the front door.

"Goodbye." She shut the door. Locks it.

My chest quivers as my stomach turns upside down. I start to panic cuz this all feels like juvie.

I suppose our relationship was a ticking bomb. Sooner or later, it was going to explode. With fire and fury. That's what happens when you hold emotions inside.

I knock on the door gently, whispering so the neighbors don't know what's happening, "Ma, stop. Just let me back in. Please, I really need to sleep soon. Don't do this right now. I can't afford this."

After a few minutes, there's still no answer. I give up.

I'm done knocking. I'm done begging her to want me even if I'm not the perfect daughter.

*Screw her.* I've held on to hope for far too long that she would return to normal again.

I open my backpack, scrambling through the clothes I managed to stuff in quickly. Relieved I packed my cell phone, I frantically text Coach and my friend Gina.

**Me:** Carlos, can u please help me? I need a ride. Something happened at my house.

**Me:** Ginaaa can I stay at ur place tnite? Pretty plzzzz. My mom and I got into an argument. Can hitch a ride to ya.

Less than one minute later, Coach pings me back.

**Coach:** Coming right now. Meet me at the back of your apartment complex. See you soon!

I grab my things and make my way to the back alley where the shadows of trees shroud the area in darkness.

Pacing back and forth, I keep a close eye out for Ma, worried she might change her mind and see Coach picking me up. That would make her furious, but what does she expect? That I'd bang on the door for hours until she feels like she's tortured me enough?

**Coach:** Pulling up. Get in quickly.

When his red truck comes around the bend with the headlights off, I wave my hands in the air. I swing the door open and jump inside the passenger seat in one smooth motion.

"Thank you for saving me!" I sigh in relief.

Coach circles around the complex to exit and asks me, "You and your mom fighting again?"

I just say, "Yup." I don't want to get into the details. Sometimes he can be a little paranoid that Ma or someone else suspects something between us.

I already told him about the issues between me and Ma when we talked about what happened to her in 2006. He doesn't *not* like Ma. He just says she's complicated.

"You can't have these things happening right now. Does she know that you have a big meet coming up?"

"Duh," I say. "She knows, but why would she care?"

I buckle my seat belt as he turns onto McPherson Street.

He put his hands over my head, caressing my hair. His touch makes me feel less stressed out.

"You get your mind ready for regionals, it's important. Don't worry about anything else." He keeps stroking the front part of my head in a circular motion.

I turn to Coach, smiling and nodding. "Okay, I'll try, but I didn't bring my running shoes." I try to forget that I just got kicked out of the apartment and tell myself that everything is gonna be fine, as long as I have him.

"Don't worry about it. Where to now?"

I take out my cell and see if Gina texted back.

"My friend Gina said I can come over in forty-five minutes."

*She's probably sneaking me in through the window.*

"Okay, I can take drop you off then."

We stop at a red light.

"You're gonna be fine. Just breathe," he says, comforting me.

We drive north and cross Highway 35 until we park on the backside of a Motel 6. It's not the type of motel you'd check in to for a long stay, but it's nice to know he's surprising me with a room. This will save me from having to embarrassingly explain to Gina about what happened at home. And I'll get my own bed, so I'll be ready for practice in the morning.

Slipping a blue baseball hat over his dark brown hair, he lowers the visor to conceal half of his face and says, "Give me a sec, Kris."

I nod—"Okay"—and watch as he disappears to the front entrance of the lobby.

**Coach:** Booked room 103. Meet me on the opposite side. Make sure to hide your face from cameras.

Cautiously, I get out of the truck, glancing in all directions, hoping no one will see me, thinking about why he said to avoid cameras. I'm tempted to sprint to the room, but I fight the urge.

What would people say if someone spotted me? *Walk normally. Walk normally.*

I can imagine my face plastered under a headline. *Kristy Gonzalez seen at a motel with Coach. Inappropriate relationship. An investigation is underway.*

Everyone and their abuelas read the local newspaper. The whole city will find out and talk about me. Who knows what people would say?

I tilt my face toward the ground, dodging a security camera before arriving in front of room 103, relieved to get there and get some sleep.

"Come in, come in." He hurries me inside and checks if anyone saw me going inside.

I scan the room. TV. Mini fridge. Red-colored curtains. Two beds. No frills. I push down the top of one of the mattresses and it creaks.

*This will do for now.* "Which one do I take?" I ask, since we've never slept on the same bed.

"Sit," he says smoothly, taking a seat on one of the beds. I do as he asks, and he rests his hands on my lap.

Taking out my phone from my pocket, I say, "Need to text Gina and tell her I'm not coming."

"Don't." He takes away my cell, tosses it onto the other bed and says, "I'll take you in a bit."

"Huh?"

He climbs on top of me, his weight squishing my chest. Turns out, he only booked the room for one hour.

# ONE STEP CLOSER

**It's day one of the regional track-and-field championship meet in** San Antonio, Texas, and things aren't going well.

I crossed the finish line in fourth in the 100-meter-hurdles prelims with a time of 15 and change. I felt it, *knew* I was way too slow.

*How did I four-step two hurdles?*

I don't even wanna look up at the stands, but I do, and catch Coach shaking his head. Which only means one thing: He's pissed off.

I pretend like it's all good, despite knowing I'm capable of running faster than Regina, who won our heat. Her times are usually 15 seconds and up. I've run 14s in the last couple of meets and was seeded in third place coming into regionals.

We all know the rules: Only the winners of each heat will automatically qualify for the finals, followed by the next five fastest times. My time places me in ninth place, leaving me outside of the qualifying group. I'm out.

"Congrats, girl!" I say to Regina.

She's like 5'9". Long, lean limbs. Pretty light brown hair. High ponytail with a pink ribbon. She can step over hurdles like they are the size of a six-inch cone.

"Thanks, girlie." She smiles, happy she's moving on to the next round.

She's got the most perfect, flawless smile, which makes it a little bit worse.

Unlike me, I got fangs like Dracula. They're sharp as a razor and noticeable; people often jokingly say I'm a vampire. What's worse is that my real name is Elvira. Like the fictional horror movie lady from the '80s who called herself "mistress of the dark" and wore a black wig and had big breasts.

I really don't like my real name. Or my teeth.

Sometimes, I wish Ma had money for braces, but I haven't even been to a damn dentist in many years. She used to get her teeth fixed across but after what happened, we will never dare cross the bridge into Mexico again.

*Oh well.* Who cares . . . having a nice smile won't help me get back to the state championships.

"See you next time," I say to Regina.

I wave at Regina as she runs to her coach and parents in the stands. She probably thinks I'm too short for the event.

I walk off the track, getting mentally prepared for my next race. The 300-meter hurdles. Now that I can't qualify for the 100-meter hurdles, this race is my last chance to make it to state. I walk into the bathroom. Sitting on the toilet, I face-plant into the palms of my hands.

*Carlos is probably looking for me. I don't wanna face him yet.* I take a deep breath. Try to think positive.

*I need to kill it on the 300-meter hurdles. That's what I need to do.*

I leave the bathroom, ready to face him.

"What happened to you, huh? ¿Te olvidaste how to hurdle o qué?" he's asking me in front of everybody on the stands. "Your splits were way off." He's shaking his head, scratching his dimpled chin and clicking his stopwatch. I look off into the distance, past his shoulder, avoiding eye contact with him.

"Well . . ." My mind wanders off as he's analyzing my splits to each hurdle. I shrug. "I guess I just freaked out."

That's my best excuse.

"You can't afford to freak out with these stakes on the line."

"I just felt too much pressure."

He launches into one of his favorite quotes. "Pressure is something you feel"—he points directly at his chest—"when you don't know what the hell you are doing. And did I not prepare you for this meet?"

"Yeah, you did," I say timidly, feeling his anger shoot through my body.

He lifts two fingers up stuck together.

"You had two shots! Now you just have one."

"I know."

"Last chance or it's over for you."

I nod, feeling tense. I disappointed him badly. "I'm sorry . . ." I want to run away and hide underneath the bleachers, blame the oncoming rain, pretend like I don't wanna get wet.

"Get back out there and do your warm-up like you know what the hell you're doing. I need to see you run those 300-meter hurdles like your life depends on it. Hear me?"

"Hmm-hmm, you got it." I try to prepare for what's to come.

"Say yes or no. Not hmm-hmm."

I clear my throat and reply, "Yes. I'll run hard."

"Good, Kris. That's the only thing I expect of you."

Coach sends me off into the battlefield, never once wishing me luck. He doesn't believe in luck. He thinks everyone was born with the will to control their own life. Their own race.

I start my warm-up. Practice alternating legs just in case I gotta take an extra stride between hurdles and lead with my less dominant leg. Which could end in disaster!

"First call for the girls' three-hundred-meter hurdles," an announcer calls out.

I head to a tent to check-in and grab my hip number. I'm on lane number four, heat two. There are three full heats, and the fastest eight girls will qualify to the finals tomorrow.

*Oh my god.* I can't help but notice Christa Hall. She's wearing a bright red uniform that's the color of blood. I feel like she's gonna eat me like a lion on the track. In one freaking bite.

Christa is running in the heat before mine. Gives me plenty of time to study her blocks from the sideline. She's got long legs, about four inches more than mine. The muscles in her arms are well-defined. Her white spikes are slick.

Her game face is relaxed and calm.

Bet she's free of anxiety, considering she can outrun all of us with her eyes closed. Perhaps this race isn't as important to her, since she's already been recruited to run for Baylor University. Must be nice knowing all these coaches want you, and not the other way around.

I daydream of what it would be like to be her for just a second.

"Runners, on your marks," the announcer calls, interrupting my thoughts. I watch Christa press down on her blocks with her right foot. Her muscular legs extend perfectly on her running blocks. I hope someday I look as good as she does crouched low like that.

"Get set . . ."

*BAMMMMMMM!*

The gun cracks, and she's off like a cheetah. No one can catch her.

Christa easily wins.

"Heat two, next!" the announcer calls out, while the next heat waits on the sidelines. My heart begins pounding again.

I adjust my running blocks and take one start, running between twenty and thirty meters as a warm-up. *I'm ready. Let's do this.* I slap my thighs and my face, trying to hype myself up.

Standing behind my blocks now, I shut my eyes. I envision running through all eight hurdles and finishing in the top two. *I'm qualifying for finals in less than one minute.*

"Runners, on your marks."

I take one glance at the girls racing against me.

"Good luck!" a few of us exchange words with each other.

I set in my running blocks and do my typical ritual of seeing the hurdles through tunnel vision. Then I drop my head. Eyes down. Elbows locked. Knee on the ground.

"Get set." Inhale deeply. Backside up.

"Go!" Exhale out.

*Run, hard!*

Forty-four seconds later, I win my heat. I'm off to the finals.

The following day, I'm back in the infield warming up, scoping out my competition.

Some of the girls I had been doing research on for the last few months are the same girls who advanced to the finals with me. I remember their exact PRs and know how fast most of them are in an open sprint.

I think I can beat them, as long as I run a clean race.

"First call for the 300-meter-hurdle girls' finals, please check in." The announcer voice makes my stomach turn. Soon, I'll be in the death zone.

I check in and take my hip number, lane number five. Great lane. Way better than ending up on the outside lane on a staggered race where you can't see anyone running against you until someone either passes you or you realize what place you're in as you come around the curve into the homestretch. By that point it might be too late to shift gears.

Once I place the sticker on my hip, I keep moving around until they call our heat. From the corner of my eye, I see Christa. She's doing high knees. Her face is relaxed, like she's gonna bake a cake, not run an agonizing race in a few minutes. I mean, she's one of the fastest hurdlers in the nation. She's got the scholarship. She's got nothing to lose.

*Focus on yourself. Control only what you can.* I remind myself that I have what it takes to clinch one of two spots for the biggest meet of the year—the UIL Track & Field State Meet in Austin, Texas.

To qualify for the state championships, I need to place first or second at the regional championship finals. There are four regions in Texas, so a total of eight girls compete for the state title in one final round—no prelims.

Advancing to state will help me get discovered by college recruiters. Track and field is a late-blooming sport, meaning high school athletes hardly get recruited before junior year. Which means this is the year I need to excel at the hurdles. If I wait around for senior year track season, it might be too late cuz the state championship meet takes place the last month of the school year. By then, most universities would have already recruited their incoming class, leaving less scholarship money available for late signees. And I need a full scholarship. There's no way Ma could ever afford to pay for school.

Today, Christa will take first, no doubt, unless she false starts or something goes terribly wrong.

And me? Coming out of the prelims, I'm sitting in third place, just trailing behind Makeda Campbell, who won her heat yesterday, too. She's a much better technical hurdler than I am, but I'm faster in an open sprint. I can't afford too many mistakes.

"Girls running the 300-meter hurdles, please come to me," one of the officials calls out with a clipboard.

As I huddle around the official with my competition, she calls out Christa's name.

"Christa, lane four."

Then me. "Kristy Gonzalez, lane five."

"Got it."

Once she makes sure all of us eight hurdlers are present, we walk over to our designated lanes. I feel the nerves kicking in, my stomach becoming queasy.

*You can do it, Kristy.*

I adjust my running blocks, taking a few starts to see how the blocks feel. Feeling quick and strong, I'm ready. *All set.*

"Runners, on your marks."

I tuck jump, wiggle my legs, and do my tunnel vision ritual as I sit in the blocks. I clear everything from my sight and mind except for the first hurdle in front of me.

"Get set."

Leaning forward, I inhale deeply. Hold it. Wait for the gun to pop.

*BAMMMM!*

I explode off the blocks, feeling my wheels turning quickly. I tackle the first hurdle effortlessly, and I'm running strong.

Hurdle two. Clean.

Hurdle three. Clean.

I'm first to all three hurdles.

Hurdle four. Clean.

Now, this is where the fight begins—out of the curve and into the homestretch. Out of my left peripheral, I see a red uniform one stride ahead of me. It's Christa, charging the hurdles. She's fierce.

*Stay with her. Stay with her.*

I try to stay as close as I can to her, pumping my arms and quickly striking the rubber track with my little feet.

Hurdle five. She's in first. Me in second. Her hurdle technique is a lot smoother than mine.

*Hold off.*

I look straight ahead and there's three more hurdles, and then the finish line. *I want it. I need it.*

Hurdles five to six, I feel my form breaking.

*Don't cross the midpoint, stay on the balls of your feet. Push, off your feet. More force. Lift the knees.*

These cues go in and out of my thoughts as I enter the DEATH ZONE.

Hurdle six—I attack with my left leg and clear it. Phewww.

I'm staring down hurdle seven. *Damn.* I'm slowing down. My mind and body aren't working together.

*Move faster.* That thought seems to take a little bit longer to register with my muscles. That's how I know I'm getting tired.

*Don't stutter. Don't. stutter.* I fight the urge as I'm four strides away from attacking the next obstacle.

*I can't help it.* The hurdle seems to grow taller and taller, like I won't be able to clear it. I'm not confident I can make it with my less dominant leg on this one.

I stutter over hurdle seven. *Dammit.* I put more effort into the ground to get back into my cadence.

*C'mon, this is what I came for.*

Hurdle eight, the last one.

I'm hurting. My body is running out of fuel. Bet the crowd in the stands can see it as I clench my teeth and scrunch my nose.

Last hurdle, here we go. I'm three strides behind Christa, who is untouchable.

*Don't give up. You're not a quitter.*

I really wanna stop sprinting and fall to the ground, to catch my breath, but that's not an option. I have no idea how far the other girls behind me are.

Hurdle eight—here it comes. It looks gigantic. It's just an illusion when you're low in the tank.

*Attack it. Show them what you're made of.*

I can't feel my body. How am I supposed to lift my knees and take off over the hurdle?

I have no idea, but I manage to clear the last hurdle with my strong lead leg.

The crowd is chanting, roaring. Hands clapping. *This is it.*

The pain in my navel returns, more intense than ever.

*Goooooooooo!!!!!!*

I pump my arms, drive my knees, and sprint to the white line.

*I want it.*

I can feel that ticket inching closer and closer the more I spring my body forward. I fling my arms in the air as I cross the finish line in second place behind Christa.

As I slow to a walk, I feel disoriented, both pain and joy coursing through me. I shut my eyes and tilt my head back. Faintly, I pick up the sounds of feet pattering across the finish line behind me.

*Thank you . . . Stars. Even though I can't see the stars, I thank them for guiding me, for watching me.*

My life changed in 44.12 seconds.

*Yes! I did it. I'm heading to state.*

# TWO STEPS BACK

**A woman walking around Riverbank Track comes up to me and** Coach during the middle of our practice.

"Can you take a photo with her?" She points at her six-year-old daughter in the distance.

I smile at the little one running toward us.

"Sure."

She's a bit shy.

"Mira, like this," she says to her daughter, crouching slightly forward in a standing start. "You're gonna take a picture with her, mija. She's the girl in the newspaper. ¿Te acuerdas? The one that jumps really high."

"Come . . ." I bend down, and motion her to come stand next to me.

I ask, "What's your name?"

She tells me, showing her pearly white teeth minus one missing front tooth. Now I feel shy, too. I'm flattered some random person wants to take a photo of me with their child.

The little girl looks up at me, analyzing my face. "Are you really the girl in the picture?" Her voice is soft and pitchy.

"Hmm-hmm ..." My eyebrows arch. "If she was jumping like super high over a hurdle ..." I smile at her. "Then it was me."

Yup. That's me in the newspaper photos, jumping at least a foot over the high hurdles. I swing my leg at the hurdle instead of driving my lead knee straight into the crossbar. I'm scared I won't clear the hurdles. In actuality, a good hurdler will skim the top white, plastic crossbar.

At least some nonhurdlers think my technical flaws are cool.

"Say cheeseeee ..." Her mother elongates the letter *e*, which forces me to smile big.

"Cheeeesssee," all of us sing in sync. The woman snaps a photo with her cell phone.

"Muchas gracias."

"You're welcome." I giggle and turn to Coach. I want him to know that people are noticing our hard work, but he's doing something on his phone.

The woman presses her child close to her body and says, "I bet your parents are super proud and supportive of you."

I stop smiling, feeling my throat get tight. I wish I felt that were true in my heart.

"Hmm-hmm." I nod. Uncomfortably, I rush out, "Thanks, ma'am. I gotta go run now. Got state soon."

I manage to wink at the little one as she prances away. I walk toward Coach. He's looking at his watch now, waiting for me impatiently.

"Sorry, Coach," I say, ever so often glancing back at the track, noticing the mother twirling her daughter, then locking hands.

I wish me and Ma were still like that.

"Kris, you ready or what?" Coach asks monotonously, distracting me from going down memory lane.

"Yup."

"Warm up those hip flexors again," he orders me even though I had just done that before I took the photo.

I'm lost in my thoughts, wondering if the little girl's mother would be as excited about taking a photo with me if she knew about my secrets.

"Carlos?" I want to ask him what people would think if they knew about us. But I know this is an unspoken rule. We never talk about these things at practice.

"What next?" I turn around to look at Coach. His eyes are glued to his phone.

He's nodding his head like something bad happened.

"What?" I inquire.

He shows me his phone.

*The H1N1 influenza virus outbreaks hits Texas. The WHO organization increases the pandemic alert from Phase 3 to 4.*

"Kristy, the state meet is now in June," Coach says.

State is now a month later. I shake my head and say, "This isn't how things are supposed to be." Our training plan was developed for me to peak the week of the state championships, which should've been this weekend.

"We'll just have to adjust our training plan."

"But I feel at my best shape ever! Swear I feel like I can PR again right now. How can this be happening?" I complain. I just wanna freaking get this season over with already and know if I'm good enough to run at a university.

"There's nothing we can do," he says, looking at his watch. "One month will go by fast. I promise." I notice he sounds uncertain.

"What if the meet gets canceled?" I ask.

"Then we wait until next season."

Next year's state meet will take place around the time I graduate from high school. Hopefully, someone might be interested in a late recruit.

All this bad news makes me wanna slack off, so I loosen my ankle, point my toe, and clip the sharp edge of the crossbar of the hurdle, knocking into it.

"Now, don't get lazy on me, keep that foot dorsiflexed," he says as the hurdle rocks back and forth.

"But what if..." I mutter my words and get my thoughts together. "What if there's no next year?"

"You're just being paranoid. Just focus on June fifth," he says.

I finish warming up and try to agree with Coach, "Prolly right."

"Follow me," he says, walking over to the starting line of the 400-meter dash.

"Hey, Mr. Reina," Coach waves at the old security guard, who's been a big supporter for the both of us now that we train after school. My high school practice finished for the season, and no one else from Anderson High School or from our city qualified for state.

Finally, Coach and I get to train in the daylight.

With Riverbank Track being one of the only public tracks in town, it gets crowded once it's opened to the general population after the school year.

At times, I need to scream, "Runner, runner!" as I run between hurdles on lane two cuz groups of people walk mindlessly on the inside lanes. It's dangerous at times running full speed and having to swerve around people, but that's what you gotta do around here.

"See anything new?" Coach asks, pointing in the distance.

I hardly ever pay attention to the first curve on the track cuz I never run that part in the 300-meter hurdles.

"Yeah, uh-huh." I bob my head and ask him, "You set up the 400s?"

My mood shifts into a mixture of nervousness and excitement.

Coach has been toying with the idea for weeks about setting up the 400-meter hurdles to help me build stamina for the 300s, as well as prepare me for the next level—running at the collegiate level.

"You ready to be a chingona o que?" he asks, signaling it's time to move up to the grueling 400-meter hurdles.

"Well . . ." I start to mentally prepare myself for the extra two hurdles and 100 meters. "I guess since we have another three weeks to train now."

"Whenever you're ready. Let's hit it. I wanna see you run a fast one. Pretend this is a time trial," he says.

Time trial? "Ala, okay . . ."

"Run fast, kid!" Mr. Reina yells from his chair.

*Great.* I got way too many eyes on me now on my first attempt. Everyone and their mothers and abuelas take advantage of the public track to exercise. It's like I'm putting on a show out here when I practice during the day. That's what happens when there's only one public track for the entire city.

*Oh no. Shitttt.*

I spot two of those girls from the yearbook committee who also happen to be members of Las Marthas. One of them stuck gum in my hair during lunch last semester.

*Ugh.* They're walking across the track now.

I pretend like I don't see them, but I feel this anger grow inside of me.

"Let's go, Kris. What are you waiting for?" Coach's voice echoes around the track, loud enough others can hear. I bet *they* can hear, too.

I channel my anger, feeling my feet ready to patter down lane number three as I get in a three-point stance.

My body is charging with so much adrenaline, I'm shaking.

"GO!" Coach yells.

I push forward, not knowing what to expect as I start off my run on a curve, but all I can hear is them being mean again, calling people names as I head toward hurdle one.

My feet are moving quicker than ever. I was right. Earlier today, I told Coach that I'm sure I can pull off a big PR soon. I feel it.

*Freak. Slut.* I can hear them making their usual comments.

I'm peeling out, sprinting crazy fast.

Hurdle one is approaching faster than anticipated.

My strides are off. I can't slow down now. *Here it comes.*

I clip the hurdle and next thing I know, I tumble to the ground, rolling to break my fall like a gymnast.

"Get up and finish!" I hear Coach yell.

The adrenaline helps me get back up, propelling my body back in motion. I run—can't let those chicks think I'm weak.

I attack the next hurdle smoothly.

*"Winners never quit and quitters never win."*

I sprint down the homestretch with Vince Lombardi's quote stuck in my head. It helps me survive the death zone.

Crossing through the final line, out of breath and my knees wobbling, I hunch over my body. My hands squeezing my waist.

"Oh . . . my . . . god," I manage to say between deep breaths. I just completed my first 400-meter-hurdle run. Feels like I ran ten races in one.

Coach is standing over me, arms folded across his chest. Can't ever tell if he's angry at me or what.

"But I finished . . . I finished it, Coach," I say either way, wondering if he's upset that I hit a hurdle.

Clicking his stopwatch, he analyzes my splits. "Let's see . . ."

Meanwhile, I begin to feel my body again after my heart rate starts to chill out.

"Aouwww," I moan lowly, trying not to be a big baby. There's a throbbing pain somewhere around my knee, but there is no way I'm gonna let those chicks see me cry.

Just act cool, like it's nada.

"Kris-ty . . ." Coach says in two syllables. "You just ran that in sixty-four and change even with the fall."

"I did?" I ask, surprised. "Is that good?" I'm trying to conceal my pain.

He smiles, nodding his head. But now I'm dying here.

My knee wants to give out, so I allow myself to fall, butt first to the ground. That's when I notice that my right knee is covered in blood. It's dripping down to my shin like water. Loose rubber pieces from the track are stuck deep in my skin.

I scrape some off them off. Just grazing the top of my knee hurts.

I turn to Coach quickly, then back to my leg, wondering if he is thinking what I'm thinking. *It doesn't look good.* My knee is swelling like an eggplant. Egg-shaped, purple and green.

I don't want anyone walking the track to know I'm hurt, so I whisper, "Carlos . . ." I slip and fix it, "I mean Coach. I'm hurt. It hurts. Gacho bad."

In this moment, I wish he could wrap his arms around me, tell me I'll be alright, and fix me. But he can't. We can't. He can't play that part in front of everybody here.

"Aver. Let me look. Stand still." He tries to get me to stop fidgeting, but now I'm nervous, thinking, *I'm done. I fucked up. It's my fault.*

Coach has me lying down. My back itches from the dirt.

"How does this feel?" Coach tries to straighten out my leg, gently pushing down my knee.

"Please, stop. Stop. Stop." I can't.

"And this?"

"Coach!" My knee is painful to the touch.

"Chinga, Kris . . . ," he says, inspecting my knee more closely.

"What? It's gonna go away soon, right?" I hold my breath.

"No sé. Looks pretty banged up. Pero you were flying down that curve like I've never seen you run."

*Ugh.* I cover my face, wishing I could go back in time and not let those chicks get into my head. Something about those bullies just makes me wanna attack the hurdles like it's them.

"I'm so stupid," I whisper to myself. This is the same knee I banged up a few years ago when I wiped out on my skateboard on a five-foot quarter pipe. When that happened, I'd fallen on the cement, landing knee first—and something inside my knee popped. It took weeks to walk normally again.

"It's a dislocated patellar." I reveal the diagnosis to Coach after visiting the doctor's office with Ma. She scolded me the entire time, disappointed I might need surgery. It's my fault I've messed up my knee too many times. Add that to all the other injuries I've gotten from sports and the medical bills keep piling up. My dad's insurance only covers a portion of the costs.

I ask Coach to pick me up near the apartment when Ma leaves. Making my way downstairs is a workout, since I can barely move my knee. It feels like triple jumping down a slope and hoping you won't break your skull.

"Is it really as bad as the doctor said?" I ask Coach, hoping he'd say all doctors in town just exaggerate. They don't know athletes like we do. We push through pain and discomfort.

"How's it feeling now?"

"One through ten . . . like a six." Maybe more like a seven. The pain in my knee has only gotten worse since yesterday.

Coach pushes down the sides of my banged-up knee, and I get the chills. There's a soft, grating sound whenever he does that.

"Owww. That hurts."

"Yeah . . . well. Looks no good."

"Stop." If this is his first joke with me, it's a bad one.

"I think you should rest, let it heal for a few weeks."

"A few weeks? How? I don't have a few weeks," I say in disbelief, biting the bottom of my lip, trying to hold back defeat. "That's not happening. We gotta practice. Like right now. I can't waste time. This is my chance . . . You *know* that!"

"Let's take a few days off and evaluate next week. We got time. State isn't until next month. You could be alright by then." I look for a glimmer of hope in his voice, but it's full of uncertainty.

"This can't be happening to me." I open the passenger door. We're in the empty parking lot of a fast-food restaurant where we sometimes park to chat in private.

"Kris . . . ," Coach says, his eyebrows arched high. "You need to rest and keep off that knee! You're gonna mess it up more."

I give him the side-eye before reaching to grab the handle above the passenger door. I'm gonna walk normally, without my knee buckling and throwing me off-balance. *I can do it. Just watch me.* I muster the courage, pulling my body upward and out of the passenger door. I plant my left leg down on the ground first, then slowly straighten out both my spine and right leg.

"Come back inside," Coach begs me. He's worried about my knee, but probably also that someone might recognize us hanging around in an empty parking lot.

"You always say pain is weakness leaving the body, and I'm not weak!"

As soon as I try to strike my right heel flat on the ground and put weight on my feet, my knee gives out, forcing me to hold on to anything I can—the door panel.

"Te dije. Just rest." He's upset with me, but I'm more upset at myself.

Coach gives me a hand, pulling me inside his truck and telling me, "Let's keep icing it off and on. It'll get better. If you were good enough to make it to the state championships, then you're sure as hell good enough to suit up to compete. Got it?"

"Yeah, okay, if you say so . . . ," I say, thinking that if it's impossible to walk, how the heck am I gonna run and clear the hurdles? Coach is nuts.

Three weeks later, the state championships arrive with my knee still not fully healed. I fight through the pain and run the race anyway. I finish in seventh place.

*Dammit. I freakin' blew my chance.*

# STEVEN'S ADVICE

"Kristy, great to meet you! Come in," the new girls' track head coach greets me.

"I'm Coach Cortez." He introduces himself and we talk for a few minutes. I quickly realize he isn't another male coach with an ego problem, and any worries I have about him disappear.

"Hey, umm . . ." I scan the room, relieved that Miranda isn't anywhere to be seen. He's only coaching the boys' team from now on. Good. He held me back for too long.

"By any chance, have you gotten any mail for me?" I ask. It feels as though I've been holding my breath ever since state last season. I came in last place. I'm just hoping that a university wants to recruit me anyway.

"Let me check," Cortez says.

"Okay," I say as I watch him scan the pile of mail.

"Nope. Nothing has come in since I started working here," he says, and it hurts.

"Can you, like, double-check?" I'm thinking there must be just ONE recruiter out of the hundreds that were in the crowd at the state championships that noticed I was injured. Couldn't they tell by the way I crouched uncomfortably in the running blocks, struggling to keep my right knee on the ground?

Cortez keeps looking.

Didn't anyone notice I might have more in the tank? Impressed by how I was the only Latina out in that field? Or that I was the shortest hurdler from a border town?

"Nope," he says as he lands on the last white envelope, his eyes reading the recipient's name.

*No one saw anything in me*, I guess.

"Alright, Coach. See ya around," I say, trying not to look too sad knowing that this time around, I didn't get recruited. High school seniors across the nation should be signing their letters of intent by now, committing themselves to their universities.

I walk out of Cortez's office and scroll through my phone contacts, searching for "John."

**Me:** Carlos! No letters. Ughhhhhh.
**Coach:** It's still early signing, wait a little. Did you post the YouTube Videos and created a BeRecruited account already?
**Me:** Yup. I'm on it.

I delete the texts, hide my phone in my back pocket, and head over to the parking lot, trying to avoid the security guards in golf carts patrolling the area.

I'm supposed to be at lunch hall. Instead, I'm meeting with Steven. We're sitting between two parked cars, catching up away from everybody.

"Was up, dude?" I pat him on the back.

He chuckles. "What's going on, girl?"

"Nada. Just lots of things happening, ya know?"

He replies, "Yeah, same here." Steven talks about his issues at home. He's struggling to get along with his father. I suspect his father is an alcoholic like mine.

"Can't wait to go to college and live it up," Steven adds with a cool tone.

I sigh, "Same . . . but that's if I even get the . . ."

"What?" Steven's eyes meet mine. "What do you mean? You made it to state last year. You were literally the only one in town to do that."

"Nah, doesn't work like that. I wish," I say. "I . . . I actually blew the race."

No one at school really knows what happened during the race. Not a word in the newspaper about my injury. Coach wanted it that way. He said it's best not to say anything or people will think I'm a loser.

"Pos, what are you gonna do?"

"Wait until the end of the season?" The season starts in three months.

"Hmm," Steven murmurs, probably realizing that I'm running out of time. "So how's it going with Richard?"

"Oh my god . . ." I roll my eyes and add, "I hide from him now that Miranda left me alone."

"Don't get why those other girls haven't said anything," Steven wonders.

I could probably explain why to Steven. I'm no different than those girls.

Maybe Richard's victims needed something from him, like I did.

A safe place? Money? A grown-up to hear them out? A better grade? Keep them on the varsity team?

Steven's head tilts. "No more old, creepy-ass men, then?"

"Mm-mm . . ." I mumble, "Nah, not really."

"Not really?"

"Yeah."

"What does that mean?" he laughs awkwardly, sensing something's up.

I lift my right hand and start to bite my nails hard.

"What . . ." Steven gives me a look, like he knows *it's* right there at the tip of my tongue if it weren't for my damn fingernails.

"Nada."

"Tell me."

Would he be my best friend if I lied to him? *Dammit.*

"Dude?" I remove my index finger out of my mouth and stick out my pinkie.

"Promise you won't tell anyone. Not even Gina."

"For sures. I won't tell a soul." He pinkie promises me.

I stare off into the distance, noticing the barbed wire that encloses our campus like the basketball court in juvie.

"IsCarlos," I say in one word.

"Who?"

"My private coach. That's his first name."

I feel my heart dropping to my feet. What if Steven won't believe me?

"Kidding me?"

"No. Super serious."

"Damn. I knew it."

"What do you mean?"

"Ever since he became your coach, he's all you talk about. And that's *when* we even hang out. You're always busy practicing . . ." He pauses before lowering his voice. "I don't know. It's like you're different. And I just felt something was going on but couldn't know for sure what it was."

Maybe Ma was right. I have changed, but . . . I thought for the better, no? I turn my head away from Steven, feeling embarrassed.

"Ay, I'm sorry . . . ," I add, "I don't know, but feels so wrong now, ya know?"

I lean into Steven, wanting to give him the play-by-play of the details about what Coach and I have done, but I can't. What if he judges me cuz I've chosen Coach over him and all my friends? Can I tell him that Coach won't let me see my friends? He's like, "You need to prep for next spring season or else your times will suffer."

I just don't wanna piss Coach off, especially now that he's helping with my recruiting. We've been filling out the prospective student-athlete questionnaires from my top schools.

Steven gives me that look, like he knows what I'm trying to explain with my eyes. "Kristy, you should report his ass and find another coach," Steven says with a solemn look on his face.

"N-no, I can't," I stutter.

"He's controlling you. Don't you see?"

I imagine telling Coach I want out. No more living in the shadows. No more living a lie. I wish I could, but who else would train me? How else am I going to be able to earn a scholarship? How else will I leave all of this behind for good? And I wonder what Coach would say or do if I told him it had to stop.

"Okay, so what are you gonna do, then?" Steven asks.

Guilt starts crawling inside of me. Suddenly, I feel like a traitor.

*Carlos would hate me if he heard me talking about him like this.* I shake my head, biting my lips, wishing I could figure this out without pissing everyone off.

Steven looks worried. "Don't wanna see you get hurt. You said he's told you his cousin can make people disappear."

"But I think his cousin was kidding." Like, why would Coach hurt me? After everything we've been through, and everything I've told him about my life. *Nahhh.*

"People don't joke about that," Steven says.

"Dude. Never mind. Just forget it. I'll figure it out."

"You realize you're like the girls Richard messed with, right?" he asks.

*Carlos isn't like Richard, though.* I think it through. *Steven wouldn't know. He's not there.*

I shake my head again, regretting I said anything.

"He is. Only he's better at fooling you," Steven continues.

*No, he's not. Or at least, I think. Ugh. Well, maybe so. But doesn't he love me?*

"Steven . . . ," I start saying, "if it wasn't for him, I don't know if I would've become this good."

"No, Kristy." Steven places his hand on my shoulder. "You've always been fast, don't forget."

I think back to eighth-grade year, walking in as the new student at Ridge Middle School and becoming best friends with Steven. He always bragged about how he was friends with a track star. That year, I won every sprint race. Back when I didn't have any hurdles.

# HITTING THE BRAKES

Coach picks me up just behind Ma's place. He's driving me to another motel in broad daylight. I run through a bunch of excuses to end these secret outings between us.

*I don't wanna do this anymore...*

*I wanna date guys my age...*

*I'm graduating soon and leaving...*

*We're gonna get caught...*

*My mom found out...*

"We're starting practice at five thirty a.m. on Tuesday. Need you to get mentally ready. None of these parties y nada. Focus. Do you understand?" he demands.

"I told you. It was Amanda's birthday get-together. That's it."

Her party was the first time I had gone out—like, at all—since we started training a year ago, and now I'm getting reprimanded for it.

"Don't you wanna make it back to state?" I hate how he switches between the Coach I know and need, and the Carlos I wanna leave.

"Yeah, more than anything!" I answer truthfully, envisioning getting back to state, killing it on 300-meter hurdles. At the same time, he has hijacked my free time. Somehow, though, his words have a powerful way of reeling me in, making me doubt my decisions and what's best for me.

He adds, "You got to make better choices." He says things like he's wiser than me. Does being older automatically make you smarter?

Coach goes on and makes it clear that if I wanna make it back to state, I'm not allowed to have a life outside of track. Not even during the offseason.

"But I actually miss chilling with my friends. I wanna see them before the season starts."

In three weeks, my final spring season of track and field will begin, and when it does, I'll be completely busy until I wrap up with state. Hopefully. By then, I'll be cap-and-gown ready, graduating from high school, and on my way to study at a university. Doubt I'll have the opportunity to say goodbye to my closest friends now. I haven't even spoken to Rudy since I made that first call to Coach in his bedroom.

Coach turns right into a quiet street and says, "You'll forget about everyone here when you leave."

*Will I?* I don't think so. I still miss Ghost Town, Tita, La Machas, Tío's gritos, Myra's eccentric style and smooches, Bubbles's altar, and my friends from South Middle.

He slows down before reaching a hump on the road, turns his head toward me, and asks, "You sure you want that scholarship?"

"Yeah! Duh . . . more than anything in this world," I answer. This is how he always gets me to agree.

"That's right. You know what you need to do. This is business," he says, patting the top of my head and messing up my ponytail.

I brush him off, pretending to scratch my ear. The way he touches me now isn't rainbows and butterflies. The only sparks I feel are of fire and fury, feelings of mistrust and anger.

*He's messing with my head.* Why would someone who cares about me not let me have fun? Why would someone who cares about me always check where I'm at? Follow me to make sure I'm not lying about it? Constant texts? Hundreds of missed calls? Like I'm not trustworthy? Like I'm not allowed to live my life?

Steven's words dance around my head. *He's controlling you. Don't you see?*

Something tells me that Steven is right.

*Oh shit.* It's taken me eleven months to realize it. Maybe I just hate to think I could end up as a victim. Like I'm supposed to be smarter, tougher than that.

We come to a red stoplight.

Hands on the steering wheel, Coach rests his eyes on the light.

*Okay, just do it. Tell him. If I don't say it now, I never will.*

"So . . ." My voice cracks, attempting to pick one of the many ways I should start this uncomfortable conversation.

"What's up?" His reply is upbeat. He can't sense my hesitation or he's messing with me.

I stare at the red light, hoping it never changes color. Hoping someone will open the door. Hoping someone will take me from him. Hoping someone will get me that scholarship right this second. So I never have to see him again.

*Green light.* The wheels start to move again. Soon, I know we'll end up at a seedy motel off Highway 35, the same highway that leads to the very place Ma went missing nearly four years ago.

"I was gonna say . . ." I struggle to speak, wishing I could just have the guts to speak my mind. Tell him I'm done with feeling like

I have no choice when it comes to our secret meetings. That what we've been doing has really messed with my head. This isn't right. There's something really wrong.

*C'mon.* It's time to change gears. No more living in hiding. No more lying to myself. Lying to Ma. Lying to Gina. Lying to the newspaper. Lying to my entire community.

My finger taps against my thigh. I ease into the conversation. "Coach Cortez is like super chill. He told me I don't need to practice with the school anymore. Just with you. And he trusts you know your stuff."

"That's badass. He won't get in our way like Miranda. Plus, Cortez knows he isn't a hurdles guy. He's got no choice if he wants a chance to win a district title. That's for sure."

"Makes sense . . ." It occurs to me that it was training with Coach that brought me Miranda's wrath. Which led to me having to listen to Richard's disgusting stories. Now I feel so stupid for reaching out to Coach in the first place.

He parks at the back of the motel in an empty parking lot.

"What were you gonna say?" he's asking.

I unbuckle my seat belt, tighten my fist, and muster the courage to look at him in the eye like one would look at an angry tiger, ready to run from danger.

My mouth opens, "I, um . . . I . . . I can't do this hiding thing anymore. I kinda wanna date guys my age . . ." And the words tumble out before I can stop myself. "But we can still train. We got one more season to dominate together."

I guess that's 50 percent truth, 50 percent lie. Somehow, I think I've mastered lying these days cuz I'm scared the truth comes with consequences.

"We're gonna break more records, too. I feel it . . ." I close with that so he's happy.

Suddenly, he steps on the gas, and his truck sprints forward. He's going really fast. I can't even think. What's happening?

Then he brakes. It's sudden. My body flies forward like a rag doll. One loud thump.

"What the f—"

Feeling confused, I rub my forehead and think, did his foot slip on the gas pedal or did he do it on purpose?

Quickly, I buckle my seat belt back on, scrambling to push my back into the passenger door, as far away from Coach as possible. I sit there stunned, unsure what to say or how to feel.

Tears form behind my eyes. *He's not the person I thought he was.*

Then I snap like a firecracker. "The hell is wrong with you? Are you insane?" I pull out my cell phone from under me. I try to text Steven for backup, but Coach snatches my phone out of my hands.

He leans over his seat, grabs my shirt in his fist, and glares at me with empty, shallow eyes. Worse than an angry tiger. "Don't play with me," he growls.

*Oh no.* I shake my head, though. I'm not playing. I'm dead serious.

"Who's been here by your side this entire time? No one. Just me!"

"You . . . you . . . I know . . . you have, Carlos, but . . ." I stutter in fragments, wishing I could escape and go somewhere safe, but where? I don't know where to go.

To Ma? She will ask more questions than I can answer truthfully. She won't understand. To Ghost Town? I haven't been back since Ma and I left. To Abuela? I haven't talked to her in a while, and she barely scrapes by on food stamps. To Dad? I don't even think he would know what to do with a kid he hasn't raised.

I think back to Ma's promises from when I was a kid, about how we'd have a better life in the north side, but to me, things have always seemed worse, not better, than the barrio.

Coach is fuming, I feel his presence like a hot oven. Burning my skin. Hurting me.

"But why can't we just go back to how things were?" I ask desperately.

"Goddammit." He slams his closed fist against the steering wheel. It makes me jump. "I've taken out credit cards just so you can have the proper clothes . . ." He starts counting with his fingers. "Shoes . . . comfortable hotel rooms . . . good quality food, because eating all that greasy shit you've had your whole life isn't gonna help you run faster."

He's right about my eating habits. I've never felt this healthy physically.

But sometimes I miss my abuela's tortillas, bean-and-cheese tacos, and the Mexican feasts that brought me and my family in Ghost Town together. Now I'm far gone from my roots. I don't even know who I have become.

"What was I supposed to do?" I ask sharply.

*Say no?* He knew I needed new spikes and sometimes money for food, things Ma couldn't provide for me at times. I never needed that much more. I thought he meant it when he said if I ever needed help, I could count on him. But really, it was just a front so he could take advantage of me.

"I can pay you back. All of it. I promise. Just tell me how much."

I fumble through my words, trying to quickly lay out a plan to reimburse him, reminding me of having to collect Mom's ransom. Money neither me nor Ma have been able to repay.

"This is how you wanna pay me back?" he asks, jerking me back into the present. I feel anger building up inside of me when I rub the bump that's forming on my forehead.

"I'll pay you right away when I get a job if you want!" I add, pretending like I don't know it's not about the money.

"Ice it when you get back, Kris." He ignores my question.

As if this was just like my knee injury. I should've known better. He wasn't any different than Richard.

"I did it so you could chase those dreams of yours. Opportunities that not many kids around this town have," he explains.

I flashback to one of my first races, where I ran into Mindy, who used to train with Coach. They used to be super close, just like Celine.

During her senior year and my freshman year, she was crowned district champion in the 100-meter dash, edging me out of first place by .02 seconds. I wanted to be her. She was always sweet, full of light, and one of the smartest kids in her high school at a campus with over four thousand students. Everyone said she was going places, someday. But I saw her recently. She was barefoot, walking on the underpass of Highway 35. Her beautiful thick hair was so disheveled, I hardly recognized her.

*I wonder what happened to her? Could I end up just like her?*

"You really want to throw everything away before the finish line? How stupid *are* you?"

His words cut me deep. I begin sobbing, and tears pour down my face. I don't know what to do or what to say. I don't want to throw my dreams all away. I'm so close to the finish line. But I don't want this, either.

"I don't. Please, stop." Maybe at the end of the day, I do end up fucking things up.

*No. No. He's messing with my head still.*

He scratches his chin, nodding his head and staring out the window.

"If you're going to act like this, don't expect me to help you anymore. We're shutting things down. Practice is over."

"Wait. Wait. Wait. No. No. No," I plead. "Please!" I panic, and my whole body starts to shake. I don't have another plan. I don't have a backup hurdles coach.

"Go be with some kid. See what they can offer you. You're gonna realize quickly how much you need me. I promise you."

"I know you've helped me tons." I'm trembling. I never thought he'd say this. I thought . . . I thought he cared. "I know . . . But what about the college recruiters? And FASFA?" Coach has all the information about the college coaches and everything I need for my financial aid application.

"What about it?"

"I need the info. Like the passwords."

"Don't know what to tell you, then."

I try to take back what I've said and hurriedly spit out, "I changed my mind. I'm sorry. I . . . I just can't think anymore. I'm stressed about this season and worried someone is gonna find out. I'm sorry, Carlos. Please. I mean it."

Coach places his hands on my shoulder. I try not to pull away, remaining still. I'm feeling small again, like I need him. Yet I loathe his touch now.

"Nope. How could you be so ungrateful? After all I've done. I can't trust you!"

I think back about Ma and all the times she said I was an ungrateful huerca. A mal creada. There must be something wrong with me if the two people closest to me think I'm ungrateful.

What am I supposed to do? I'm not perfect. I'm just a kid.

"Please, don't . . . don't say that to me. Please."

A deep sob escapes from my chest, I can barely breathe from crying, and I'm pretty sure I look ugly now. All these emotions of betrayal, anger, sadness, confusion, heartbreak, hurt, loneliness swing back into me like the time Ma sent me to juvie.

*I can't stop practicing the hurdles or I'm doomed. I need a coach. I am grateful.*

I try to find the strength in me to stop crying, to be strong, and somehow pull myself together. *I'm courageous. I can roar louder than him. I'm a barrio girl. I can do this.*

I turn my sad face to a poker face. I make the switch like I'm an actress playing in a dramatic novela. Calmly, I clear my throat and press my nails deep into his skin, and I say, "You're right. I'm just being stupid."

"You're going to go back home and think about this long and hard. We either stick to *all* our training regimen or we're finished. Call me when you figure it out."

# ON MY OWN

**I'm staring across the Riverbank Track into the darkness and the** empty alley where Coach used to park his truck every morning before practice.

*C'mon. Carlos. Don't leave me like this. Just say you're sorry and make things right.*

I touch the screen of my phone again and wait, pulling and stretching the cuffs of my sweatshirt like mittens and shuddering against the bitterly cold wind. Maybe he will text me saying he forgot his coffee. He got a flat tire. His alarm didn't ring.

When the clock strikes 6:00 a.m., it hits me. He's not coaching me unless I give him what he wants. And what he wants is not okay.

I gaze up at the stars. *Hey, it's me again. Remember me? What was I supposed to do? Give me some answers, please.* Talking to them makes me feel a little less lonely.

Maybe I should've sucked it up, like Ma used to tell me whenever things got tough. Maybe I shouldn't have mentioned dating guys my age at all. My words can be lethal sometimes, I know, but I mean I thought someone who's thirty-seven would understand a confused seventeen-year-old girl.

I think in circles about last week. *Focus.*

I place hurdles around the track and others just off the side of the track for skipping drills. *I guess this is it.* I'm on my own. Breathe in. Breathe out. Everything's gonna be alright.

*Tap-tap-tap.* I lift my lead leg straight, up, down, and over the top of the hurdle, gliding my body counterclockwise around the hurdles. My muscles are tight. It's way too cold.

I can faintly hear Coach in my head saying, "Good. Keep that core nice and tight," as I finish up my final hurdle drill variation—leg swings over the top hurdle, hands flat, leaning against the wall.

Truth? Training without a coach isn't the same. But I can't waste a day of practice. The new season is around the corner. I can't just quit now.

I walk to the start of the low hurdles. Take off my sweatpants and sweatshirt. Slap the back of my hamstrings. *Wake up.* Need my mindset right. I squint into the darkness to see the eight hurdles on the track, and I can barely make out a feeble outline of the distant metal objects. I place my body in a standing running stance and wait to hear his voice to give me a countdown and say, "Con ganas. Finish strong."

*What if I won't ever be the same hurdler without him?* Worse, what if I end up as a could've, should've been hometown story?

*She was never the same after she stopped training with Coach . . . He could've taken her all the way . . . She's a quitter . . .*

I look at the broken rubber of the track, noticing how rugged it is and how it once was a prestigious stadium. Someday, all of this will be a memory of the past. Will I regret if I just quit right now?

As I clench my fists tight, doubts seep into my head. I don't want to end up like Miranda, someone who's bitter for not reaching their full potential. Even if I don't get that scholarship, at least I tried going through these challenges off and on the track.

*Ready. Set. Go.* I take off, barely running full speed.

The first hurdle rises on the horizon. I lead with my left knee, come off the ground. I clear it. Off the first hurdle, a crisp wind weaves through the track, pushing against my chest. I fight it.

Swinging my arms and lifting my knees in between hurdles. My legs feel abnormally tight. Like I'm being pulled down by gravity more than the usual. My feet trudge forward like flat tires . . . slowwww.

Hurdle two: I'm four strides away. Images and sounds of the past begin to creep up in my mind like a monster.

*You're gonna throw it all away before the finish line?*

I struggle to maintain my technique, but I hurdle away from his voice. CLEAR! Off to the next.

I keep accelerating to hurdle three. Then four. *You're so ungrateful.* His words really struck a nerve. *Maybe I am. Maybe I am not.* I can see my breath in the air. I'm struggling to fill my lungs. *You'll see how much you need me.*

I soar out of the backstretch, into the death zone, gasping for air. I jump over hurdle seven, instead of stepping over it. I worry I might slip back into old habits again and feel my confidence unraveling. It seems like everything I worked hard for is slowly slipping away. *You're too short to be a hurdler. You're not good enough. You're not getting out.*

I feel the burn throughout my body.

Hurdle number eight. I run toward it, feeling afraid I won't be able to attack it without falling. About ten feet from the hurdle, I come to a complete stop. Face-to-face, I stare down the last obstacle. Somehow, I see his face.

Not giving a damn if the world can hear me, I scream at the hurdle . . .

*"I hate youuuu!!!!!!!!!!!"*

And burst into tears.

With the pink hues of the sunrise in the distance and the stars disappearing, I hunch over with one arm resting on my knee and the other grabbing on the plastic crossbar of the hurdle. I feel defeated. Stuck. *Fuck it. Fuck it.* I feel like I don't have any other option but to call him.

My hand grips the cell phone tightly.

"Carlos? Um . . . we're all set. Call me back soon." I leave a voice message, feeling ashamed that I've given in to whatever Coach wants and needs from me.

"The day after I left him a voicemail, he called back and all he said was, "Let's get to work, then," without bothering to ask a single question. We went straight back to training twice per day. Pretended like nothing happened in his truck. I didn't feel like I had any other choice but to surrender to his rules. *I won't let him bring me down.*

"Remember who you are . . ." Coach breaks the silence, starting in on one of his classic pep talks in his truck before a race. "And what you're made of." He jolts me from ruminating on why I'm here with him again.

"Mm-hmm . . . ," I reply, looking out the window toward the track. Little does he know I don't need his reassurance anymore. Things are just the same, but different, now.

I've started to ask myself: What do I want? What do I need?

I still feel like I need a coach to help me reach my goals, but I also want my old life back.

I've started spending more time with my family and hanging out with my friends. And Carlos doesn't like it one bit. He still calls me constantly and expects me to ask him permission to see my family or friends. I've even caught him following me a few times. But I don't care anymore if he's upset with me, I go anyway. He just wants to control me, but these days it's just about me and my one-track mind. He won't derail me from reuniting with everybody I love, and he certainly won't derail me from reaching my hopes and dreams. I'm fighting for myself.

"This is it, verdad?" Coach asks, sounding sentimental.

"It is . . . ," I reply coldly. It's our last Border Olympics, and our two-year "partnership" is coming to an end soon. I'm weeks away from potentially qualifying for state. This chapter in my life is nearly finished.

"This is the end, Coach," I say, imagining how my life will be when all of this is over soon.

"Well . . . it's been one heck of a ride, Kris . . . ," he says, tapping at the newspaper sitting between us. According to a local sports article published this morning, Coach and I built the most successful sports partnerships in town.

But did we?

Well. It depends on what they meant by *successful*. Sure, I won races and earned over one hundred medals. I even broke old records. Got invited to the Latin Hall of Fame. But personally, it was an unhealthy partnership and relationship.

"Yup . . . ," I reply, thinking back to Steven recently calling it a case of Stockholm Syndrome. That I bonded with my captor. And that's when I realized, I needed to set myself free. It felt like no one was going to rescue me.

I toss my shoes over my shoulder and swing the door open. "Bye, Coach." I don't call him Carlos anymore. Nope. Not. Ever. Again. Carlos is dead.

"I wish you the best, Kristy."

"Thanks. And it's Elvira," I say proudly for the first time.

I walk toward the track, wishing he would just disappear into the distance forever. My mind still wrestles between how I can feel grateful that he coached me, awakening my inner strength, and also angry that he kidnapped my body. He stole me away from the people who loved me. All I wanted was to feel loved and accepted, the way Ma used to show me before that *night*. Somehow, Coaches' approval gave me what I felt was missing. I mean, he could've become the role model I needed during a tough time in my life, but instead, he turned into an extra hurdle down the homestretch.

*I don't need him.* I squint my eyes and get tunnel vision, prepared to soar to the top. When I first joined track and field, I saw competitive running as a way to escape scary things. These days, I don't run from my fears. I run toward them.

*"Runners, on your marks . . . get set . . . go . . ."*

I'm off into my own world. It's just me and the hurdles. I can hear my breath. I can feel the air pushing back on me. I can hear all the voices of doubt. *You're too short. You're too weak. You're not good enough.* But I'm not listening anymore.

A few moments later, I end up having one of my best performances at Border Olympics. I win each event: 100-meter dash, 100-meter hurdles, 300-meter hurdles, and long jump. I even shatter my own city records. Afterward, I'm awarded with the MVP trophy for totaling the highest points of any individual.

I step down from the podium and jog toward the bleachers to Ma. She's sitting in the first row of the bleachers with Rafael.

"You were right," I blurt out, saying it out of nowhere just to get it out of my system. I should've listened to her about being careful who to trust. I wanna tell her about Coach.

"Rafael, come back!" She's distracted, yelling at my speedy four-year-old brother. I'm watching Ma keep a close eye on Rafael. He's running across the bleachers giggling and mimicking like he's a runner. My brother is full of energy and joy.

"Mami! Sista! Look at me!" He squeals.

I'm starting to understand why Ma was distant and cold when she got back. Being taken hostage can feel a lot like someone kidnapped your heart and mind.

I think about Ma and what she had to go through when she got kidnapped. How she had to endure all the pain and the aftermath that ensued. She lost faith in many people and despite her distance, she tried to be there for me as best as she could. She tried to protect me.

It all makes me wonder. How can people that supposedly love us hurt us?

Rafael returns to Ma's side, and she gives me with one of those looks like, *¿Qué dijiste?*

"Nada. Never mind," I tell her before she asks any more questions. I'm not ready to tell her. Rafael needs Ma to be healthy. Not be more stressed.

"I'm a runnerrrrrrrr," Rafael shouts, running off again, and Ma forgets I even brought anything up. And I'm relieved she does. I just wanna forget about this, too.

By the time Rafael tires out, I scoop him up to take a picture, remembering how far we all have come. I hope someday, Ma and Rafael are proud of me, and forgive me for being distant, too.

Maybe one day they will understand the sacrifices I felt I needed to make to create a different path than any of us could ever imagine. Opportunities I desperately want and feel like I deserve.

I hope all of this was worth it, and my dreams come true.

# THE LAST HURDLE

**I'm in my hotel room, opening a manila folder that contains the** meet schedule, four pins, a few sticky hip numbers, and my last high school race bib number: **#2848**.

Head down, trying not to poke my skin, I carefully pin the bib to my uniform with safety pins. I try to position the number in the middle of my torso. Not too high. Not too low. It nearly covers my entire stomach.

I take a glimpse of myself in the mirror. I'm championing my navy blue, gold uniform one last time. *Kodak moment. This is it.* I snap a mental picture in my head. Someday when I'm older, I'll want to remember this day. The day I woke up back at the 2010 UIL Track & Field State Meet my senior year!

Four varsity seasons. Fifty track meets. Three city records. Many medals and thousands of hurdles later, my high school track-and-field journey is coming to an end. *Deep breath in. Deep breath out.*

There's nothing more I could've done to prepare myself for my final races—the 100-meter hurdles and the 300-meter hurdles. I've given it my best at practice. I stuck to the training plan despite all the challenges I had to face.

After the knee injury and seventh-place finish at state last year, I vowed to return back here strong and healthy. And this time, I'm more confident than I've ever been in my life. *No matter what happens next, I know I am good enough.*

I decided to drop out of the open 100 to focus on the hurdle races since they are final races, back-to-back. Even though I'm seeded in last place coming into the races, I know I belong here. All that matters is that I give it my best.

I compete in the 100-meter hurdles first. Off the blocks, I react late to the sound of the gun. About .24 seconds slower than my average split to the first hurdle. Despite the hiccup off the blocks, I set a new PR with a time of 14.40 seconds and a seventh-place finish. I'm happy with my performance.

The 300-meter hurdles, my signature event, is up next.

I head to the warm-up area west of the legendary Mike A. Meyers Stadium on the campus of the University of Texas in Austin, Texas, to go through my warm-up routine. My fellow competitors are there, too. The field is riddled with the state's finest track-and-field athletes. Everyone's on their A-game, preparing for the showdown of their life. A once-in-a-life opportunity for many.

About an hour out and I'm working on alternating legs over four hurdles when a UIL official carrying a clipboard makes an announcement. "Attention! Girls running the 300-meter hurdles, please form a line in the order of your lane assignment."

I take one final acceleration sprint for about thirty meters and close shop. *I'm ready.* I'm first in line to get my lane assignment. I got lane two. I'm actually relieved about my lane placement this year.

There's just something about a tight curve that makes me feel like I can charge the hurdles like a bull.

While the rest of the girls line up, I notice Laurie Barry. Like me, she's qualified in both hurdle races this year. We're the only returning female hurdlers from last year's state championships in the 300-meter hurdles, but unlike me, she did well, finishing first in the 100-meter hurdlers and second in the 300-meter hurdles. She's a beast, and running in the same race as her is exciting.

"Okay, girls! Please, follow me."

I begin to lead the way, and we head over to the track like a pack of wolves. Although I'm the tiniest wolf with the slowest qualifying time, that's okay with me. I'm proud of myself for making it back to state. I'm the only athlete at state that qualified in my three combined events. It's a huge accomplishment for anybody who has made it this far.

I follow the familiar path, leading the girls toward the exclusive gate entrance meant only for those athletes competing next. I anticipate how again I'll walk into the most beautiful track and field I've ever seen in my life in front of twenty thousand spectators.

*Click. Click. Click.* Our cleats scrape the ground, grinding and scratching the cement. The crowds look like a vast river, steadily making their way to their seats. We march our way past. People gaze at us. *This is it. Take it all in.*

When we reach the gate, my armpits begin to sweat gacho bad.

It's a mix of nerves and the sweltering Texas heat. Earlier this afternoon, the temperature hit over ninety degrees. The turf's temperature adds another twenty degrees, too. The track can feel like it's overheating. But a hot day makes for fast times down at the UIL Track & Field State Meet.

I'm biting my nails now. There's a part of me that wants to give in to the old, familiar feelings of panic and anxiety like so many races before. My heart is pumping. *I'm good enough to be here. I deserve to be here.* I remind myself that negative thoughts don't define me.

I don't fight my nerves anymore. I allow them to come and go like a wave with each positive affirmation I tell myself, setting them free. *Breathe in. Breathe out.*

"Remember to leave all your belongings in the black box as you enter the field," an official reminds us.

"Y'all ready or WHAT?!" another official exclaims. All of us got our game faces on.

For some, clinching the state title is like winning the Olympics. The Lone Star State has a big track-and-field culture. The state breeds some of the best high school boys' and girls' competitors in the country, many of whom end up becoming world-class athletes and qualifying for both the NCAA championships and Olympics.

Among many Texans, there's a popular adage: "Everything is bigger in Texas." But maybe it should be: "Everyone is faster in Texas."

An announcer with a deep Texas twang blares through the speakers. "Up next, we got the girls' three-hundred-meter hurdles on the track."

I peel my eyes away and glance up at the jumbotron. Smack-dab in the center of the first backstretch of the track, the clock reads 7:05 p.m. Just below the time, over ten camera people position themselves for our race. I even notice an ESPN camera. Everyone is talking about how this event could be one of the fastest girls' 300-meter-hurdles races in Texas high school history.

Walking with my head held high, I lead the hurdle group onto the track as the parched summer breeze sets in and the shadows of the crowded stands shade half of the 400-meter track. The bleachers begin to rattle, and fans erupt into chants and cheers. There's an electrifying energy in the air. And with the backdrop of the Texas capitol under clear, blue skies, it feels like a dream.

In this exact moment, I imagine the ground rumbling, tilting the tectonic plates with all the different sounds vibrating around me. Super track fans in Texas are the loudest. They're like a modern version of spectators during a gladiator fight, and it sorta makes me feel like I'm a young gladiator at the Colosseum. But of course, I'm not a gladiator. I'm a young Tejana from a border town who had to battle real life hurdles.

Now I'm at the top of the world. In MY world.

Running became a safe place for me, a place to retreat from everything and everyone. It's where I've taken all my feelings and experiences and transformed them into something positive. While there has been so much I couldn't control, running is one thing I could. I don't worry about anybody trying to come in between me and my dreams anymore. I determine how I perform and what will become my destiny. *I can do this!*

I'm mentally prepared to face my final hurdle. All my hard work has paid off and today, I'm representing myself, which means I'm also representing puro Ghost Town, South Middle, the rucas, Anderson, my community, and all the kids who dream big. Soon, I'll be carrying their voices and stories on the soles of my spikes as I cross the finish line and beyond. Because if I can do it, anyone can, too!

*It's my time to shine!* I squint my eyes at the bleachers. Among the thousands of people up in the stands, I search for family and friends who came to support me. They are my biggest supporters, wearing T-shirts that say RUN, KRISTY, RUN! *Thank you.* I smile and mouth the words, hoping they can read my lips.

An official escorts us into our lanes.

"On lane number two . . ." Our names and accomplishments are announced over the loudspeakers.

To hear them trumpeted to this arena, to know that the people watching this can hear what I managed to accomplish, is incredible. They might not know who I am, where I come from, or how I got here, but I do. I'm a barrio girl.

I drift back to the night Ma was kidnapped four years ago.

I think about how her survival depended on my little size 4 feet, racing to come up with the ransom money so I can cross the finish line in time. That was all a horrible nightmare, but this was a moment I discovered the resilience I've always had deep within me. It taught me to look fear in the eye and to run toward my problems, not away from them. If I do that, I can overcome anything.

Today, I will harness that same strength to help me over the last hurdles.

A white flag comes up. *This is it.* The UIL officials are ready to start the race. I stand still behind my blocks. Taking in the silence and zoning in.

"RUNNERS . . ."

"ON YOUR MARKS . . ."

I walk around my blocks and stand up tall a few feet in front of the metal apparatus.

My eyes look up ahead. There. They. Are. The hurdles. *Hi.* I greet them like they are my friends now. Not my enemies. It was all perspective.

I squat down with both of my hands flat on the ground and crawl backward into my blocks to stretch out my calves and muscles. Then

I settle comfortably into the blocks and take one last glance at the hurdles. Tunnel vision. *I'm not afraid anymore.* My eyes focus on the rubber ground, and all I can hear is my breath going in and out of my nostrils.

"GET SET . . ."

I suck in one quick, deep breath and shift my body slightly forward. I wait for the sound . . .

*BOOM!* The starter pistol fires. I push off the running blocks and dash toward the first hurdle faster and more explosive than ever. Somehow, I attack the hurdle with my right lead leg without any hesitation.

I step over the hurdle, maintaining my speed, and return to my seventeen-stride pattern. The next hurdle arrives; I attack it with my dominant leg fiercely. I keep sprinting in a hip-to-pocket arm-swinging motion, trying to maintain my top speed.

Driving my lead leg into the third hurdle, the first obstacle on the curve, I can feel a couple of bodies clearing the hurdles at almost the exact same time as me. Nope. I'm not dead last. *Trusts in your steps. Trusts in your rhythm.*

Hurdle three, clear! Laurie Barry is out ahead. She's on another playing field, leading the pack about two strides in front of everybody. But everyone is running their own race, I'm gonna hold on!

Hurdles four and five come and go by in a flash. *Keep moving.* I emerge out of the curve, into the infamous DEATH ZONE and homestretch. The hurdles only seem to be getting taller, but I run toward them; there's no way of turning back. The sounds of the wild crowd cheering and stomping come and go with each breath, propelling me forward.

I stutter-step coming into hurdle five, but I don't let the stutter get to me. *Keep going!* I got no idea what place I'm in or who's right up on me. All I know is that I'm moving faster than I've ever been able to.

It's all clear now as I leap hurdle six, out of the curve and into the homestretch. I got a chance to finish in the top half. *Finish strong.* I dig deeper than I ever thought I could. Like if I could reach for my heart and run with it in my hands like a baton right about now, I would.

Hurdle seven, clear. Up ahead is the last hurdle to my final race, but it's becoming more challenging to keep my form. My mind wrestles with different thoughts. *I wanna slow down. I wanna stop. I wanna give up.* My thighs are on fire. My body is screaming, help!

In the past, there were instances in my life where I've felt it might've been easier to quit than to fight for what I felt I deserved: a fair chance to succeed. But every single drop of sweat, every single tear, every single real-life hurdle—all of it prepared me for this very moment. *Don't run from the pain. It's okay to be afraid. Embrace this challenge.*

I'll never know what I'm capable of if I don't give it my best. I got one last hurdle, and I won't give in to the pain or the fear. I'm leaving it on this track. It's now or never. My mind can overcome anything.

Without stuttering, I lift my dominant leg and leap over hurdle eight. I push forward into my final stride, gritting my teeth. I am stronger than ever.

As I approach the finish line, I realize that everything I have ever needed was inside of me all along. Regardless of place and time, I've already won—

I AM A CHAMPION.

# AFTERWORD

## HURDLING'S LIFE LESSONS

I can still see the illuminated track at Mike A. Myers stadium in Austin, Texas, with the Capitol building shining in the distance. The sounds of the crowd wildly cheering fresh in my ears and the tingling sensation from the hot, dry air filling my lungs. There I was crossing the finish line with my hands high in the air and my eyes glued to the performance board.

A wave of emotions cascaded down on me. Difficult memories from the past flashed before my eyes. Ma doing all she could to get us out of the barrio. Running as fast as I could to raise the ransom. Saving Ma from kidnappers. Landing in juvie. Surviving abusive coaches. These were challenges my family and I had to face, sacrifices I had to make for a fair chance to succeed. Despite the obstacles off and on the track, I crossed the finish line at the UIL Track & Field State Meet in the 300-meter hurdles with a personal record time of 43.65 seconds, putting me in fourth place in Texas and top twenty in the nation.

Although I did not win the race, no number of medals or awards would change what really mattered to me in that moment. The lessons I learned about myself and life through my track-and-field journey were most important. Three lessons from those years stand out in my mind that help guide me today.

LESSON #1: I learned the first step on any journey is to begin. I remember coming in second to last place in the 100-meter hurdles as a freshman in high school. I doubted I could be a competitive hurdler. I feared the height of the hurdles. What I learned is that fear is a normal response when facing any new challenge. The fear told me to quit, but another voice in my head told me if I didn't try, how would I know what I'm capable of?

LESSON #2: The second big thing I learned was to confront challenges head-on and giving it my best without worrying about the outcome. Hurdling taught me it's okay to fall. When you're continuously faced with hurdles, quitting only seems easier than to keep running toward a place that may or may not exist at all. But by failing and trying again and again, I developed resilience. Without it, there's no way I could have made it to where I am today.

LESSON #3: Lastly, the third major lesson I learned was not to allow others to define who I am, who I could become, and what I could accomplish, or rely on them to determine my value. It's easy to fall prey to your own doubts, and to what other people think or say about you. I learned to ignore them because all that truly matters is that you believe in yourself and give it your best.

At the state meet, I recall telling myself while walking off the track, "For the rest of my life, nobody can ever take away this moment from me. When I'm older, I'll look back with admiration and appreciation for what I accomplished."

Today, I live to say it's true. I am proud of Kristy. She is my hero.

# MY COLLEGIATE SCHOLARSHIP EARNED AND LOST

When I made it to the bleachers, I noticed a stream of college recruiters gathered around me. Schools like Rice University, University of Houston, North Texas, UTEP and University of Mississippi were proclaiming their interest in having me join their teams. That's when I knew! Finally, I got scouted! I was going to have the opportunity to receive a college education with an athletic scholarship. Later I learned colleges had been interested in me all along. After I graduated from high school, I got called into the coaches' office. Our new varsity head coach handed me a stack of opened envelopes that were hidden in another coach's desk—Miranda or Richard, I didn't get an answer. All I knew was that these recruiting letters addressed to me had been mailed to my school around my junior year, even before I began private sessions with Coach A.

By the time I got a hold of these letters, it didn't matter. I had already committed to run at the University of the Incarnate Word (UIW) because they offered me a full athletic scholarship. I accomplished my big goal!

During my first semester, I lived with seven girls in an open dorm room. I trained every day at 5:30 a.m. with my new team and took eighteen credit hours in order to complete my five-year program in four years, since my scholarship only lasted that long.

However, it did not take long for my mental and physical health to suffer. I ended up in the ER twice. During those visits, doctors discovered that I suffered from polycystic ovarian syndrome (PCOS) and was anemic. I had scar tissue from multiple ruptured cysts on my ovaries. This could have been the cause of the stabbing pain I felt during practices and after races. Looking back, I wish my coaches would have recognized that my pain wasn't for attention. I wish they had the knowledge to understand female student-athletes can be suffering from health issues that can impact their performance.

Somehow, I still managed to pass my classes and powered through my first indoor and outdoor season. At the Lone Star Conference Championship Meet, I earned podium finishes. I ran a strong 400-meter hurdles resulting in a second-place finish. I made the finals in the 100-meter hurdles and long jump. I also led my team to victory in the 4×100 meter relay. I wrapped up that first season by breaking the school hurdle records and qualifying for the 2011 NCAA Outdoor Track and Field Championships.

I opened my sophomore indoor season strong, breaking my own school record in the hurdles. However, I was struggling with intense backaches. My head coach told me that it was all in my head, often complaining that I was losing my toughness. Soon, I began losing sleep, terrified I'd lose my scholarship if I didn't perform well. I kept competing as hard as I could. I felt that I had to fight for my education. My scholarship. My future.

After the Texas Tech Invitational indoor meet, I set a new school record while struggling to leap each hurdle.

Less than twenty-four hours later, I woke up unable to get out of bed. Every step shook my spine, leaving me in excruciating pain. The results of an MRI confirmed my worst fears. I fractured my spine in my L3, L4, and L5 vertebrae. It was the type of injury that usually resulted from force trauma. However, there wasn't a specific incident that I could think of that could have caused it.

Instead, it was an accumulation of years of pushing my body beyond its limits, and if I didn't want to risk becoming paralyzed, I would have to stop leaping over obstacles. "You won't be able to run the same again," the doctor said, while strapping a back brace around my waist with Velcro. I had to wear it for months to reduce my mobility and stabilize my back. During my recovery, I fell into a deep depression. I thought I had lost a part of who I was. I realized running had given me a sense of purpose. Running was the only thing I felt like I could control. In a way, hurdling was a form of escaping the bad stuff happening around me.

I persevered through the physical pain and existential turmoil, determined to return to the team for my junior year. Early in that season, I was injured again and forced to quit the team. I lost my athletic scholarship.

In addition to a newfound lack of identity, the absence of track left me with a lot of time alone with my thoughts. Everything from my past came back to haunt me. I quickly discovered that nobody could outrun pain or trauma. Not even a runner. For the first time in my life, I decided to put my physical health and emotional well-being first. I knew I needed to liberate myself from all the pain, memories, and suffering I carried with me. It was time that I confront my past and finish writing my story.

## NEW YORK CITY AND MY NEXT CHAPTER

I moved to New York City in May 2013 to chase my next dream. I would complete the book that I started while I was in juvie. I would bring to light all the darkness I had been living in. When I arrived in the Big Apple, I had no connections. No friends or family. No writing degree. Not even a college degree. What I did have was trust in my resilience and determination to lead me where I was supposed to go.

A few months into my move across the country, I jumped back into the sport of track and field. Except this time, I was the one running the drills in the Upper West Side at the Calhoun School. It was there I discovered my passion for coaching, and it inspired me to launch my own youth track-and-field club team. I recruited athletes from all socioeconomic backgrounds. Our program grew to over one hundred athletes from all boroughs. Within our first year of operation, the program helped qualify athletes to the USATF Youth National Championships. It was also during this time that I went back to school, determined to complete my studies, and finish my degree.

In December 2015, I was finally able to say, "I'm a first-generation college graduate." I walked down the stage in my cap and gown to receive my bachelor of science degree, with Ma and the rest of my family looking on with pride.

Shortly thereafter, at just twenty-three years old, I was given an opportunity to coach track and field at the University of Pennsylvania alongside Coach Joe Klim. In addition, I was put in charge of the Young Quakers, a mentorship program for youth athletes from low-income communities in West Philadelphia. By the end of that first season, we were able to help qualify a relay team for the Penn Relays where they competed in front of thirty thousand spectators and finished in second place.

The following season, I received a job offer at the Armory Track, the most prestigious indoor track-and-field facility in the world, located in Washington Heights, New York City. It's home to the National Track and Field Hall of Fame and NYRR Millrose Games, and more than one hundred thousand athletes come through its gates to compete each year. I had the honor to work with hundreds of athletes of different skill levels and age groups. It proved to be the greatest privilege of my life.

The experience also taught me so much about young people, coaching, myself, and my past.

What stood out to me was there are many kids struggling with the same obstacles I had to overcome in my youth. Problems stemming from socioeconomic conditions, familial conflict, systemic disadvantages, and abuse by adults in positions of power. The latter inspired me to reflect on my own experiences with my coaches.

## GROOMING AND ABUSE IN SPORTS

A few years ago, I received a call from my mother asking if I'd heard about the anonymous tips that had been received by the local news channel. Young women accused a high school coach of sexual misconduct and abuse. It was Coach Richard. Two teenage girls from other cities in Texas had finally broken the silence, one of whom was his own niece. He was eventually charged with numerous crimes, convicted, stripped of his teaching credentials, and required to register as a sex offender. But he took a plea bargain and was able to avoid any time in prison.

I'm shocked that a coach like Richard would be hired not only to teach high school students but to coach a girls' sports team. He was hired at our school, despite numerous misconduct accusations at two previous schools. How could our school administrators look past this information? It caused me to doubt that the adults who were supposed to protect the student body were dependable.

When I was a teenager, I felt forced to listen to the awful things Coach Richard told me, and I was afraid to speak up. I feared the administration who hired him despite knowing his history would once again look past any accusations and he would not be held accountable for his actions. It wasn't long after these experiences that everything unfolded with Coach A.

For a decade working on this manuscript, I refrained from diving into what happened between Coach A. and me. I simply wanted to forget about it and write this book without that part of my story. I felt ashamed that it happened to me, like it was my fault that it happened. In the back of my mind, I could hear voices telling me that I'm not grateful for the coaching and gifts that Coach A. had given me. Voices that told me there was nothing wrong since I was seventeen years old, the age of consent in Texas. The voices insisted that I must honor our secret or otherwise be labeled as a traitor.

However, coaching my athletes really influenced my decision to include this part of my life in the book. I also watched the rise of the #MeToo movement that empowered women to speak out against abuse in their work environments and in sports, as recently witnessed with the USA women's gymnastics team. The outpouring of collective courage and accountability resonated with me. But I also knew we were leaving out the most vulnerable group of people who needed their voices to be heard, too.

I decided I needed to be a voice for my athletes and others like them who had been sexually harassed, assaulted, or abused in the spaces they should feel safe. I wanted to be a voice for change, and this provided the motivation to keep pushing for this book to be published.

## GROOMING PROCESS—STATUS, AUTHORITY, POWER

To better understand what happened to me, I conducted thorough research on sexual abuse in sports, reading scholarly articles and interviewing victims of all ages and genders. The research I found only made me realize the dire need for this subject to be openly discussed despite how uncomfortable it may feel.

Reviewing the research provided me with a greater understanding of how I became a victim and why I remained silent for so long. The first major takeaway from reviewing literature that resonated with me spoke to the nature of the coach-athlete relationship, especially at the level I was training. "Intense relationships between coaches and athletes seem to be a prerequisite for promoting young athletes' success in sport. At the same time, such close relationships carry risks for negative dependencies, misuse of trust, and commission of abuse."[1]

I learned the biggest risk factor in these abusive relationships was power. The psychological power that enables an authority figure to coerce and manipulate the victim. The social power that insulates the perpetrator from criticism and influences the victim to remain silent for fear of not being believed or losing the opportunities that come with the sport. Finally, the threat and act of physical power through violence.

The coach's position of power is derived from the "closeness of the relationship, the legitimate authority of the coach and the coach's expertise and previous successes, and the coach's ability to control access to the athletes".[2]

Looking back into my own experiences, I see that Coach A. used his credentials and reputation as a locally renowned coach to gain my trust while I was going through an incredibly difficult period of life.

---

1 Sonja Gaedicke, Alina Schäfer, Brit Hoffman, et al., "Sexual Violence and the Coach-Athlete Relationship—a Scoping Review from Sport Sociological and Sport Psychological Perspectives," *Frontiers in Sport and Active Living* (May 2021).
2 Ashley Stirling and Gretchen Kerr, "Abused Athletes' Perceptions of the Coach-Athlete Relationship," *Sport and Society* (February 16, 2009).

He weaponized that trust and my vulnerability, wielding them as power over me. It wasn't until our last few months when everything came crashing down between us that I was finally able to recognize he had been taking advantage of me.

I had never heard of the term "grooming" and didn't know that it describes "strategies consciously used by abusers to persuade [victims] to engage in sexual activities."[3] I also had no way to know how to identify what grooming looked like. One recurring characteristic of the grooming process is the "coaches' development and building of friendships with their victims, which impede athletes' recognition of coaches overstepping boundaries. These efforts include compliments and presents from coaches, phone calls, invitations to coaches' homes, isolation of athletes, and having secrets with coaches."[4] I now clearly recognize this was exactly what Coach A. had done to me.

## WHY IT CAN BE DIFFICULT TO SPEAK UP AND WALK AWAY

Because he had threatened me if I ever tried to leave, it was extremely difficult to walk away. There weren't any resources in my community that I knew of for girls in my situation. Once I finally did try to confront him in his truck outside the motel, he turned violent, confirming my fears. Then his behavior escalated from manipulation and control to include intimidation and stalking. I felt trapped, scared for my future and my life. Leaving abusive situations is never easy.

---

3 David Finklehor. *Child Sexual Abuse: New Theory and Research.* (New York : Free Press, 1984).
4 Sonja Gaedicke, Alina Schäfer, Brit Hoffman, et al., "Sexual Violence and the Coach-Athlete Relationship—a Scoping Review from Sport Sociological and Sport Psychological Perspectives," *Frontiers in Sport and Active Living* (May 2021).

Especially when you're a teen and you don't feel safe to speak up. I felt like I couldn't trust any of the adults around me.

The coach-athlete nature of the relationship made the situation more confusing, challenging, and traumatic for me. I feared the consequences of standing up to someone with authority, status, and power. Today I know that each of these factors prevented me from leaving the abusive relationship. Again, the research I discovered helped explain what I was going through. "Coaches develop social capital to increase their status within the community and build a shield of immunity against accusations. Consequently, it becomes difficult for athletes to report abusive coaches without endangering their own trustworthiness and sporting career."[5]

I succumbed to these fears, too. I was scared no one would believe me if I spoke up about what was happening. I feared retaliation from my former high school, friends, family, and community for speaking out against someone so respected and well liked in our community. I was scared that everything I had worked so hard for would be taken from me. I feared that my scholarship and the accolades I had earned would be stripped away. I also worried that I'd bring more problems to my family if I spoke my truth. Given everything that they had already been through, I wanted to remain quiet for them, too. Even today as I write these words, I am worried about how some people will respond. But what I am most scared of is staying silent and potentially putting other potential victims at risk.

When I was younger, I was critical of decisions I made about the inappropriate relationship with Coach A. Through my therapy sessions and research, I learned that it's okay to have made mistakes. It's

---

5 Kristine Bisgaard and Jan Toftegaard Støckel, 2019, "Athlete Narratives of Sexual Harassment and Abuse in the Field of Sport," *Journal of Clinical Sport Psychology* (May 31, 2019).

okay not to know what to do. But it's not okay for anyone to blame a teen who has been groomed by an adult into a sexual relationship.

## THE RESPONSIBILITY OF ADULTS AND HEALTHY BOUNDARIES

Neuroscience research shows that human brains don't "mature" well into adulthood, including the prefrontal cortex, which is one of the final areas to develop. This area of the brain is responsible for complex cognitive behavior, including "planning for the future, decision making, goal-directed behavior, and emotions."[6] One study stresses the importance to "understand consent as a contextual, multi-layered, complex process."[7] The emotional and psychological capability to comprehend the short- and long-term consequences of consenting to a sexual relationship develops with the prefrontal cortex into adulthood.

Despite the fact that the age of consent in Texas is seventeen, the law doesn't account for or consider the scientific fact that teens, whose brains are still developing, do not have the same abilities as adults when making decisions about informed consent. With the additional power imbalance that exists between teen and adult, especially coach and athlete, it is always the responsibility of adults to establish and protect healthy boundaries in relationships with student-athletes.

Now I understand how as a teen, I was doing the best I could to

---

6 Stacey Bedwell, "Do Teenagers Really Make Bad Decisions?" Frontiers for Young Minds (September 27, 2017), kids.frontiersin.org/articles/10.3389/frym.2017.00053.

7 Sonja Gaedicke, Alina Schäfer, Brit Hoffman, et al., "Sexual Violence and the Coach-Athlete Relationship—a Scoping Review from Sport Sociological and Sport Psychological Perspectives," Frontiers in Sport and Active Living (May 2021).

survive, to create a better life, and trusted Coach A. was doing the same for me. I felt he was like family, and according to the research, "When coaches take on roles as best friends, brothers, sisters, and parents, it becomes harder for athletes to identify the boundaries where the relationship turns abusive."[8] All of these studies have helped provided a framework to express what young Kristy felt then. The relationship with Coach A. was inappropriate, abusive, and harmful.

## STEPS TO ADDRESS THE PROBLEM

Currently, Texas law requires all school employees to participate in training concerning prevention techniques for and recognition of sexual abuse and other maltreatment of children. But this is not enough. We need to provide young people with education, preventative tools, and resources to help protect them. While many nonprofits exist to support educators, families, and adults in the protection of children, there need to be more programs aimed directly at providing guidance, assistance, and support to kids themselves. We need these programs to be promoted and widely available at schools.

I believe we also need stronger screening systems in place at schools that stop predatory adults from gaining access to students through hiring or volunteering in the first place. Schools also ought to provide better protection for whistleblowers to encourage reporting inappropriate or harmful incidents. Lastly, there should be

---

8 ibid

greater oversight of extracurricular programs. In my experience, the coaches at my school operated with complete freedom and impunity.

## CHANGING AN UNHEALTHY SPORTS CULTURE

Sports culture too often demands student-athletes to harness unhealthy aggression, strive for dominance, and repress emotions or anything perceived as weakness. It can adopt attitudes that are detrimental to the emotional health of student-athletes and can also be sexist. Popular slogans such as *Have some balls* and *You run/ throw/jump/hit like a girl* are just a couple of examples of these attitudes in action. All of this deeply impacts how young boys and girls view themselves and others. I believe this type of culture creates the expectations that make it clear that doing anything traditionally considered feminine, like speaking up about pain, especially mental or emotional, is considered weakness, and that athletes should fake their way past it.

## WOMEN IN SPORTS LEADERSHIP POSITIONS

Finally, our sports programs across the country need more women in coaching and leadership positions. For example, women account for only 19 percent of coaches in track and field. This is an important step to advance gender equality, but it also can change the culture in sports. I wonder how our sports culture would change if at least half of leadership positions in female team sports were filled by women.

Would the lives of our female student-athletes be positively impacted? Would my high school experience have turned out differently?

I dream that one day our sports organizations will cultivate a healthier and safer culture for female athletes.

## KIDNAPPINGS IN MÉXICO

Years ago, I learned hours before Ma was kidnapped, the perpetrators pretended to be wedding guests and spoke with Ma's friends. The original plan was to take one of Ma's friends hostage. Except when things didn't go according to plan, they kidnapped Ma instead.

The ringleaders who orchestrated the kidnapping were sentenced to fourteen years in prison. Meanwhile, another co-conspirator is currently in prison awaiting sentencing in the US. I also learned there were other victims held captive with Ma. But no one else filed charges. Unfortunately, stories like ours are common along the border. When people found out about my mother's story, other kids reached out to me to tell me about their missing relatives. They all expressed fear of speaking out.

Beginning in the mid-2000s, the number of kidnappings-for-ransom crimes started to dramatically increase. It was also around this period that the victims transitioned from high profile, wealthy victims to victims of all socioeconomic statuses. These crimes most often go unreported for a variety of reasons, including a lack of confidence in the Mexican police and government. The National Institute of Statistics and Geography (INEGI) of México provides an annual crime and victimization report. On average, there have been an estimated 84,658 kidnapping victims each year over the past ten years.[9] It is also estimated that only 1 percent of all perpetrators are arrested and convicted for their crimes.[10]

## NARCO CULTURE AND THE MEDIA

Whenever I see the glorification of Narco culture in Hollywood, I deeply worry how our youth might perceive crime and violence. Movies and shows tend to idolize the kingpins but offer portrayals of their lives that are far from the full truth. The reality is violence destroys families on both sides of the border. Given how media shapes culture, there are consequences for the stories we tell and consume. Humanizing cartels and their use of ferocious violence makes it more difficult to change the culture. Movies and shows can make them seem more acceptable, or inevitable, and consequently audiences may believe the cartels' crimes are acceptable, or at least inevitable, too. For American audiences, this is also portrayed as a problem "over there." But for Americans like me and many others along the border, this problem exists in our communities, too.

The poverty level in my hometown is one of the highest in Texas.[11] Nearly 30 percent of households run by single mothers.[12] These circumstances can leave kids, especially boys, vulnerable to organized crime. For example, two local teenage boys rose the ranks as hitmen for a notorious drug cartel right around the same time that Ma was kidnapped.

9 National Institute of Statistics and Geography (INEGI), *National Survey of Victimization and Perception on Public Safety* (2022).
10 Rory Smith, "Mexico Has a Kidnapping Problem—and It's Getting Worse," Vox (May 11, 2018), vox.com/2018/5/11/17276638/mexico-kidnappings-crime-cartels-drug-trade.
11 US Census Bureau
12 City of Laredo—Open Data GIS Portal

One of them was known for his athletic accomplishments and had big dreams. He was raised by a single mother in an impoverished barrio and ended up in juvie just like me. However, after leaving juvie, he was lured into one of the cartels. At just nineteen years old, he ended up in prison with a life sentence. During an interview, he admitted to the fateful murder of my thirteen-year-old friend and classmate, Rodrigo. He explained he was enticed and motivated by the power he felt and the wealth he gained through his crimes.[13]

I often wonder how different the lives would be for these boys, Rodrigo, my family, and my community if drug related violence hadn't flooded into our barrios on both sides of the border. I do know the problems of kidnapping, drugs, and violence are all interconnected. They are problems for both Mexican and American citizens, and problems both governments of the United States and México should be doing much more to solve.

## MISSING WOMEN

There's a scene in Part I where Ma is driving us to our new house in the north side when Kristy notices a group of people picketing on a street corner. These people were the families and friends of local missing women. Frustrated by the lack of answers and actions from both the US and Mexican government, they took their voices to the streets. At the time, it never crossed my mind that Ma would become one of those missing women less than a year later.

Today, there are thousands of missing Hispanic and Mexican women along the border. The women come from all economic

---

13 Dan Slater, *Wolf Boys: Two American Teenagers and Mexico's Most Dangerous Cartel* (New York: Simon & Schuster, 2016).

backgrounds but are predominantly low to middle class. Each day, I consider myself fortunate my mother returned. Not all families are as lucky as mine. There are many who are still missing and may never found.

## MA'S LIFE

What happened to Ma was horrific. To this day, I cannot fathom what she had to experience. Like so many other victims of violent crimes, Ma's life has never been the same. However, my mother embodies resilience and strength in her life after surviving the traumatic ordeal. It's apparent in my two teenage brothers, whom she has raised with her husband, even after what she endured. She finds her peace baking into all hours of the night, making the best baked goods in our border town.

I now know that Ma's kidnapping and the emotional and psychological wounds that resulted were the main cause of the deterioration of our relationship. I think back to the night that I was sent to juvenile. Now I'm able to see that I was calling out for help that my Ma couldn't provide because she also needed help for herself. Without access to mental health resources, we both suffered. Unfortunately, I ended up being sent to juvie instead of getting the love, care, and support I desperately needed at the time.

## JUVENILE HALL

The juvenile hall I was sent to was shut down, only to make way for a new one to open. Although I spent just a few days there, my time in juvie was a nightmare. I never forgot the pain I felt lying there all alone, cold, and hungry with so much uncertainty. I felt like I had been locked away in a dark closet because adults didn't know how to help me.

This experience made me realize that if I wanted to survive and live a different life than the one I was born into, I needed to learn how to create my own path. And really embrace that I am the navigator of my own ship. Without any role models, road map, or guidance. I needed to do anything and everything I could to make my own way in this world.

The experience also taught me the American juvenile justice system wasn't set up to help me or any child become a successful adult. When I reflect about how I ended up incarcerated, I know juvenile hall was the last place I should have been. It wasn't designed to provide the help, support, and resources I needed. Instead, it was as if I was being punished for my trauma and the lack of mental health resources in my community. I see how I became a stronger person from these experiences, but I also experienced trauma, pain, and suffering in the process. It doesn't have to and shouldn't be this way.

## IMPACTS OF YOUTH INCARCERATION

Studies show that incarcerating our youth can have negative impacts for their rest of their lives. Nearly half of juvenile detainees are reported to feel hopeless or have thoughts of death within six months prior to detention, and incarceration only exacerbates problems. Some researchers have found that incarcerated youth experienced three to four times the suicide rate of the rest of our youth community.

The current methods of response to suicide at juvenile correctional institutions is greatly flawed. Placing a child who expresses suicidal thoughts in isolation is incomprehensible. Detention should not be a "dumping ground" for young people who are struggling with their mental and emotional health.

## BETTER SOLUTIONS FOR AT-RISK YOUTH

To help our youth live healthy lives and reduce recidivism, we need to do better. We need to reimagine what solutions can be offered to troubled youth who come from communities where their problems and needs are often ignored. We must rally around our most at-risk children and ensure our communities provide them with the tools and resources they need to overcome their obstacles and thrive. This includes access to mental health resources, healthy meals, mentorship programs, and extracurricular activities to cultivate skills and express themselves. Building a strong support system and positive influences around our most vulnerable kids can enable them to see other possibilities for their lives and to feel supported, prepared, and motivated to achieve their dreams.

## TRAUMA AND HEALING

While writing this book, I read my childhood journals to help me write the manuscript. To write this story in my most authentic teenage voice, I had to relive memories that I wished I could have kept locked up. I wished I had tossed the key in the deepest part of the ocean, to a place where there's nothing, not even life. Only darkness.

As I read those journals, there were days I woke up crying. I went to bed crying. There were times I didn't think I could live another day. There were many moments I felt like I was making a big mistake by removing the bandages I'd covered myself with for far too long and exposing my life. Traumatic stress can have long-lasting impacts on the brain.[14] Thankfully, as an adult, I have been able to work with a therapist, which has helped me persevere through all of this as best as I could.

I've been writing my story for more than fifteen years, and what I now realize is that this journey has been one of self-liberation and self-love. I learned that keeping everything hidden away and swallowing my voice only kept me in the shadows, running away from my fears. To be truly liberated, I had to expose the real hurdles in the dark.

## FINAL REFLECTIONS

I am stepping out of those shadows and illuminating everything I've been battling. My story is now available for all to read. The book will make its way throughout the world just like Gerda Weissmann Klein's book.

I hope each of the adults who read my story understands that we have the power to protect, help, and support our children to leap over whatever barriers are in their way. We must listen to their experiences and stand with them. All it takes is for one person to make a positive difference in their lives.

Finally, to my young readers: You are brave. You are loved. You are not alone. I believe you ALL have the strength to face your fears, overcome any obstacle, and step into your light.

Today, I am free.

---

14 Dorothie Cross, Negar Fani, Abigail Powers, Bekh Bradley, Clinical Psychology and Practice (May 20, 2017), onlinelibrary.wiley.com/doi/full/10.1111/cpsp.12198.

# ACKNOWLEDGMENTS

Immeasurable gratitude to everybody who supported me during the development of this book and beyond.

First, I'd like to thank the people on the front lines who shaped me as a writer. To Ross Klavan, whose mentorship, support, and guidance have been a great source of encouragement. I'm astonished when I look back at how far I've come since we sat on the rooftop of a New York City skyscraper to discuss my first draft. I was twenty-one and unsure about my ability to convey my own story well enough to secure a book deal. Your first words were, "You ought to write it yourself no matter how long it takes. It's YOUR story!" This is some of the best advice I've ever received. Thank you!

I'm forever indebted to Charles Salzberg for inviting me to join the New York Writers Workshop. For seven years, I rewrote, edited, and polished draft after draft under your instruction at the JCC in the Upper West Side. Despite all my run-on sentences, spelling errors, and tenuous grasp of the most basic grammatical rules, you believed in me and my story. As you say, "Elvira is my most improved student I've had in my decades of teaching." My growth as a writer is a testament to hard work, perseverance, and infinite patience of a great teacher like Charles. I'm thankful for all the insights I accumulated from you and your students over those years.

The completion of this book would not have been possible without the loving support of my writing "aunties": KC, Karen, Cynthia, Phyliss, Terry, Judy, Liz, Coree, Carol, Wendy, Esther, Vivian, Robbie, and Jack. To the teachers who inspired me to reach for the stars. Miss Alegria, Ricardo Nuño, Dr. H. Cuellar, Mr. Paul D. Lack, and Mr. Bohan. To Alicia Ruiz Elementary and United South Middle Schools. It brings me great comfort and relief to know there are many educators around the world whose mission is to empower our youth by encouraging them to dream big because anything is possible. I see you!

Thanks to the Aguilar, Gonzalez, and Ramos families for shaping me to become the woman I am today and, most importantly, for giving me the most epic childhood memories. *Puro* Ghost Town.

I am forever grateful for all the generous individuals who helped me bring my mother to safety. To Vane and Lorena for standing by my side during a very traumatic time in my life. To Sarita, for being the most loving and strongest woman in the barrio.

I would like to express my deepest appreciation and love to my friends for their continuous support during the writing of this book and throughout my many other endeavors. Liliya. Kayla. Diana. Caitlin. Brian. Tim. Alexander. Erik. Ricky. Kikeh. Isela. Jameson. Sergio. Sonia. David. Elizabeth. Julio. Shaneve. Jared. Steven. Ben. Cheers to my sk8ter friends and Exodus skateboards: Jesse, Tony, Dereck, Robert, and the rest of the crew.

Thanks to my therapist Laura for helping me process difficult memories and guide my personal growth. I would also like to thank

Mr. And Mrs. Garibay for photographing my running journey in high school and offering to share the images with my readers.

Big shout-out to the following organizations that helped shape me as a coach and gave me the opportunity to make a difference in the lives of hundreds of athletes: The Nike Track & Field Center at the Armory, University of Pennsylvania, Calhoun School, Riverdale Country School, and NYC Junior Sprinters Track & Field Club.

To my dearest Coach Klim, you are the definition of a leader whose coaching philosophy I deeply admire, and I hope that I have become a better coach because of you. To the incredible teams at the Armory Foundation, InsideOut Writers, Las Comadres, When We Band Together, and Pigmentocracia, I appreciate all the efforts your teams put in to try to make a difference in people's lives.

Much of this book was written at public libraries and it was incredibly helpful to have resources at my disposal. During many writing sessions, I would gather not only inspiration but hope from browsing the books, dreaming one day my story may end up among them. I would like to especially thank the following libraries: Stephen A. Schwarzman (New York City, NY), St. Agnes (New York City, NY), Riverside (New York City, NY), Buena Vista (Burbank, CA), Lloyd Taber (Los Angeles, CA), Joe A. Guerra (Laredo, TX), and the J. Erik Jonsson Central (Dallas, TX). These public spaces are an education lifeline, source of community, source of job opportunities, and a haven for so many. For places like my own hometown, where half of the county lacks basic literacy, we would be putting more underserved children at risk with funding cuts and full closures. We must preserve and expand access to our public library systems through unwavering support, patronage, and funding.

I don't know where you Rucas are at today, but I want to let you know that you're always in my thoughts and I'm thankful for our "secret" conversations. Perhaps without breaking some rules in juvie, this book may have never existed.

Gerda Weissmann Klein, what a resilient, incredible human being. She inspired much of who I am today. May her name and glory live in this book forever!

Zeynep, my literary agent, I appreciate how hard you worked to help me get this book into the hands of the best team. Thank you for believing in my story.

At Roaring Brook Press, I want to thank my incredible editors Connie Hsu and Nicolás Ore-Giron for being delicate and compassionate with the development and completion of this book. Kate Sullivan, thank you for your incredible insights. To the many of you at Macmillan who have contributed to this book's journey, I'm grateful for your help. Jackie Dever and Avia Perez, thank you for your care and attention with the copyediting. Big thanks to Aurora Parlagreco and Israel Vargas for their vision, talent, and collaboration in the making of the design and artwork for this book. Because of your dedication and hard work, young girls and boys of all shapes, colors, and sizes will go to bed at night dreaming of the endless possibilities, knowing their voice in this world matters, too!

To our youth around the world. This shout-out is dedicated to you. I thank you for being yourself. For standing up for what feels right. For fighting the good fight. You are the captain of your own ship. You can steer wherever your heart desires. Keep going. Don't give up. I believe in you.

Lastly but most importantly, I would like to express my sincere gratitude to my readers around the world. Thank you so much for giving Kristy and many young girls like her a chance to be heard and feel seen. From the bottom of my heart, I thank you for making my wildest dreams come true.

# BIBLIOGRAPHY

Bedwell, Stacey. "Do Teenagers Really Make Bad Decisions?" *Frontiers for Young Minds*, September 17, 2017, kids.frontiersin.org/articles/10.3389 /frym.2017.00053.

Bisgaard, Kristine, and Jan Toftegaard Støckel. "Athlete Narratives of Sexual Harassment and Abuse in the Field of Sport." *Journal of Clinical Sport Psychology*, 13, no. 2 (2018): 226–42. doi:10.1123/jcsp.2018–0036.

"City of Laredo-Open GIS Data." *City of Laredo—Open GIS Data*, open -laredo.opendata.arcgis.com/.

Cross, Dorthie, Negar Fani, Abigail Powers, Bekh Bradley. "Neurobiological Development in the Context of Childhood Trauma." *Clinical Psychology and Practice*, 24, no. 2 (May 20, 2017): 111–124. onlinelibrary.wiley.com/doi/full /10.1111/cpsp.12198.

Finklehor, David. *Child Sexual Abuse: New Theory and Research*. New York : Free Press, 1984.

Gaedicke, Sonja, Alina Schäfer, Brit Hoffmann, Jeannine Ohlert, Marc Allroggen, Ilse Hartmann-Tews, and Bettina Rulofs. "Sexual Violence and the Coach-Athlete Relationship—a Scoping Review from Sport Sociological and Sport Psychological Perspectives." *Frontiers in Sports and Active Living*, 3, (2021). doi:10.3389/fspo.2021.643707.

National Institute of Statistics and Geography (INEGI). "National Survey of Victimization and Perception on Public Safety." 2022. Translated: "Encuesta Nacional de Victimización y Percepción sobre Seguridad Pública, inegi.org.mx/contenidos/programas/envipe/2022/doc/envipe2022 _presentacion_nacional.pdf.

Slater, Dan. *Wolf Boys: Two American Teenagers and Mexico's Most Dangerous Cartel*. New York: Simon & Schuster, 2016.

Smith, Rory. "Mexico Has a Kidnapping Problem. And It's Getting Worse." *Vox*, Vox Media, May 11, 2018, vox.com/2018/5/11/17276638/mexico -kidnappings-crime-cartels-drug-trade.

Stirling, Ashley and Gretchen Kerr. "Abused Athletes' Perceptions of the Coach-Athlete Relationship." *Sport in Society*, no. 2, Informa UK Limited (February 2009): 227–39. doi:10.1080/17430430802591019.

"U.S. Census Bureau QuickFacts: Laredo City, Texas." *Census Bureau QuickFacts*, United States Census Bureau, census.gov/quickfacts/fact/table /laredocitytexas/IPE120221.

# RECOMMENDED READING

Here are some of my favorite books I've read over the years. These stories provided me with examples of perseverance, courage, and determination. I encourage you to check them out if you're looking for more books full of inspiration. I hope these stories remind you of your own infinite potential and the endless possibilities for your life.

- *All But My Life* by Gerda Weissmann Klein

- *Undefeated: Jim Thorpe and the Carlisle Indian School Football Team* by Steve Sheinkin

- *Up from Slavery* by Booker T. Washington

- *Wolf Boys: Two American Teenagers and Mexico's Most Dangerous Drug Cartel* by Dan Slater

- *Who Was Amelia Earhart?* by Kate Boehm Jerome

- *Soul Surfer: A True Story of Faith, Family, and Fighting to Get Back on the Board* by Bethany Hamilton

- *The Body Keeps the Score* by Bessel van der Kolk

# RESOURCES

988lifeline.org

athletehelpline.org

uscenterforsafesport.org

thearmyofsurvivors.org

projectella.org

# ORGANIZATIONS

National Sexual Violence Resource Center—nsvrc.org/survivors

National Alliance on Mental Illness—nami.org/Home

National Institute of Mental Health—nimh.nih.gov/